THE FACE OF TRUTH

THE FACE OF TRUTH

A Study of Meaning and Metaphysics in the Vedāntic Theology of Rāmānuja

Julius J. Lipner

State University of New York Press
Albany

First published
in USA by
State University of New York Press
Albany

For information, address State University of New York Press,
State University Plaza, Albany, N.Y. 12246

Printed in Hong Kong

Library of Congress Cataloging in Publication Data
Lipner, Julius.
The face of truth.
Bibliography: p.
Includes index.
1. Rāmānuja, 1017–1137. 2. Vedanta. I. Title.
BL1288.292.R36L57 1986 294.5′2 84–24075
ISBN 0–88706–038–2
ISBN 0–88706–039–0 (pbk.)

10 9 8 7 6 5 4 3 2 1

The face of truth is covered by a golden bowl. Uncover it to my view, O Pūṣan, for the sake of truth's law.

(*Īśa Upaniṣad*, 15)

Contents

Preface

Many people, especially in the West, have been led to believe – though it may be this trend is slowly being halted – that there is no such thing as a tradition of critical Hindu theology. I understand 'theology' here in its broad sense, to include hermeneutics, theorising about the nature of religious language, philosophical theology, doctrinal theology and so on. Thus some believe that Hindus, being 'mystical-minded', have never been seriously concerned with the systematic inquiry into religious matters, and that, accounting this a virtue, they have sought always to play down and relativise the intellectual side of faith, preferring to lay emphasis on the way to salvation and its underlying practice. Others hold on the contrary that Hindus are by and large 'worldly minded', following a religion designed to ensure worldly success and security, with the other-worldly dimension of no more than marginal concern. As generalisations both these views are quite false. Hindus, no less than Christians, have a long, varied and profoundly serious tradition of theological inquiry, and it is one of the chief purposes of this book to give evidence of this by examining in some depth the Vedāntic theology of Rāmānuja (eleventh – twelfth century CE). The concern with Vedānta is especially to the point for it is the broad tradition of Vedānta which in one form or other has offered (and continues to offer) to perhaps the majority of literate Hindus the psychologically live options for religious theory and experience.

By one fell stroke too I seek to disabuse those scholars who maintain that all the sustained critical work of the Hindu tradition is 'philosophical' in nature. In the end, for the most part this may well turn out to be a verbal quibble, but the time has come, I believe, to rehabilitate 'theology' as an apt description for a substantial part of the intellectual tradition of the Hindus.

Many Westerners also believe – alas, this is true for too many of the modern Indian intelligentsia as well – that the great Advaitin Śaṃkara is representative of Hindu religious thinkers. Now this belief too strikes me as manifestly indefensible. No doubt Śaṃkara is central for our appreciation of the religious teaching and theological development of Vedānta, and indeed for Hinduism's self-understanding today, but he is hardly representative of Hindu theologians or even of Vedāntins. There are other religious thinkers who have influenced greatly the theological scene in India and who deserve more than a courteous look-in; they deserve to be with Śaṃkara in the centre of the stage. Rāmānuja is one of them, and another important concern of this book is to foster a paradigm-shift in the appreciation of Vedāntic theology by bringing about due recognition of Rāmānuja's contribution.

There is a further consideration, one which touches me both personally and professionally. This concerns the question of inter-religious dialogue, especially between Hindu and Christian points of view. I am heartened that increasingly, not only in the Divinity Faculty of Cambridge University, where I teach, and in other departments of religion in Britain, but also in India, students and experts in the various religious disciplines are coming forward, actively interested, as I am, in furthering Hindu–Christian dialogue. Indeed it is in partial response to this interest by non-Indianist colleagues that I have written this book, both to inform and to stimulate the process of dialogue. The theology of Rāmānuja I believe lends itself peculiarly well to furthering Hindu–Christian understanding, and though it has not been my primary concern by any means to spell out the possibilities for dialogue in this regard – for this book is primarily Indological in character – in my treatment of many topics I have sought to be sensitive to the needs of dialogue and on occasion to intimate where it might bear fruit. (For my views on the relationship between Hindu and Christian thought see my 'Through a Prism Brightly', in *Vidyajyoti*, Apr 1980, pp. 150–67.) In any case, it is my hope that non-Indianist philosophers of religion and theologians will find much to interest them in this book, and in writing certainly I have had an eye to such readership.

Of late, two or three works have emerged on the theology of Rāmānuja. It may be asked if there is room for another. Let me answer this question in more than one way. First, it seems to me that the number of potentially worthwhile studies on Rāmānuja is indefinite. A glance at any of the standard works will show that Rāmānuja is acknowledged to be, even if this is not yet a popular acknowledgement, one of the main religious thinkers of the Hindus; yet compared to some of the main religious thinkers of the West he has been hardly studied. It seems to me at least as short-sighted to ask if there is room for another book on Rāmānuja as it is to ask if there is room for another book on Augustine or Thomas Aquinas, for example – Western theologians on whom worthwhile studies continue to appear, based rightly on the assumption that the rich veins of their thinking will not soon give out. So it must be with Rāmānuja.

Secondly, further to these remarks, this book is intended to be a work of original presentation and research. Throughout I have sought to deal with matters not taken up or analysed in depth in previous Rāmānuja studies, or to illuminate by a new approach. But to say this is not to deny that this book is primarily a critical exposition, rather than a critique, of Rāmānuja's thinking (though on occasion I have indicated where criticism might be made). To my mind, though Rāmānuja's theology is profound it is extremely difficult to comprehend systematically. Rāmānuja does not sit lightly to learning; his thought is often condensed and sometimes obscure (both these features are reflected in his Sanskrit expression). Thus it seemed to me more important at this relatively early stage of Rāmānuja studies to concentrate on critically expounding Rāmānuja's difficult thought than to give it a critique, and though I have made no concessions to rigour in analysis I have tried always to be clear. Nevertheless, while I hope that this book will be read by the layman and scholar alike, I am aware that it will not be an easy book for those who have not acquired some facility in the critical method. Again, it has been my intention to provide a basis for a creative understanding of Rāmānuja's thought in terms of which bridges might be built between it and Western expressions of philosophy and theology. A critique would have undermined this project. Finally, an exposition-*cum*-critique would have doubled the length of this book and I have had to be mindful at all times of the limited space at my disposal.

This book focuses on two aspects of Rāmānuja's thought, and on their relationship. The first aspect, the subject mainly of the first two chapters, concerns the question of 'meaning', with special reference to Rāmānuja's understanding of the nature of sacred language and of divine predication in the context of the opposing views of the Prior School of Exegesis (i.e. Pūrvamīmāṃsā) and Advaita. The impression is widespread that questions relating to scriptural hermeneutic and the theory of (sacred) language were of secondary concern for the master Vedāntins; this impression is false. Such questions were of fundamental importance for the Vedāntins, for on their answers were constructed the various Vedāntic theological edifices. A book on the theology of Rāmānuja, for instance, which does not give due consideration to his views on the nature and interpretation of the sacred word is like the wonderful aerial assembly-hall of the god Śakra – it hangs in mid-air. I have sought to avoid such an architectural marvel.

The second aspect concerns Rāmānuja's metaphysics in its wider theological perspective. To this end a metaphysical inquiry into Rāmānuja's view of the finite self and its salvation as well as of the nature of the supreme being is undertaken. A unifying chapter is devoted to Rāmānuja's theological method, while the work as a whole seeks to show the relation between the two aspects of his thought mentioned above.

A note about the critical apparatus of the book. All the translations from the Sanskrit are my own; however, limitations of space have on occasion made it necessary for me to give in the notes not the whole Sanskrit text translated but such words or portions of it as are likely to prove in my judgement of most interest or contention to Sanskritists. Inevitably here I must accept a charge of arbitrariness on my part; but in mitigation let it be said that in many cases, because of the importance of the quotation or the difficulty of the Sanskrit, or both, the Sanskrit text has been given in full, and in any case in every instance full references to the text in the Sanskrit original are provided. In deference to non-Sanskritists I have confined the Sanskrit as far as possible to the notes (to make for easier reading of the book), and have provided a full glossary. Full bibliographical references of works mentioned are to be found not in the body of the text but in the Bibliography at the end. There is also a list of abbreviations used, with their uncontracted equivalents.

This book is the fruit of early critical studies in Christian and Hindu thought in India and England, and of continuing years of research during a full teaching-programme as a University lecturer. In the process I have acquired a lasting admiration and affection for the man with whom I have wrestled in this book. I pay warm tribute to all my teachers, especially to Frs R. De Smet SJ, J. de Marneffe SJ, A. Sabino SJ, and G. Koelman SJ – all of the Jnana Deepa Vidyapeeth in Pune, India (formerly the Pontifical Athenaeum); also to Professors K. K. Banerjee (now deceased) and P. K. Sen and other staff members of the Philosophy Department, Jadavpur University, Calcutta; and finally to Professors H. D. Lewis and D. Friedman (the latter now deceased), formerly of King's College, University of London.

Their wisdom, learning and kindness continue to inspire me. A number of other persons, some of whom must remain unnamed, have helped my writing of this book by their constructive advice and criticism. Special thanks in this regard are due to my learned friends Brian Hebblethwaite of the Divinity Faculty of Cambridge University and Fr George Gispert-Sauch SJ of Vidyajyoti Institute of Religious Studies,

New Delhi, though of course the responsibility for what has finally appeared in print must remain mine. And here I must record how much I owe to John Hick, with whom friendship continues to deepen over the years, for encouraging me to persevere when I most needed encouragement. Finally, my thanks to my friend Raymond Allchin of the Oriental Studies Faculty of Cambridge University for suggesting the short title of this book.

But above all my warmest gratitude to my wife Anindita and to my children, Tanya and Julius, who for so long and with (mostly) unfailing patience and fortitude put up with the continuing drama of my battle with Rāmānuja. Conscious that I owe them much, I dedicate this book to them.

Cambridge J. J. L.

1 Language and Meaning

In this book we shall be studying the theology of Rāmānuja, a Tamil Brahmin from South India. Rāmānuja (traditional dates: 1017–1137 CE)[1] was a man of deep faith in God[2] and wrote essentially as a theologian: that is, his main concern as a thinker was to reflect systematically on the nature of God and God's relation to the world. To this end he was also a philosopher in the commonly accepted sense of one seeking lasting and fundamental knowledge by the light of reason. But his philosophy was at the service of his theology and to do justice to both aspects of his approach we may call him a philosophical theologian.[3] We shall not spend time in describing his life or the social milieu of his times, interesting and important though this may be. Much of the former appears to be shrouded in legend, and adequate biographies to suit all tastes, in potted or more extended versions, are not difficult to come by.[4] At the risk of seeming insensitive to Rāmānuja the man, I suggest we devote all our energies to examining Rāmānuja the thinker – and this for a number of reasons. In the first place, his thought has made a lasting impression on the multi-faceted phenomenon that is Vedāntic Hinduism and continues to mould the religious perspective of many; secondly, I believe that Rāmānuja's thinking is likely to influence deeply theological, especially Christian, speculation beyond Hindu cultural boundaries. We shall not be able to go into this in detail though I hope that in treatment and content this book will be seen to have potential for inter-religious, especially Hindu–Christian, dialogue. On occasion I shall try to make this outward-looking aspect more explicit. Finally, it is Rāmānuja's thinking that presents the evidence we may rely on best to assess his contribution as a man of God towards enriching our lives. This work therefore is a critical tribute to Rāmānuja as thinker.

Traditionally, nine works are attributed to Rāmānuja. These are the *Vedārthasaṃgraha*[5] (i.e. the Summary of the Meaning of the Vedas, which I shall refer to as the Summary), the *Śrī Bhāṣya*[6] (his main commentary on the *Brahma Sūtras* – I shall call this the Commentary), the *Bhagavadgītābhāṣya*[7] (his commentary on the *Bhagavadgītā*), the *Vedāntasāra* (i.e. the Essence of the Vedānta), the *Vedāntadīpa* (i.e. the Vedānta-Lamp[8]), the *Gadyatraya* (a trio of devotional prose hymns), and the *Nityagrantha* (the devotee's Manual of Daily Worship[9]). In his book *The Theology of Rāmānuja*,[10] J. B. Carman points out that 'the traditions of both Vaḍagalais and Tengalais' – the two schools into which Rāmānuja's sect split some centuries after his death – 'have always ascribed just these nine works, and no others, to Rāmānuja' and that 'there is complete agreement between the two schools that Rāmānuja wrote (only) nine works, all in Sanskrit'.[11] Basing ourselves on this traditional judgement we may, in the first instance, disregard as unauthentic any other work ascribed to our theologian.

The first five listed are works of theology proper and will receive our main attention. While scholars are agreed that the first three of these are indisputably Rāmānuja's, the authorship of the *Vedāntasāra* and *Vedāntadīpa* has been disputed on various grounds. Nor has the authenticity of the *Gadyatraya* and *Nityagrantha* remained unchallenged.[12] Since Rāmānuja's philosophical theology is comprehensively expounded in the first three works listed, it is to these that we shall turn most. However, in my opinion no compelling reasons have been advanced to substantiate the claim that Rāmānuja himself did not write the *Vedāntasāra* and *Vedāntadīpa*, and on occasion I shall refer to them.[13] But with respect to the last two titles the position is different. I believe that the case for not accepting them as Rāmānuja's works, though not proven, is stronger. Of late a number of attempts have been made to establish this case, apparently with some measure of success. I shall have some observations of my own to offer on the matter in Chapter 6 and for the time being we may leave this issue. Fortunately, these works contain very little if any explicit theologising, their main purpose being either devotional or ritualistic. However, the doctrinal implications that these hymns may be made to yield through their evocative imagery and other considerations can lead to important shifts of emphasis mainly in our assessment of Rāmānuja's ethical stance, and for this reason it is appropriate I think to consider the question in Chapter 6, which treats of the means and goal of salvation. It is as well to note here that on substantial issues Rāmānuja's undisputed theological writings, at least, readily lend themselves to being treated as a systematic whole, for on such issues his thought is remarkably uniform. It is only occasionally then that we shall find it useful to advert to a minor change of expression or idea.

We can now take note of the broad conceptual framework in which Rāmānuja theologised. This framework was moulded by factors which at once both channelled and restrained his thinking. To begin with, Rāmānuja, like rival Vedāntin theologians in relation to their own religious traditions, believed that the religious community (*saṃpradāya*) to which he belonged alone preserved the correct interpretation of the scriptures. This was the Śrī Vaiṣṇava community[14], and he is acknowledged by the members of that tradition to be the sixth[15] *guru* in their succession of *gurus*. If one's own longstanding hermeneutic tradition was *the* authoritative one, others were deluded in making the same claim for their line of teachers.

For the classical Vedāntins and their followers theologising was a serious business, and the passionate search for truth from the scriptures could be pursued only by one pure in spirit and free from deviant views. It was no virtue to be seen 'doing theology in an original way', to be offering a new interpretation of the ancient wisdom. In spite of interpretative rivalry, among the schools teaching-pedigree was respected. Theological originality, expressly claimed as such, lacked authority and therefore any claim to illumination in the eyes of the faithful and of rival teachers. The professed aim of the sound exegete and theologian (unlike that of, for example, the poet, the dramatist, the military strategist) was not innovative but essentially preservative: his to perpetuate in an increasingly relevant and perhaps systematic way the teaching that had been handed down – not to change it. It was more important to be regarded by one's contemporaries as standing within the continuum of tradition than to be credited with an 'original' but deviant mind.

Rāmānuja gives regular expression to this idea. In the opening dedicatory verses of his works he often acknowledges the spiritual and intellectual debt he owes to his predecessors, especially to Yāmuna (a noteworthy theologian in his own right and Rāmānuja's penultimate *guru* precursor). We have in the Summary, 'Triumphs the sage Yāmuna by whom has been dispelled the deluding darkness [of falsehood] spread out in the world and lacking [the light of] scripture and reason'.[16] Nevertheless, in spite of the binding respect a theologian had to show his teaching-tradition, he had ample scope if he was so minded to contribute fresh insights, by the creative organisation of his material, the penetration of his arguments and even by doctrinal innovation. Amid the wastes of sterile glossary and arid commentary characteristic of much of Hindu theology, there is often original illumination. Rāmānuja is a beacon in this regard. But such originality had to be cloaked by the pretext of only bringing to fruition or reflecting faithfully what was already in the tradition from the beginning.

So far as Rāmānuja's approach was concerned, his starting-point for the theological enterprise was not inference or any other form of sense-based (*vyāvahārika*) experience, but the standpoint of faith. This faith was based on a particular exegetical tradition of the scriptures, but it was the scriptures which Rāmānuja, in common with the *ācārya* or teacher theologians of the other schools, acknowledged to be the original source for the knowledge and attainment of man's supreme end, the ultimate reality, Brahman. In his commentary on *BrSū*, I.1.3, for instance, Rāmānuja rejects any sort of perception or inference as a valid *pramāṇa* (source of knowledge) of Brahman. On the contrary, he asserts, the sole such *pramāṇa* is scripture.[17] This is because only scripture can make known an object totally different from the objects of the other (sense-based) *pramāṇas* – a being whose 'proper form[18] being opposed to everything repugnant is an ocean of unlimited, eminent, unmeasured, noble qualities, comprising omniscience, omnipotence and so on. There is no question [for such a being] of even a trace of the defect of likeness with anything known from the other *pramāṇas*.'[19]

But the faith of the Vedāntins was not a blind, irrational faith. Though reason on its own was a treacherous guide in matters theological, directed and illumined by scripture it had a very important part to play in the systematic inquiry into Brahman. Even Śaṃkara, whose emphasis on the utter transcendence of the Absolute could be expected to have belittled reason's role in our knowledge of Brahman, makes this clear by explicit statement and the pervasiveness of his critical approach. He says, 'Granted that it is the Vedānta statements which express the cause of the origin etc. of the world, inference too, provided it does not become opposed to the Vedānta statements, should not be rejected for strengthening our grasp of them, since argument can be reckoned helpful to the canonical scriptures.'[20]

Rāmānuja no less. His powerful use of argument especially to attack opposing viewpoints can be readily appreciated by even a perfunctory reading of the Summary and the Commentary. When the need arises, this tool is made to support and augment his own exegeses and conclusions. For Rāmānuja scriptural interpretation must make sense, and must be seen to make sense. While countering an Advaitic opponent he states, 'Not even for ratifying canonical scripture should what is wrong or contradictory be postulated.'[21] The course of this chapter and indeed of the book will illustrate how in Rāmānuja's case reason could be made to bolster and illuminate scriptural faith.

As noted before, Rāmānuja wrote his works in the Śrī Vaiṣṇava stream of devotional theism, which acknowledged Viṣṇu-Nārāyaṇa as supreme Lord. This stream was fed by many sources in Hindu tradition.[22] Chief among these were the religious fervour and verse of the Tamil saints (the Āḷvārs), the religious works of the Pañcarātra tradition, the voluminous literature of folklore and law (the *Śrauta, Gṛhya* and *Dharma Sūtras, purāṇas*, and *itihāsas* or 'epics'), and most important, what came to be called the *prasthānatraya* or three foundations of Vedāntic theology: (1) the *Upaniṣads* or culmination of the Vedas, (2) the *Bhagavadgītā*, and (3) the *Brahma Sūtras*. We must also not forget here the influence, positive and negative, exerted on Rāmānuja's thinking by rival views, which we shall take up presently. By Rāmānuja's time all these factors had given rise to a school of theology which revealed more and more explicitly and systematically its philosophical dualism. One pole of this dualism was the absolute principle, the supreme Brahman. The other was the finite, dependent order, and the two were sought to be preserved in an equilibrium which distinguished but did not separate them.

However much Rāmānuja may have imbibed and expounded Āḷvār and Pāñcarātrika spirituality later in life, especially after his conversion to the Śrī Vaiṣṇava community and the acceptance of its *ācārya*-ship, we are unable to say how much he was influenced by these traditions during his formative years. We cannot trace the precise impact of these writings in the development of his theological outlook. Rāmānuja's relationship with the Pañcarātra system is intriguing. According to W. G. Neevel it was a central if not the primary task of Yāmuna (Rāmānuja's *ācārya* precursor) to build upon 'a long and substantial tradition that was attempting to work out a harmonization between Pañcarātra and Vedānta' and indeed to show that 'even in the cases where there is a (seeming) contradiction or conflict, the injunctions of the Pañcarātra Āgamas are independently authoritative as equally valid alternatives (vikalpas) leading to the same end'.[23] This cannot be said to apply to Rāmānuja. Far from strengthening the impression of a 'harmonization' of Pāñcarātric and Vedāntic thought, throughout his writings he appears to retreat from this tendency, so great is his desire to make acceptable to the orthodox the Vedic credentials of his system. Thus, while Rāmānuja may well have endorsed the authoritativeness of Pañcarātra as a source of scriptural truth, he does not make much of it, and there is very little explicit identification between his views and those of Pañcarātra. Even in his most extended treatment of the teaching under *sūtras* II.2.41–2 (*Th*, II.2.42–3) in the Commentary, he keeps his distance from this school by such expressions as 'Thus they say' (*iti vadanti*), 'in this system' (*asmin tantre*), and 'the Sātvata scriptures . . .' (*sātvataśāstra-*).[24]

Again, there seems to be no explicit reference to Āḷvār works in Rāmānuja's writings, and this too is significant. However much it may (or may not) have been his intention 'to introduce the educated leadership of all Hindu society to the double tradition of Sanskritic and Tamil Vaiṣṇava theism, the Ubhaya Vedānta',[25] we have seen that all the works traditionally ascribed to him are in Sanskrit, their philosophical theology being grounded in the *prasthānatraya*.[26] The tenor of Rāmānuja's thinking and the tradition that all his works were in Sanskrit make it clear that, if he wished to publicise the Tamil Vaiṣṇava sources, he wished more to establish as universal a base as possible for his system. For this it was necessary to write in the *lingua franca* of orthodox Hindu scholarship – Sanskrit – and to appeal to sources with the widest scholarly and religious authority. This meant that, in the main, Rāmānuja attacked his opponents on common ground in so far as they sought similarly to accredit their views, and that he used common sources to state his own case.

We noted earlier that Rāmānuja's thinking was also influenced by rival points of view, and that this influence need not have been only negative. Countering the *pūrvapakṣin* or opponent was an essential part of Vedāntic method, and theologising was carried out with the aid of vigorous and often aggressive polemic. Indeed, the history of the Vedānta schools may well be described as a history of theological and exegetical controversy. The fact that Rāmānuja was first a disciple of Yādavaprakāśa, as also fully conversant with the views of Bhāskara, Yādava's counterpart – both being proponents of a form of theism in the tradition of Bhedābhedavāda[27] – must be borne in mind when assessing his theological stance. Certainly the influence these two thinkers exerted on him was not an entirely negative one.[28] Still, after Rāmānuja's induction into the Śrī Vaiṣṇava sect the philosophical shift in his dualist position must have been considerable, for though his thought has affinities with Bhedābhedavāda (and much depends on the precise meaning we give to this term) he himself was in no doubt as to his theological differences with those like his former mentor. This is seen from the stringent critiques of Bhedābhedavāda we encounter in his works.

The chief opposing views Rāmānuja dealt with were Advaita, Pūrvamīmāṃsā (i.e. the 'Prior School of Interpretation'), Bhedābhedavāda and Sāṃkhya, and, if it is true that Śaṃkara's writings represent a ceaseless battle against the Buddhists and Pūrvamīmāṃsakas, it seems equally true that it was to counter mainly Śaṃkara's awesome metaphysic and exegesis that Rāmānuja theologised.[29] Nevertheless, so far as the nature and use of language, especially scriptural language, were concerned – our chief interest in this chapter – both Śaṃkara and Rāmānuja had a common foe in a very influential contemporary view on the interpretation of the sacred texts. This was the Prābhākara school of Pūrvamīmāṃsā. Both used a common approach and sometimes common arguments to repudiate the Prābhākara, but differed significantly between themselves, as theologians within the same Vedāntic tradition, on the nature and scope of divine predication and other aspects of scriptural exegesis. In the remaining portion of this chapter we shall be largely concerned with Rāmānuja's understanding and rejection of the Prābhākara view of the nature of language, especially scriptural language. It is only on this basis that we can then go on to consider his theory of divine predication through which knowledge of Brahman is gained, and then the metaphysics of his system which itself could be shaped only upon the proper understanding of the scriptures. Our first step must be to discuss preliminary matters, not so much about the meaning of the scriptures as about scripture's origin and components (i.e. words and sentences).

Both the Prior and Later Schools of Interpretation (i.e. Pūrvamīmāṃsā and Uttaramīmāṃsā or Vedānta) are agreed that the canonical scriptures or Vedas are *apauruṣeya* or 'impersonal' as to the origin and disposition of their language. This does not mean that the Vedas have no personal *promulgator(s)* but that no personal agent, supreme or otherwise, has determined of his own accord the referential relation between Vedic words and their objects (i.e. the denotativeness of words), and the order in which these words occur in the Vedas.[30] There are important differences between the two camps as to the relative importance of the two main sections of the Vedas, the earlier ritual portion (*karmakāṇḍa*) and the later knowledge portion (*jñānakāṇḍa*), but there is no disagreement about the fact of *śruti*'s[31] impersonalness. Further, it was an accepted correlate of the Vedas' impersonalness that they are eternal.

To appreciate Rāmānuja's position here it will be useful first to outline his understanding of a characteristic Vedāntic belief: the recurrent production and destruction of the manifest world, and so apparently of the Vedas as a part of this world. He seemed to accept without question the tradition that the world periodically underwent two sorts of dissolution (followed by a reconstitution of things). One was a 'qualified dissolution', the other a 'great dissolution'. In the first, certain created entities of the celestial order were exempt from the periodic merging of determinate being back into the bosom of the ultimate Brahman. Chief among these was the demiurge Brahmā (not to be confused with Brahman), also called Prajāpati and Hiraṇyagarbha. In the second, every finite entity was 'reabsorbed' into Brahman, its ultimate source. In both cases, apparently, the Vedas suffered dissolution too, in so far as they were a part of the determinate, manifest order. Thus we are faced here with the question of what it means to say that the Vedas are 'eternal'. Again, it was part of the myth (though Rāmānuja did not necessarily regard it as such) that the Vedas were promulgated at the beginning of a world reconstitution, either by Brahman, in the case of a 'total' reconstitution, to Brahmā and then on to the primeval seers of mankind, or, in the case of a 'partial' world creation, by the latter agents themselves. What does this make of the Vedas' 'impersonalness'?

This is how Rāmānuja describes the actual process of the world's production (and the Vedas' promulgation) after a great dissolution:

> When a [great] dissolution comes to an end, the Blessed One, the supreme Person, remembers the previous configuration of the world, and having resolved, 'Let me be many', he diversifies [into individual entities] the whole aggregate of enjoyables [i.e. non-conscious beings] and their enjoyers [i.e. conscious beings], previously collapsed in himself as but his residual power. Having created as of old the Mahat etc. [i.e. the cosmic material principle(s)] and the Brahmā-Egg [or universe itself] right up to Hiraṇyagarbha, and having manifested the Vedas in their traditional order, he imparts them as before to Hiraṇyagarbha, instructing him as to the production of the world comprising the forms of the gods etc., while he himself remains as its inner Self.[32]

There is also a description of the production of the world after a partial dissolution,[33] in which Brahmā is again said to remember the powers and generic configurations of the primeval seers of a previous world-order and on this basis to fashion the individual forms of their successors. These seers, specially endowed with the requisite powers, directly perceive the Vedic texts without previously having studied them, and reproduce them unaltered in accent and form to be transmitted to posterity.

We can leave for a later chapter the interesting metaphysical questions raised by these mythic descriptions as to the immediacy and absoluteness of Brahman's creative causality and so on. Here we note that for Rāmānuja (and the other Vedāntins) Vedic promulgation, rather than being a genuine composition of the sacred texts, is the faithful reproduction of a physical medium (i.e. the Vedic words, sentences, sounds) that has always pre-existed. It is the empirical manifestation repeatedly in separate space–time continua (the periodically reconstituted worlds), by personal agents – the promulgators – of a transcendent deposit of truth. Even Brahman, the supreme Person, is said to remember[34] the Vedas in their form 'of old'. Thus, for Rāmānuja, the personal promulgation of the Vedas is compatible with their eternity and impersonalness ('impersonalness' being understood, as noted before, in the sense of there being no personal determiner of the denotativeness of Vedic words and of the order in which these words occur in the Vedas).

We shall come more specifically to the concept of 'impersonalness' in due course; let us say something more here about the Vedas' eternity. Since the world-cycles are beginningless as a process and potentially endless, they are in this sense eternal, and the empirical manifestation of the Vedas is also eternal in this sense.[35] But in what sense, we may ask, do the Vedas pre-exist (and indeed post-exist) eternally, and 'where' do they do this? Rāmānuja would answer that the Vedas in some way exist continuously, eternally, in the mind of Brahman – their source and goal – who is eternal. Just as during a great dissolution the aggregate of conscious and non-conscious beings remains deindividualised and collapsed in Brahman, in potency proximate as it were to individuation, so too the Vedas repose deep within the consciousness of Brahman in potency proximate to their pre-established empirical form. When the time for re-emitting the world arrives, they are evoked or manifested (Rāmānuja uses the Sanskrit term *āviskṛ* in this context) rather than composed by the supreme Person who transmits them via Brahmā and the ancients to mankind.

Rāmānuja appears to base the eternity of the Vedas on the natural eternity of Brahman. Brahman is their chief end; they exist to reveal him and to show the way to him and as such are dependent on him. Rāmānuja says,

> The Vedas in the form of injunctions, explanations and chants make known Nārāyaṇa, the highest Brahman's, proper form, the form of his worship and worship's special fruit. Like the supreme Person then, the collection of words called 'Veda', which makes known his proper form, his worship and the latter's fruit, is eternal.[36]

We may say, in fact, if a distinction current in mediaeval Christian scholasticism is helpful here, that the Vedas are rooted in Brahman's essence rather than in his will. Their periodic empirical manifestation (as of the world) may depend on the divine will, but their content – their structure and form – by revealing the divine essence (so far as this is possible) is directly rooted in it and cannot change since the divine essence at heart is unchanging. In short, if the supreme being is to be revealed through language, it must be in the form of the Vedas as we have them.

By this we are apprised of the primacy, indeed uniqueness, of Sanskrit, the language of the Vedas. As the sacred language Sanskrit was the paradigm of all language both for the Earlier Exegetes (the Pūrvamīmāṃsakas) and the Later (the Vedāntins). As such Sanskrit was more than worthy to be the language for pan-Indian Hindu culture and scholarship. Both types of exegete found Vedic words 'telling' in more than one respect. Auditorily speaking, it was crucial not only to receive and pass on the correct pronunciation (and sequence) of the canonical texts but also to accent them properly. For, as part of the sacred ritual ordained by the scriptures, the Vedic utterance correctly expressed was a necessary if not the sufficient condition to bring about the desired fruit of the sacrifice, promised by the scriptures. This harks back to the earlier emphasis, in the history of Brahminism, on the ritual as embodying its own dynamic and latent *brahman* or power which was released under controlled conditions by the officiating priests or brāhmaṇas (i.e. Brahmins) for establishing and maintaining macrocosmic and microcosmic order (*ṛta, dharma*). The Pūrvamīmāṃsakas stopped here. They were not particularly interested in the existence of a supreme entity or in divining its nature. For them the Vedic sacrifice and its various scriptural fruits were paramount, for, by putting into practice the rituals enjoined by scripture, the overall fruit of the preservation of cosmic order and the particular fruits of human welfare in this post-mortem lives, were guaranteed. All else was of secondary importance. Thus the Pūrvamīmāṃsakas studied the sacred texts as centring on the (mainly sacrificial) ritual, and analysed language in so far as it made the proper performance of the ritual possible. They developed basic rules for scriptural exegesis which in large measure were adopted by the Vedāntins.

The Vedāntins for their part had a totally different perspective on reality. They regarded the ethic underlying the sacrifice–fruit concern of the Pūrvamīmāṃsakas as a morally self-centred one, and valuable only as a stepping-stone to its own transcending. It was only after an individual had had his fill of this ego-centred ethic and become weary of the potentially endless stream of physical rebirth (*saṃsāra*) in which it enmeshed him that he was prepared to make the sacrifice that really mattered – that of his ego – and adopt a Brahman-centred way of life.

This won for him the fruit of such sacrifice: in this life liberating insight into the ultimate reality that was Brahman; and a *saṃsāra*-transcendent state, actual Brahman-realisation (whatever this was interpreted to be in the different schools), after death. Thus the Vedāntins were concerned primarily with the knowledge and attainment of Brahman, and to this end, as their name implies, concentrated on that part of the Vedas, the so-called 'knowledge section', which satisfied their concern: the *Upaniṣads* or Vedānta.

The two exegetical camps differed radically in their appreciation of the sacred texts in spite of their common recourse to them, yet both were to a great extent 'word-mechanics', intent, like all professional exegetes, on constructing systems of scriptural coherence, in which the analysis and interplay of semantic units were vital. Because of the differences, the Pūrvamīmāṃsā hermeneutic largely adopted by the Vedāntins was made to serve quite different Vedāntic ends. The seven-membered rule of Pūrvamīmāṃsaka exegetical technique was accepted in principle by the Vedāntins but applied to very different effect as they arrived at the *siddhāntas* (conclusions, final positions) of their various theological schools. Van Buitenen notes that this rule was embodied in the following statement:

> 'Initial and concluding statements, repetition, novel element of teaching, reward, description and argumentation are the characteristics by which the right interpretation is determined.' Most important are upakrama (introductory statement) and upasaṃhāra (terminating statement): the latter may never be in conflict with the former in order to establish the ekavākyatā[37] of a context.[38]

Though Rāmānuja too was influenced methodologically by this technique, he forcefully rejected the language-theory that the Prābhākaras, especially, associated with it.

We can now examine more closely the concept of the 'impersonalness' (*apauruṣeyatva*) of the Vedas as Rāmānuja seemed to understand it. We have already noted that for him impersonalness has two connotations. First, it refers to the precise sequence of words in the Vedas in their Sanskritic form; secondly, it refers to the denotative relation between Vedic word and its object. The latter sense should be emphasised, for it is usually either overlooked or unrecognised in such discussions and has important implications for Rāmānuja's theory of language, as we shall see later. As to the first sense Rāmānuja says,

> This is what the Veda's impersonalness and eternity mean: that it is by the specific sequence [of Vedic words] remembered by mental impressions generated in due order by preceding enunciations that [the present sequence] is enunciated. This applies equally to us and to the Lord of all. The difference is this, that the supreme Person irrespective of mental impressions himself apprehends [the sequence] directly.[39]

In other words, after partial dissolutions, the enunciation of the Vedic texts takes place by means of innate mental impressions (*saṃskāras*) in the minds of the promulgating seers. These, untutored, perceive with their mind's eye the precise form and sequence of the (Sanskritic) words that make up the *śruti* or canonical scriptures. Even the Lord himself follows the pre-established sequence, except that in his case, being perfect and omniscient, he intuits the Vedas rather than relies on the cognitively less perfect method of beholding innate mental impressions. Of course, the Lord takes the initiative of promulgation at the end of a great dissolution of the world. But in either case there is no question of the original composition of the scriptures. We have already considered the question of the Vedas' pre-existence and conformity with the Lord's essence, and of the sacrosanct nature of the Sanskrit language that the quotation implies. Let us here deal with the difference between the Vedas' impersonalness (in the first sense mentioned above) and the 'personal' (*pauruṣeya*) nature of ordinary, everyday (Sanskritic) parlance. The difference is that in ordinary speech, though the words used may be the same, the order of words is different from that of the *śruti*, an order depending on the personal determination of the speaker.[40] As such, ordinary speech does not have the normative authority or liberating power of the Vedas, and is accounted 'personal'. While there is a sharp contrast in a number of ways between Rāmānuja's (i.e. the classical Vedāntic) notion of 'revelation' and that of the great semitic religions, there is a strange similarity in the stress (at least with Islam) that the sacred word is at its most potent in the original language and form. This stress on the potency of the Sanskritic word is more clearly seen under the second aspect of impersonalness, which we shall now consider.

That Rāmānuja regarded the denotativeness of Vedic words, i.e. the referential relation between Vedic words and their objects, as part of the concept of impersonalness cannot be gainsaid. For, in each case, this referential relation, like the sequence of Vedic words, is an eternally fixed and determined one, and has not been established by any personal agent. As such it is part of the 'impersonalness' of the Vedas. In this connection

Rāmānjua quotes with approval *sūtra* I.1.5 from the *Karmamīmāṃsā Sūtras* – a seminal text for the Pūrvamīmāṃsakas especially – attributed to the sage Jaimini. This *sūtra* states, 'The relation of a word with its object is innate.'[41] Rāmānuja goes on to say,

> Just as fire has the natural power to heat, and the senses, like the eye etc., have the natural power to produce their specific cognitions, the [Vedic] word too has the natural power to denote . . . The power to denote is natural for such [Vedic] words as 'ox' because no [person-made] convention is known [regarding the referential relation between Vedic word and its object], there being no interruption in the beginningless deposition [of this connection]. Hence as in the case of fire's power to burn, and the senses' power to make known, we must acknowledge the [Vedic] word's power to denote.[42]

The analogies cited to illustrate the kind of denotative power of Vedic words are significant. Heat is *natural* to fire; part of what we mean by 'fiery' is 'hot'. Nobody can decree a change of this meaning. In the same way revealed words are naturally related to their particular objects. As such they have inherent meanings. There has been no pact or unilateral decision, there is no convention (*saṃketa*) known, human or divine, for establishing the relation between the Vedic word and its referent. Rāmānuja contrasts the conventional basis of gesture-language and personal appellations (such as 'Devadatta') with the inherent referentiality of Vedic words. In the former case we know either from tradition or through more direct evidence the determiners of the convention; in the latter instance we cannot, because there is no such determiner.[43]

This idea is elaborated in the Commentary in the context of children learning the use of Sanskrit. The point is carried in so far as the words learnt originate in the Vedas. The learning-situation, we are told, begins with 'ostensive definition', i.e by pointing at objects with the finger.

> Mother, father and others point with their finger to objects, i.e. to mother, father, uncle and others, the moon, animals [tame and wild], man, bird, snake, etc. intending, 'Now learn this' and 'Follow that.' The children, taught often enough that particular words relate to particular objects gradually perceive that cognition arises of its own accord[44] with respect to these words and objects. Not perceiving any other relation between word and its object and there being no knowledge of a personal determiner [of this relation], they are in no doubt that the application of such words to their objects is [denotatively] secure.[45]

It may not seem a very strong argument to say that Vedic denotativeness is inherent because we do not (and cannot) know of a personal determiner of this relationship; this argument may well sound circular. But it was part of the mystique of the Vedas, and it strengthened their authority, to give them a semi-autonomous status, even though Rāmānuja as a good theist sought to place their ultimate authority and source in the supreme being, Brahman.

However, as we have noted before (see n. 30), it was not any sort of Vedic word that had this innate referential power. In this context Rāmānuja speaks somewhat obscurely of 'naming' words; 'obscurely' because he does not explain what he means by 'naming' words, presumably because he took it for granted that his readers would understand his meaning. Nevertheless, from the examples Rāmānuja gives (see, for instance, the previous quotation) and from the early Pūrvamīmāṃsaka context out of which the discussion arose we may take it that the 'naming' word (*nāmaśabda*) was paradigmatically a (Vedic) substantive denoting a type of material entity, e.g. 'ox/cow', 'man', 'god', 'Indra' (as a type), 'stone'. Every naming-word had a pre-established referentiality to a particular object. Now Rāmānuja does not say explicitly whether the denotativeness of such substantives as *ātman*, referring to *non-material* substantival entities, was pre-established. We may take it that it was, and this point will become clearer when we discuss in a later chapter the mode of predication for Rāmānuja, especially in its theological context. A further question arises here: what exactly was the object of the naming-word, and indeed of all substantives referring to substantival existents, so far as Rāmānuja was concerned? We shall take this matter up in part later in this chapter, and in a wider context subsequently. For the time being we may understand by 'object' of a naming-word at least the natural (substantival) referent it denotes.

We can proceed now to Rāmānuja's treatment of the Prābhākara view on the nature of language, especially Vedic language. As noted before, the Prābhākara position in this respect was a very important one in Rāmānuja's (and Śaṃkara's) time and shaped almost on its own, through the dialectics of agreement and disagreement, the Vedāntic approach to the question. We shall see that it has contemporary relevance as well.

Rāmānuja states the Prābhākara view thus:

> Because it is impossible to learn the denotative power of language except through its use by one's elders, and since this use depends on

> the cognition of what-is-to-be-done [rather than of what-is-the-case], language as a [distinctive] source of knowledge [pramāṇa] concerns what is to be done. Therefore the Veda's purpose concerns only what is to be done. Thus the Vedānta texts cannot be regarded as the *pramāṇa* for some full-blown entity, the highest Brahman [which is not something-to-be-done].[46]

In other words, all language, including the Vedas, is essentially prescriptive rather than fact-assertive. Language has more or less point the more or less prescriptive it is. It fulfils its truest end when it enjoins action rather than describes what happens to be the case. The Vedas, as sacred language, indeed the paradigm of language, share this basic characteristic and are concerned essentially with action, especially the proper performance of the sacred ritual. They cannot be used as an authoritative source of knowledge for the existence and description of some transcedent full-blown entity such as Brahman. This would be to pervert their true end, which is not descriptive of reality, the asserting of what is the case, but prescriptive – the enjoining of action. Their paradigm linguistic form is the injunction (*vidhi*), mainly to sacrifice, and this is best expressed in the potential or optative mood (*vidhiliṅ*) in the Sanskrit. Other linguistic forms, such as explanatory statements (called *arthavāda*) or invocatory chants (*mantras*),[47] have point only in so far as they serve to accomplish, directly or indirectly, ritual action. In terms of the current debate in the West about the nature of religious language, the Prābhākara stance is a 'non-cognitivist' one.[48]

In what follows we have drawn together for cumulative effect the various strands of Rāmānuja's argument against the Prābhākara, taken from different places in his writings. We may discern two aspects to this critique: one negative, the other positive. In the former, Rāmānuja challenges the coherence and propriety of his opponent's view; in the latter, positive steps are taken to show that the Prābhākara understanding of the nature of language, especially Vedic language, is wrong.

Starting on the negative side we shall consider Rāmānuja's rejection of the basic feature of performability, which, it is claimed, invests language with purpose in general. The method followed is the usual one of classical Hindu discussion, the debate progressing through argument and counter-argument till the final position (the *siddhānta*) – the author's own – emerges as the culmination of the process. The opponent starts[49] by saying that performability can be explained in terms of the objective of the act of willing. What is this objective of the willing-act, asks Rāmānuja? That for the sake of which the action is done, the object of desire, answers the Prābhākara. The object of desire, counters Rāmānuja, distinguishing, can be either some thing or a state of affairs, i.e. the objective object (e.g. a post-mortem paradise, the birth of a son, a devoted wife), or the subjective object, i.e. some personal experience (e.g. joy), which incites the agent to desire the object. Action cannot have the first as its end, for to say that the objective object is action's concern is to make action subordinate to a state of affairs or the already existing thing in so far as action would be directed to such. Language, including the Vedas, whose purpose is to enjoin action would then need to be basically as fact-assertive as prescriptive in that it would have to assert and describe the factual end of action. And this would run counter to the Prābhākara position. The opponent is manoeuvred into accepting the second alternative – that is, into saying that the desired object for which action is primarily done is the subjective object, the agreeability generally experienced by persons doing voluntary action. Now, says Rāmānuja, warming to his theme, only pleasure is agreeable to man, nothing else. Even the cessation of pain is not what is agreeable, merely what is desirable; the desirable is not necessarily the agreeable. But, since it is also desirable to have pleasure, agreeability is often confused with desirability. In other words, in Rāmānuja's view, the discussion boils down to saying that for the Prābhākara the chief concern of action, and by implication of language, is agreeability, is pleasure. This was a derisory conclusion for an orthodox Hindu to maintain (and the Pūrvamīmāṃsakas prided themselves on being orthodox Hindus), for it made him a crypto-hedonist and an ally of the despised materialists (*cārvākas*). Under cover of unbounded reverence for the sacred ritual and the writings in which it was commended and enjoined, was not the Prābhākara saying that the chief concern of holy scripture was the pursuit of pleasure? The conclusion is that the Prābhākara cannot offer any acceptable explanation of the performability which for him bestows meaning and purpose to (sacred) language. So much for Rāmānuja's negative thesis. Let us now consider his more positive arguments against the opponent.

We shall examine three arguments of Rāmānuja's to establish that language, the *śruti* not excepted, is basically fact-assertive. In other words, that language, both secular and sacred, is properly used for conveying information about the existence and nature of things without in the process subserving the ulterior motive of enjoining some action. Rāmānuja does not spell out the logic of these arguments nor co-ordinate them as we have done, but I think an examination of his general position will justify our construction.

First, he shows that language is commonly used fact-assertively (and that it can be learnt in a non-performative context). He gives interesting illustrations. For example, we can consider the case where a bystander, conversant with sign-language, observes and understands a message describing a state of affairs (e.g. 'The stick is lying in the inner room') communicated by signs to a messenger for a third party, Devadatta. He accompanies the messenger as he delivers his message *in speech* to Devadatta. The bystander is ignorant of this tongue, but he rightly has no doubt, Rāmānuja points out, that the sense of the gestures – and this is a factual rather than a prescriptive sense – has been conveyed merely by the use of words. Further, if the bystander is acutely observant, he may gather that a particular word refers to a particular thing, and this has been learnt in a non-performative context. How can it be denied then that language is fitted for conveying information in its own right (i.e. is basically fact-assertive), since this situation is commonly illustrative of the use and learning of language?[50]

Though the focus of Rāmānuja's debate with the Prābhākara was the nature and purpose of the canonical scriptures or *śruti*, he was aware that the argument had to be extended to language in general, since the *śruti* was only a special case of language. Now the Prābhākaras did not deny that language could commonly be used fact-assertively, i.e. to convey information, as in the statement 'The stick is lying in the inner room.' But they inclined to the view that this was not language's most important or proper end and that language fulfilled the purpose of its existence in and through some related (course of) action (which could be deliberately *not* doing something), e.g. fetching the stick, or not beating the dog with it. The point of language was to tell you how to behave, not how things were. At least, this is what Rāmānuja understood the Prābhākara's position to be. Further, they believed that language could be properly learnt only if words were taught in connection with actions, and the learning-situation made use of prescriptive-type utterances. Thus the Sanskrit word *daṇḍa* should be learnt as denoting a stick in connection with some action, such as fetching a stick, through an injunction. The latter could be expressed either as a direct command – 'Fetch the stick' – or paradigmatically as a recommendation in the optative mood (speaking Sanskritically): 'He should fetch the stick', or 'May he/Let him fetch the stick.' If words are learnt properly only in a performative context, then, concluded Rāmānuja's opponents, making what might well appear an unwarranted leap logically, language itself has action for its chief concern and the injunction is the prime vehicle of expression. This reasoning was directed towards affirming the primacy of the sacred ritual on the one hand, and of the related Vedic injunctions on the other.

When it came to the canonical scriptures the debate assumed crucial importance. The *śruti* was accepted by orthodox Hindus to be a sound and distinctive source of knowledge (since it partook of the pramāṇic nature of language/speech as testimony) about that not cognisable from any other *pramāṇa*. The object of *śruti*, in contrast to that of the mundane *pramāṇas*, was the trans-empirical, the 'unseen' (*adṛṣṭa*). For the Prābhākaras the unseen that really mattered was the trans-empirical and (but for the scriptures) unknown (*apūrva*) connection between the sacred ritual and its fruit (which was often realised in the future, or in post-mortem existences). The *śruti* affirmed and gave knowledge of this connection so that the sacrifice, the essence of sacred ritual, could be performed. In this way the main goal of the scriptures was the performance of the sacrifice; conveying information about the existence and nature of trans-empirical entities (e.g. the gods, Brahman), even if it could be regarded as doing this, was not what scripture was about. Rāmānuja and the other Vedāntins disagreed, of course. The sacrifice was part, even an important part, of the concern of scriptural revelation; but the primary aim of scripture was the knowledge and attainment of Brahman, the transcendent Absolute. And for this end, maintained Rāmānuja, the *śruti* was essentially no less fact-assertive than prescriptive in fulfilling its pramāṇic function. 'If the Vedas are a *pramāṇa* they make known, from the collection of injunctions, explanations and formulae, a whole multitude of previously unknown and mutually compatible things as they really are; and the Vedas are a *pramāṇa* (of course . . . .'[51] It was an essential function of *śruti* to affirm the existence and nature of existing things as they really were, not only to issue injunctions about the ritual. In the *Vedāntasāra* (I.1. 21) and again in the Summary (para. 135) Rāmānuja quotes with approval the dictum of Dramiḍācārya, a shadowy, earlier teacher recognised as authoritative both by him and by Śaṃkara, which affirmed the fact-assertive nature of the scriptures: 'The scriptures state things as they really are.'[52]

Rāmānuja's next argument, by drawing out the implications of the opponent's own view, seeks to lay bare its inadequacy. The argument is borrowed from an earlier work (the *Dramiḍabhāṣya*), where it is pointed out that, even if scripture were intent on praising the sacrificial act, the praise itself would make no sense without something as objective referent. Rāmānuja elaborates on this.[53] The scriptures speak just as much of the unseen gods to whom the sacrifice is offered, and of the unseen virtues of the sacrifice, as of the excellence of the sacrificial act itself. The whole complex must be affirmed together, for *śruti's* talk of the excellence of the sacrifice is of a piece with its affirmation of the existence of the gods and the various unseen features of the sacrifice. Indeed, this affirmation enhances the excellence of the sacrifice. Thus, even if the prescription of the sacrifice were the primary aim of *śruti*, *śruti* must at the same time affirm the existence and nature of those unseen things that are part of the sacrificial complex. And, since it is agreed that the *śruti* is a *pramāṇa*, this affirmation must be veridical. The way is open then for affirming the existence, nature and importance of the supreme Brahman in the knowledge section of the canonical texts.

Well then, it may be argued, even the knowledge section of the Vedas, i.e. the *Upaniṣads*, is concerned primarily with enjoining action – the action of meditating upon Brahman. Rāmānuja has considered this objection in the Commentary and recounts a charming story, of ancient pedigree, to illustrate his response.[54] A little prince, too young to be aware of his birthright, gets lost while playing. He is found by an upright Brahmin who is ignorant of the child's parentage but who brings him up in the way of the scriptures. When the youth is sixteen he discovers who he really is and how illustrious a father he has. The King too learns that his long-lost son is safe and well and that he has been brought up in the proper manner, and is eager to see him. It is only *after* both have acquired the relevant bits of information about each other, says Rāmānuja, that they wish to and are able to establish contact. The action of meeting in an informed and whole-hearted way is logically dependent upon acquiring the right information. In the same way, it makes no sense for scripture to enjoin meditation upon Brahman, and to encourage this, without first establishing his existence and nature. The *śruti* is nothing if not intrinsically and significantly fact-assertive.

The third and final argument we shall consider probes deeper into the nature of language. We have seen that for Rāmānuja so-called naming words are innately related to their real objects. We can ask now what exactly is the object (*artha*) of a naming-word? For both the Pūrvamīmāṃsakas and the classical Vedāntins, the naming-word was directly related to its 'generic configuration' or *ākṛti*. Rāmānuja's view on what this meant was influenced by the early Mīmāṃsā metaphysic of word-theory, and perhaps the most important figure to influence the shape of this particular metaphysic was Śabara (c. 400 CE), who discussed this question in his seminal commentary on Jaimini's *Karmamīmāṃsā Sūtras*. Even then there are many gaps, and much scope for varying interpretations on important points remains. Still, by all accounts it seems that the *ākṛti* is a real entity of tenuous metaphysical status, a sort of composite, class-contour or concrete universal in virtue of which members of a particular class become individuated. The (Vedic) naming-word is related directly and innately to its own *ākṛti* and through the *ākṛti* immediately (but not innately) to all the real individuals subsumed by the *ākṛti*.[55] The non-innateness of the relation between word and its individual referents (rather than *ākṛti*) makes it possible for these referents to come into existence and perish, as individuals do, without affecting the pre-established and eternal nature of the relation between the word and its *ākṛti* in the first place. (We can assume that, as in the case of the Vedas themselves, this relation exists, during a dissolution period, in a potency proximate to its realisation.) There are grounds for saying that for Śabara, as for Rāmānuja, only substantival material entities are subsumed under *ākṛtis*, and it is not clear what *modus operandi* he envisaged for the predication of terms referring to non-material entities. In any event, for both Śabara and Rāmānuja the (Vedic) word *gau* ('ox') refers directly to the ox-*ākṛti* and through this denotes all individual (perishable) oxen. M. Biardeau has plausibly argued[56] that Śabara maintained a (subtle) distinction between the *ākṛti* and the *jāti* (generic characteristic) of an object, a distinction which was soon conflated by subsequent commentators and thinkers.

It is not clear what Rāmānuja's position is on the subtler issues (on occasion he does seem to have made the conflation mentioned above), but that he did accept the *ākṛti*-theory is clear enough. According to this theory then, certain individual (substantival, material) objects could be regarded as real (non-eternal) projections of their *ākṛti*, and as an essential part of the appropriate (Vedic) word's denotative embrace. In other words, these Vedic terms have an inherent objectivity, an inner impetus demanding fruition in the real existence of the particular members subsumed by their *ākṛtis*. The Vedic word *gau*, for instance, has an inner dynamic through its *ākṛti* towards the production of real oxen. Rāmānuja as a fully fledged monotheist rationalises this creative power of Vedic words by locating it ultimately in the essence of, and by mediating it through the will of, Brahman. Yet he reveres the mystique of Vedic creativity sufficiently to acknowledge the (at least) logical priority of the word – object (*ākṛti*) relation as a guide even for the divine will in the originative production of things, as the following extract clearly implies:

> All the Vedic [naming] words make known their objects/meanings[57] as terminating in the supreme Self. All the Vedic words having been extracted in the beginning from the Veda by the highest Brahman, he

> then created, as of old, all the kinds of being, the words being, as of old, applied as names to these beings which find their fulfilment in the supreme Self.[58]

The conclusion of our argument is this: to say thus that the Vedic word has an innate denotative power demanding fruition in the ultimate production of real things is to say that the *śruti* tends towards the affirmation of the real, that it is by implication fact-assertive.

But the preceding quotation makes a further point: that the Vedic word's denotative reach does not end in natural objects; this is only its first-order stopping-place. On the contrary, Vedic words terminate referentially in Brahman, the very ground of being. This establishes more firmly in Rāmānuja's thinking that the *śruti* has an essential fact-assertive function implied by the fact that the first-order and second-order denotative terminus of Vedic words is *being*. How exactly Rāmānuja explains this will be matter for detailed consideration in a later chapter, but we may enlarge a little here on the point of the relation between sacred language, finite being and Brahman.

Rāmānuja's broad view on this relation is well brought out in a linguistically interesting and theologically profound analysis he gives to the mystic syllable OM (also called the Praṇava). This syllable is composed of the three letters A, U, M, which in combination (in the Sanskrit) produce the sound O(H)M. It was regarded by the great Vedāntins as in some unparalleled way symbolising and expressing the Absolute. The occasion for Rāmānuja's analysis is his exegesis of a section of the *Śvetāśvatara Upaniṣad.* The analysis is involved but it repays scrutiny.

> The Praṇava has been said to be the root of the whole collection of the Vedas, and the A [the first letter of the Praṇava] is the root of the Praṇava. That is, the Vedas, but a transformation of the Praṇava, are resolved in it, their root, the Praṇava itself being a transformation of the A and resolved in the A which is *its* root. Now, since only that one who is the highest being expressed by the A, which is the Praṇava's root, is the great Lord, it is Nārāyaṇa who is the great Lord, since it is he alone who is expressed by the A, the root of the whole collection of words, and is the [ontological] root of the whole collection of beings.[59]

Not only does this statement affirm that OM as the sum of the Vedas is *the* word expressive of Brahman, but it intimates that Brahman is at the same time the principle of being and the principle of intelligibility (in and through the Vedas, the model of language and the most perfect linguistic medium of expression – hence 'Sanskrit', from *saṃskṛta* meaning 'perfect'). In other words, we have here the notion of a structural correspondence between language and reality; that is, language and reality in a real sense reflect a common *morphē* or form, converging and culminating in Brahman. We shall return to this topic later in the book.

As a result of the discussion so far we can see that for Rāmānuja the Vedas as language and as pramāṇic were essentially fitted for the conveying of information about the transcendent. They gave out a revelation which though propositional was inerrant once it had been interpreted correctly. This teaching could not be sublated by a contrary and 'higher' wisdom. By this was cut at the root Śaṃkara's distinction between a lower knowledge of Brahman based on the dualism of the Vedas and a higher knowledge which was monistic and final and which sublated the former. Rāmānuja did not deny that Veda-derived information about Brahman was indirect and imperfect. For him the liberating insight to be gained in this life was direct and presentational (*sākṣātkāra*). But it was an important part of his theological position to maintain that, so far as it went, Veda-based information was neither misleading nor errant.

To say, however, that the Vedas were inerrant, that they gave true information about the transcendent, did not lighten the task of their interpretation. It was crucial to interpret them correctly because a false understanding did not lead to liberation, man's ultimate state. As already noted, the emphasis laid on sound scriptural exegesis resulted in great doctrinal battles among the Vedāntins, and belies the widespread and superficial assumption that Hinduism has always been a doctrinally tolerant religion in the sense that in matters of belief anything would do. This is not to deny that in the main Hinduism has been intellectually a fairly open religion, at least much more so than the semitic religions (intolerance manifested itself mainly in orthopraxy rather than orthodoxy). Among the Hindus there is no history of a central, ecclesiastical magisterium empowered to promulgate sacrosanct verbal formulae, and to anathematise dissenters, as in Christianity. True, for orthodox theologians the absoluteness of the Vedas was a datum, but within particular traditions of interpretation their understanding was not tied to the infallibility of a conciliar proclamation. This made it possible for Hindu theologians, in spite of their doctrinally conservative role, to reinterpret creatively (though, as we have seen, under the pretext of faithful transmission) the deposit of teaching handed down to them, in the light of insights and conceptual models from other schools.

Rāmānuja expresses this open attitude towards rival systems (e.g. the Sāṃkhya) in his commentary, in the *Śrī Bhāṣya*, on II.2.42:

> What is rejected in the *Brahma Sūtras* in respect of the principles of being taught by Sāṃkhya is only that these principles do not have Brahman for their self (or inner principle), not the essence of the system. In the Yoga and Paśupati teachings also, it is the Lord's being only the efficient cause of the world, the contradictory conceptions about the mutually related principles of being, and those practices outside the Vedic pale that are rejected, not the essence of Yoga or Paśupati [teaching]. So it is said [in scripture]: The Sāṃkhya, Yoga, Pañcarātra and Pāśupata (systems) and the Vedas are *pramāṇas* for the Self: they must not be dismissed by polemic.[60]

Again, we have seen that Rāmānuja was much influenced by Pūrvamīmāṃsaka exegetical method. But if the quotation illustrates an intellectual openness it also indicates that doctrinal commitments within the schools were quite firm – there was no desire among the classical theologians to wallow in the amorphous soup of syncretism. Rāmānuja was keen to preserve the doctrinal rectitude of his sect, and to this end, nearer home, when it came to an opponent also professing a Vedāntic base, he was often scathing in his criticism. He reserved his choicest jabs for Bhedābhedavāda and Advaita. Thus in the Commentary, at the beginning of his refutation of the main Advaitic standpoint, Rāmānuja castigates his Advaitic opponents as thinkers deficient in logic and bereft of the Lord's grace.[61] Śaṃkara too, for all the breadth and penetration of his thinking, is unequivocal that in the end it is correct scriptural understanding and the rejection of false views that matter. 'There are many misguided teachings', he warns, 'based on [sound] reasoning and quotation, mixed with the appearance only of these. One accepting any of this without duly discriminating would be kept away from the highest goal and would go to ruin.'[62] The Vedāntic theologians made no compromise in their search for truth and were as eager as their counterparts in other religions to determine it, however elusive it might be.

We can now sum up the discussions of this chapter. After introductory comments about Rāmānuja's place in the tradition, his various works and the influences under which he laboured, we discussed the relation between scriptural faith and reason in Rāmānuja's (and Vedāntic) thought. All this was propaedeutic to the examination of Rāmānuja's theory of the nature of language in general and of the Vedas in particular *vis-à-vis* the main opposing standpoint, that of the Prābhākaras. Preliminary questions were taken up in this context too, chiefly concerning the impersonalness and eternity of the Vedas, before we proceeded to examine Rāmānuja's refutation of the Prābhākara. In the process, it is hoped, Rāmānuja's (and indeed the Vedāntic) attitude to the scriptures has been revealed. By his treatment of the Prābhākara Rāmānuja hoped to establish the fact-assertive nature of language, especially of the *śruti* in relation to the existence and nature of Brahman, man's most important and ultimate goal. Further, since the *śruti* was pramāṇic it contained veridical information about this goal. But the task of scriptural interpretation, though not an intellectually closed one, had to proceed along definite and traditional lines; it was thus that the scriptures could be made to yield the right cognition about their chief object. It is to this process and its conclusions in Rāmānuja's thought that we now turn.

2 Predication and Meaning

I

In Chapter 1 we saw how Rāmānuja sought to establish that language in general and scripture in particular are intrinsically fact-assertive and not essentially prescriptive only, as the Prābhākaras maintained. This means that the sacred texts, as pramāṇic, are able to convey veridical information about their chief object and man's final end (not determinable from any other *pramāṇa*) – the ultimate reality, Brahman. But veridical information about Brahman is not easily extracted from the scriptures: they have to be interpreted correctly. We can understand how Rāmānuja went about this only after saying much more about his understanding of (1) the general relation between language and reality, and (2) the predication of terms, especially in its theological context. In other words, in this chapter we shall focus chiefly on the way language works to yield (especially divine) information for Rāmānuja; in the process we shall get an idea of what Brahman was for him. Further, if Rāmānuja's chief opponent as to the fact-assertive nature of language was the Prābhākara, once this issue was settled the main rival position he faced regarding scriptural teaching about Brahman, within the Vedāntic camp and in terms of which he articulated his own view, was the increasingly influential one of Advaita. The Advaitic stance clearly derived from Śaṃkara, but by Rāmānuja's time (over 200 years after the master Advaitin's death) it had been developed in important respects by Śaṃkara's various followers. Thus as the discussion proceeds we shall have to keep one eye, as did Rāmānuja, on the Śaṃkarite, if not always on Śaṃkara's *pûrvapakṣa* (rival position).

Śaṃkara taught that the *śruti* points to a Brahman that is ultimately non-dual (*advaita*) – i.e. the only reality, the One without a second (*ekam eva-advitīyam*) – non-differentiated (*nirviśeṣa*) and ineffable (*avācya*), and that, simply as a stepping-stone to the liberating insight, the śruti affirms an omnipotent and omniscient Lord as the personal object of worship and devotion in the framework of an ontological dualism. Rāmānuja rightly saw that this view, which by his time had begun to bestride rivals like a Colossus, presaged the withering-away of the flowering tree of true devotion (*bhakti*). As *ācārya* of his sect he had realised that the only effective counter-measure was to construct a monotheistic system, grounded in the accepted scriptures, which was at the same time intellectually respectable and religiously satisfying. His general strategy was to show that no accredited *pramāṇa* could establish a non-dual, non-differentiated Brahman. Rāmānuja seems to have accepted only three *pramāṇas* as valid: perception, inference and the word (i.e. speech/language) as testimony. It was not difficult to show that the first two could not accomplish Śaṃkara's end. Perception's object remains within the bounds of sense, and Brahman transcends these.[1] In Vedāntic philosophy, inference arrives at its truth on the basis of perceptual knowledge and shares perception's limitations with respect to establishing a transcendent, infinite being.[2] There remains only the testimony of the word, specifically the revelation of the scriptures. It was at this point that the crux of the matter was reached.

If Rāmānuja could show that language *per se* was unable to establish a monistic Brahman, the way was open for him to interpret scripture – but a special case of language – in the theologically dualist way he favoured. In order to show this, he has recourse to his view of a structural correspondence between language and being. He argues as follows:

> Language, by virtue of its own differentiation, is capable of making known an entity-with-differentiation only, since language acts through words and sentences. Now, to be a word is to be possessed of radical element and suffix,[3] and it cannot be denied that the word, in that its radical element and suffix correspond to difference within the object, makes known a differentiated object. Further, the difference in words relates to the difference in objects. The sentence too, therefore, which is a form of association of words, is incapable of making known a non-differentiated entity, by virtue of its denoting a particular group of various kinds of object. Thus language (in word and sentence) cannot be a *pramāṇa* for a non-differentiated entity.[4]

In other words, Rāmānuja's argument, which is based on Sanskrit's being the model for language (something no contemporary Vedāntin was likely to dispute, for reasons gone into in the last chapter), is as follows. Language is composed of words and sentences. Considering the word first, it is constituted of radical element and suffix. Through its radical element a particular word keeps its root sense in various verbal forms, but through its different suffixes it undergoes differentiation as to gender, number and case. For example, take the root *jñā* (to know), which we shall see later Rāmānuja himself considers in similar context. All word-forms deriving from *jñā* share the root sense of 'know' (which is different from the root sense of 'love' or 'sleep', for instance) but differ as to their individual forms and case-endings (e.g. *jñapti*, knowing; *jñātṛ*, (masc., fem., neuter) a knower; *jānāmi*, I know). The point is that the word (e.g. the 'know' root) must be inherently susceptible of differentiation in its various forms and suffixes – e.g. 'knowing'; (sing. or pl.) 'knower(s)'; (masc., fem.) 'knowers' – in order to adequate to differentiation in its referents: (e.g. knowing-act; (one or more) knower(s); (male, female) knowers). Thus differentation in words necessarily corresponds to differentiation in referents. Now the sentence, which is at least an association of words, *a fortiori* reflects, in similar manner but in greater complexity, differentiation in and of objects. Therefore language – no less scriptural language – as constituted from words and sentences, is intrinsically incapable of making known pure, non-differentiated being, such as the Brahman of the Advaitins. On the contrary, language can act as a *pramāṇa* only for differentiated being. Unfortunately, it cannot be our business here to provide a critical appreciation of this argument. Such a policy followed consistently would result in a book at least twice the length of this one. But we can understand at least what Rāmānuja meant by affirming a structural correspondence between language and being. This ties in with his understanding of the mystic syllable OM as symbolising most potently the fact of Brahman's being, at the same time, the source and end of language and reality (see Ch. 1).

We can pursue this matter of the relationship between language and reality in Rāmānuja's thinking, in its theological context (which focused the Vedāntic concern), by considering Rāmānuja's refutation of the Advaitic view on the way language intimates Brahman, the ultimate reality. In the process we shall be apprised of not only Rāmānuja's theory of (especially divine) predication but also his view of the nature of Brahman. This refutation, in fact, takes account of the Advaitic position on (1) the word and (2) the sentence as descriptive of Brahman.

(1) In Rāmānuja's discussion, the Advaitic opponent's favourite term to designate his Absolute is *jñaptimātra* (Pure-Knowing).[5] Indeed, he argues, it is not being claimed that language either as word or sentence is a *pramāṇa* for establishing the self-luminous, non-differentiated Absolute. Such an Absolute, being self-established, has no need of a *pramāṇa*. Once all terms ratified by scripture to designate the Absolute have been purified of the various differentiations they ordinarily

connote (and which, if they remained, would wrongly colour our understanding), the self-luminous Absolute 'of its own accord stands forth'. 'Pure Knowing' is just the most appropriate expression to encapsulate the non-differentiated Absolute, once its empirical connotations of limited knowerhood (e.g. male or female) have been removed. Rāmānuja rejects this on the grounds that this term, no less than any other selected, is inherently capable of intimating only a differentiated entity. We have seen how he argues this in general. With respect to the particular term under consideration he says:

> 'To know [*jñā*] refers to awareness and as such on the basis of its radical element we know that there is a particular activity with subject and object and with a specific nature distinguishing it from other kinds of activity. From the suffixes we know of sex, number and so on. Even if knowing is self-established, it could not be established as of this nature, i.e. that it is without differentiation. In fact knowing is said to be self-established in so far as it is its very nature to be the means of [establishing] something else.[6]

No term then, not even the favourite designation of the Advaitin, can properly intimate a non-differentiated Brahman.

The thrust of Rāmānuja's argument, as I see it, is not that it is impossible for terms to be purified of empirical connotations and made to bear meaningfully upon some transcendent, perfect reality. In fact we shall see in due course that Rāmānuja himself subscribes to a view in which only a purified use of language can designate the supreme being. His argument is rather that the empirical evacuation of terms to the point of signifying absolute non-differentiation destroys the very fabric of language as we know it and by implication nullifies the *raison d'être* of the scriptures. Scripture exists to instruct us primarily about the nature of and the way to the ultimate. It can function as a conveyor of instruction only through its own adequation with reality. This it does as inherently differentiated in the way we have described. The ultimate, then, scripture's prime object, cannot be absolutely non-differentiated. For the connection between scripture as language and scripture as a *pramāṇa* for the trans-empirical ultimate would vanish. As a result scripture would lack the very basis for its own reliability as a source of distinctive knowledge about the ultimate.

(2) We come now to Rāmānuja's refutation of the Advaitic view about how sentences describing (a) the nature of Brahman and (b) Brahman's

relation to the world should be interpreted. These are the two kinds of statement at the centre of the discussion,[7] and to represent them we choose the key scriptural texts: 'Brahman is reality, knowledge, infinite' (*TaiUp*, II.1.1[8]), and 'That you are' (*ChāndUp*, e.g. VI.8.7), respectively. A crucial consideration here is Rāmānuja's understanding of the syntactical rule of *correlative predication* (*sāmānādhikaraṇya* in Sanskrit), which we shall refer to as 'CP' for short. Again it must be kept in mind that the Vedāntic discussion in this respect takes place with reference to Sanskrit. CP is a very important concept for our purposes because the main scriptural statements of the two kinds distinguished above (the ones selected as representative not excepted) conform syntactically to CP. Their correct interpretation would depend on a correct understanding of CP. Our theologian has defined CP in several places in his works, and in almost exactly the same words. In the Summary we have, 'The experts say that correlative predication is the application to one object of more than one word having different grounds for their occurrence.'[9] Now there are two levels, so to speak, to the concept of CP: (i) a grammatical one, and (ii) an ontological one.

(i) Here two or more non-synonymous terms having the same case-ending in Sanskrit are applied to the same referent. The Sanskrit equivalents of the statements, 'Brahman is reality, knowledge, infinite' (i.e. *satyaṃ jñānam anantaṃ brahma*) and 'That you are' (*tat tvam asi*) have the grammatical form of CP. Thus, in the first example, the non-synonymous terms *satyam* ('reality'), *jñānam* ('knowledge'), *anantam* ('infinite') and *brahma*, all having the same (neuter nominative, possibly accusative) case-ending, are applied to their (real) referent, Brahman, the ultimate. Where an expression occurs in which the related words in the Sanskrit do not possess the same case-ending (e.g. *utpalaṃ hrade*: 'The lotus *is in* the lake'), *vaiyadhikaraṇya* or non-correlative predication obtains.[10] The point is that the Vedāntins took the grammar of correlatively predicated statements to have certain ontological implications.

(ii) Here lies the crux of the matter. Rāmānuja argues that it is the whole point of CP that it implies differentiation not only between individual objects but also within the individual object. In other words, the correlatively predicated expression indicates that a particular thing (i.e. the referent) is the locus of a co-presence of more than one determination such that it gives grounds for the predication of several non-synonymous terms in respect of it. When we say, by way of CP, that Devadatta is young, swarthy, magnanimous and well-bred (to use an example of Rāmānuja's) we imply that one and the same object (i.e.

Devadatta himself) is the locus of the co-presence of the physical and mental attributes mentioned above. Generally speaking then, CP has an objective reference to differentiation in one and the same referent. Now, it is an accepted tenet of scriptural exegesis that the rules of everyday linguistic usage must be presumed to apply to scripture too. Thus, Rāmānuja concludes, correlatively predicated Vedānta statements about Brahman intimate that their referent is 'determined by this or that qualifier', i.e. is really differentiated.[11] It is in this context that Rāmānuja's understanding of CP differs significantly from Śaṃkara's. It was not to Śaṃkara's purpose to deny that CP intimates differentiation in the referent in everyday circumstances, but his exegeses show that in the case of correlatively predicated scriptural texts about Brahman our ordinary expectations of the rules of grammar are to be put aside. Both Śaṃkara and Rāmānuja are agreed that in the case of Brahman correlatively predicated terms are to be taken in a grammatically and epistemologically unitary sense with respect to their referent; but they disagree about these terms' ontological implications. Śaṃkara maintains that the epistemological differentiation is to be taken as a subjective phenomenon only; that is, we cannot help but think and speak differentiatedly of the really non-differentiated Absolute. But, in fact, the informed act of divine predication, by a process of the purification of its terms, should yield a predominantly apophatic understanding of its referent. Rāmānuja, on the other hand, holds that the epistemological differentiation does have objective grounds, and that there is to be a literal bias in the predication of terms of Brahman.

We can now examine Rāmānuja's refutation of the Advaitic interpretation of the *Taittirīya* text 'Brahman is reality, knowledge, infinite.' On this basis we can go on to consider his own understanding of the statement. Rāmānuja pays closest attention to the Advaitic *pūrvapakṣa* in the Commentary.[12] The opponent starts by giving examples of quality-denying and of quality-affirming texts about Brahman. He then argues that, since quality-denying texts are logically consequent upon the other, they are the more authoritative. Hence Brahman is to be understood as finally qualityless (*nirguṇa*). Now, it is significant that among the more obvious examples of the *nirguṇa* texts (e.g. 'Neither gross nor fine, neither short nor long' – *BĀUp*, III.8.8) is included the apparently positive *Taittirīya* statement under consideration. This is because, as a traditionally accepted definitional statement of Brahman, it was supposed to be among the most authoritative texts; as such for the Advaitin it had to be included among the (superior) *nirguṇa* texts. This gives us a clue as to how the Advaitin was constrained to interpret it, i.e.

apophatically. Rāmānuja then starts the Advaitic interpretation of the text, and a very sophisticated one it is too. But, for all its development in a number of ways we cannot go into here, there can be no doubt that at heart it is Śaṃkara's own interpretation as given in his *Taittirīya Upaniṣad* commentary.

The main points of the (by-now developed) Advaitic interpretation considered by Rāmānuja are as follows. First, in so far as the text instantiates CP it is meant to express a *unitary sense* (so *ekārtha*) rather than make a point about the unity of the referent. A shift has taken place here from the ontological aspect of CP towards the epistemological one. The Advaitin presses this shift home by going on to intimate that this unitary sense denotes a non-differentiated Brahman. This is argued for on the grounds that, if we gave the terms of the statement a literalist (i.e. differentiation-affirming) interpretation, then from their abstract form (i.e. 'reality', 'knowledge') we should have to infer a separate (Brahman) referent for at least the two 'positive' (qualifier) terms. The text would then be referring to two Brahmans (i.e. the Brahman that is reality, and the Brahman that is knowledge, however this might be understood) and such an interpretation would at the very least militate against the rule that CP refers to a single entity.

Then, answers Rāmānuja, in the guise of an objector, the terms of the statement, as resulting in the unitary sense that denotes a completely non-differentiated referent, would have to be taken as synonymous. In that case, what would be the point of scripture's using more than one (qualifier) term (and a scriptural statement, especially a definitional one, does not use terms idly)? Rāmānuja is trying to force the ontological implications of CP, as understood by him, upon the opponent: that is, that there are *objective* grounds for correlatively predicating apparently non-synonymous terms of the referent. His opponent will have none of it. 'Listen attentively', he says,

> as to how there is non-synonymity, notwithstanding [the text's] signifying a unitary sense. . . . We know that by definition Brahman has a nature contrary to every other kind of being; consequently every nature contrary [to Brahman] is set aside by this trio of words. The word 'reality' sets Brahman apart from 'unreal' being in so far as the latter is the substrate of change. The word 'knowledge' sets Brahman apart from non-conscious being since the latter depends on something else (i.e. consciousness) for its illumination. And the word 'infinite' sets Brahman apart from the limited in space, time and being. . . . In thus making known a single entity's nature as contrary to everything

> else, these three words at the same time have point, a unitary sense and are non-synonymous. Therefore we can say that there is but one Brahman, a light unto itself, and purged of all differentiation.[13]

In other words, the apparently positive terms 'reality' and 'knowledge' do not express what Brahman is; rather they hint at what Brahman is not, i.e. 'not non-being', 'not non-conscious'. The adjectival 'infinite' has a very important function too. It so to speak projects our understanding of the other terms into the transcendent order by removing every limitation from Brahman. The three terms taken in combination intimate an infinitely real Brahman which is consciousness itself. No doubt Brahman is absolutely non-differentiated in itself, but, since we cannot fully rise to this way of thinking, and needs must use positive language to describe the ultimate, the positive terms 'reality' and 'knowledge', duly purified, are among the best (if not *the* best) we have. There is a valid place for them in our knowledge of Brahman. Brahman is really not non-being and not non-conscious (thus the terms are not used synonymously), yet withal Brahman in itself is totally non-determinate, non-differentiated. Our thinking cannot rise to this. In point of fact, the Advaitic stance is a testament to Brahman's absolute transcendence. And to this end the terms we predicate of Brahman must be duly purified, even to the point, paradoxically, of apophasis. That is why the scriptures are there and must be interpreted correctly. They are to teach us how we are to think *about* Brahman ideally, even if we cannot actually *think Brahman* thus. In the process we have some inkling of what Brahman really is, Brahman the chief goal of human living (*puruṣārtha*). (It is to mark the contrast then between the ultimate being's transcendence in Śaṃkara's thought and the divine accessibility in Rāmānuja's that I refer to Śaṃkara's Absolute by 'it' and to Rāmānuja's God by 'he', and not because Śaṃkara's Absolute is in any simplistic sense 'impersonal'.)

But Rāmānuja, in the guise of the objector, returns to the attack. By making 'reality' and 'knowledge' abandon their proper literal meanings,[14] in that they are meant to deliver an overwhelmingly apophatic understanding of a Brahman whose nature is contrary to that of everything else, we have, he insists, a case of oblique predication (*lakṣaṇā*). The objector is not opposed to a purification of terms with respect to Brahman; he is opposed to a purification of *prima facie* positive terms such that their positive literal sense vanishes away to the point of apophasis. This can only be oblique predication, and it was commonly accepted that in the interpretation of scripture it was a grave exegetical defect to do this without good reason. Moreover, the Advaitin is compounding his transgression by taking not one but both the positive terms obliquely. The Advaitin is unabashed.[15] There is every good reason, he maintains, for taking both the positive terms obliquely, even to the point of apophasis, for this meets the very intention (*tātparya*) of the scriptural statement, 'for meeting the intention [of a statement] has greater weight than meeting the [usual] denotation [of words]. All agree that the intention of correlative predication has to do with unity [rather than differentiation].'[16] If the unity of CP can the better be achieved in non-differentiated meaning (and being) rather than the contrary, then by all means let us have it!

But this smart riposte presages the Advaitin's undoing and Rāmānuja's eventual repudiation of his position. The cumulative case against the Advaitin is too great. His interpretation flies in the face of all the accepted rules of exegesis, and he is clearly seen to be pleading a special case. The heart of Rāmānuja's repudiation is this: by having to resort to oblique meanings wholesale, by appealing to a foreclosed intention of scripture, and by shifting the onus of CP to the epistemological side, the Advaitin is really showing that he has subverted the very essence of correlatively predicated statements. For on his view 'there would be no basis for a difference of grounds in the one entity [the referent], corresponding to the terms predicated'.[17] CP affirms a real correspondence between differentiation in the terms predicated and differentiation in the referent. And this the Advaitic interpretation of the *Taittirīya* text does not do.

In his own interpretation of the text, found in the Commentary,[18] Rāmānuja tries not to fall foul of his own strictures. Śaṃkara and Rāmānuja are agreed that the passage provides a definition of Brahman. Unlike Śaṃkara, Rāmānuja tries to show that it does so not only by excluding the *definiendum* from all else but also by describing it through its essential properties.[19] Again, both the Vedāntins affirm that because the terms of the text are correlatively predicated they are to be taken in combination as a single statement with a unitary sense.[20] It is in the ontological implications of this sense that they differ markedly, as we have seen. For Rāmānuja, 'the word "reality" declares Brahman as possessing being without circumscription. By this [word] Brahman is set apart from non-conscious being, the substrate of [essential] change, and from that conscious being which is conjoined to non-conscious being [i.e. embodied selves, which for Vedānta extend from plants to the celestials or gods]'.[21] Note that the term 'reality' (and, *mutatis mutandis*, 'knowledge') both describes and excludes. It affirms fullness of being and excludes those beings associated with essential change, i.e. matter and embodied selves. The definition is beginning to fulfil both its functions.

'The word "knowledge" declares [Brahman] as possessing a nature solely of eternal and uncontracted knowledge. By this [word] Brahman is set apart from the liberated selves in as much as they once had knowledge which was contracted.'[22] The describing- and excluding-process continues. Because the *Upaniṣads* so often designate the Ultimate by the term 'knowledge' (or its cognates), Rāmānuja like Śaṃkara was constrained to give this word a special status in his language describing Brahman. In a later chapter we shall consider the matter in greater detail. Here the term is used to describe the perfection of Brahman's distinctive nature and to exclude those beings, the now liberated *ātmans* or *muktas*, which though presently participating in the fullness of Brahman's knowledge, were once in the bondage of *saṃsāra* with the limited and circumscribed consciousness this state implies. Finally, says Rāmānuja,

> the word 'infinite' declares [Brahman's] proper form as devoid of limitation due to place, time and being. Because his proper form has qualities, he has infinitude with respect to proper form and qualities. By this word are set aside the 'eternals', who are different from the two classes of being excluded by the two former words and who have a proper form and qualities of a superior kind.[23]

The eternals (the so-called *nityas* or *sūris*) are those beings enjoying the divine presence from all eternity and never in the saṃsāric condition. Rāmānuja intimates that they are the most eminent category in the kind of being from which the definition excludes Brahman i.e. finite or dependent being.

Thus Rāmānuja's exegesis, by the neat contrivance of making each subsequent qualifier term of the definition set Brahman apart from a class of being superior to the preceding one, makes the point that Brahman is *supreme* in the hierarchy of being, and *infinitely perfect* in the order of being. In other words, Brahman is at the same time the highest being and qualitatively different from every other kind of being. In this connection, note the role the term 'infinite' is made to play in the exegesis. As in the Advaitic interpretation, it is meant to give our understanding of Brahman a transcendent quality by purifying Brahman of every limitation due to place, time and being. This makes Brahman infinitely perfect in contrast to the other kinds of being mentioned. But, and this is in marked contrast to the rival view, the term is specifically made to qualify not only the divine (distinctively conscious) essence but also the divine attributes (which will be dealt with later). As a result of all this we can see that Rāmānuja's exegesis stresses both the differentiation *within* Brahman (the referent of the scriptural definition) and the differentiation *between* Brahman and finite being. Thus the ontological differentiation implied by correlative predication is given justification with a vengeance.

A final observation. To say that Brahman is meant to be purified of all empirical limitation in our understanding of the Upaniṣadic statement is to say that the statement functions by way of 'intrinsic analogy'; or rather it is to say more specifically, as Rāmānuja's exegesis shows us, that the predicates 'reality' and 'knowledge' are intrinsically analogical. That is, as predicates of Brahman they are at one and the same time to be purged of their connotations of empirical limitation and yet they retain a core of their literal meaning. And this is precisely what Rāmānuja intends. Through the use of the term 'infinite', which as a negative adjective is suited to act as the purifying element in the statement, the positive terms 'reality' and 'knowledge' are predicated of Brahman literally yet not full-bloodedly in their everyday sense. Brahman *is* real, Brahman *is* conscious, but not imperfectly, finitely real and conscious; rather he is infinitely real, infinitely conscious, or reality itself, knowledge itself. While Rāmānuja, like any true theologian who wishes to acknowledge the real transcendence of his God, recognises the need to evacuate divine predicates of imperfection, unlike the Śaṃkarites he is keen to accord them, and to be seen to accord them, recognisable literal purchase. This is why his God is at the same time Other and Supreme. The Śaṃkarites, on the other hand, overwhelmed by the transcendence of their Absolute, in spite of their disclaimers to the contrary lose sight of this positive purchase to the point of apophasis, so that their Absolute becomes so totally Other as to be hardly Supreme. The divide between Rāmānuja's theism and Śaṃkara's non-dualism, for all its subtlety at times, is both theologically and religiously decisive.

The contrast is not infrequently made between Rāmānuja and Śaṃkara that, whereas Śaṃkara sits lightly to the literal interpretation of scripture, resorting much too readily to oblique meanings (especially in the context of divine predication), Rāmānuja's reading of scripture is unswervingly (and properly) literalist. As we have seen, there is point to this contrast, at least in the two Vedāntins' understanding of divine predication. But it is worth stressing that, where it seems justified, Rāmānuja too resorts to oblique meanings. As we have pointed out, in his interpretation of the *Taittirīya* text these oblique meanings take the form of intrinsic analogy. But in his exegeses there are instances of extrinsic analogy or metaphorical predication as well. For example, when considering *TaiUp*, II.5.1 – 'pleasure is its head, joy the right wing, delight the left wing, bliss the body, Brahman the tail, the foundation' – he comments, 'since the [supreme] Self cannot have head, wings, tail, and so forth, its having pleasure for its head and so on is but metaphor, for the sake of easy understanding'.[24] Hence any pronouncement about Rāmānuja's scriptural literalism must be made with caution.

II

Nevertheless, we can examine now how with the appropriate qualifications Rāmānuja may well be called a scriptural literalist. This will emerge in our treatment of his analysis of the second scriptural text chosen for consideration: the *Chāndogya* refrain, 'That you are' (*tat tvam asi*). It will help if we call to mind the context of this declaration. Uddālaka Āruṇi, the wise teacher, asks his son Śvetaketu, who has just returned 'swollen-headed' from twelve years' Vedic study at the feet of a guru, if he asked for that teaching 'by which the unheard becomes heard, the unthought thought, the unknown known'. No doubt as Uddālaka expects, his son replies in the negative. Eventually, through a number of illustrations in which different substances merge in a common substance, Uddālaka declares the apparent identity of Śvetaketu with the subtle essence underlying the world, i.e. the Self (Ātman), summing up his teaching in the refrain, 'That you are, Śvetaketu' (*tat tvam asi śvetaketo*).[25] This refrain, then, unlike the *Taittirīya* text, is not a definition of the Ultimate, but is a statement about the relation between the Ultimate (here designated as the Self of the world) and the individual self which Śvetaketu represents. But there is another significant difference between the two texts. In the *Taittirīya* passage the positive qualifier-terms correlatively predicated (in conjunction with the referent term *brahma*) are abstract terms ostensibly signifying abstractions (i.e. 'reality', 'knowledge'). Here the two terms correlatively predicated via the copula 'are' ostensibly denote substantival being: 'That', i.e. the underlying Self of the world, and Śvetaketu. In other words, there is an entitative factor in the *Chāndogya* refrain lacking in the first text. This has important repercussions in Rāmānuja's exegesis.

If Rāmānuja's understanding of CP was a necessary propaedeutic to our appreciation of his *Taittirīya* exegesis, here we shall have to consider further, but as briefly as possible – the detailed examination will come later – the necessary metaphysical aspects underpinning his exegesis of the *Chāndogya* statement. In the process we shall need to discuss Rāmānuja's view on the denotative scope of words, in its theological context.

We start with the observation that Rāmānuja employs a central model for understanding the relationship between the supreme Lord and the world. This is the 'body–ensouler' (i.e. *śarīra–śarīrin*) model, which has a non-theological and a theological application. We shall come to the non-theological application in due course, but in the model's theological context, the world-as-a-whole (this can apply also to its individual substantival components) may be said to be the 'body' (*śarīra*) of which the Lord or supreme Self is the 'ensouler' (*śarīrin*). Suffice it to say for the present that the terms 'body' and 'ensouler' in the context of the model are technical ones and bear no obvious relation to everyday usage. To make this clear, henceforward whenever we ourselves use 'body' and 'ensouler' in their technical senses, unless their meaning is obvious, we shall write 'body_m' and 'ensouler_m' (or 'self_m'), respectively. At the very least, as we shall see, to say that the world (or an individual) is Brahman's body_m is to say that the world (or an individual) is in some respect at the same time both non-different from and yet not identical with Brahman. The point is that, within this relationship of identity-in-difference encapsulated by the body–ensouler model in its theological aspect, there obtain in Rāmānuja's thought various constituent subrelationships each with its own mode of discourse. These modes of discourse are each more or less self-contained, though they have to be integrated into the universe of discourse of the whole system. All this will be discussed later; what we are concerned with here are the various factors of the body–ensouler model, and their interplay, in Rāmānuja's interpretation of the *Chāndogya* text.

In this respect Rāmānuja appears to work with two related but separate modes of discourse simultaneously, bringing their insights together at the end within the universal framework of discourse of the body–ensouler model. One mode of discourse is 'from above', i.e. from Brahman's point of view, as it were; the other is 'from below', from Śvetaketu's point of view. From the divine viewpoint, the one all-comprehending Reality that is Brahman[26] is distinguishable, for Rāmānuja, under three aspects. First, there is Brahman in himself, the sovereign Lord, transcendent, unchanging and infinitely perfect; second, there is Brahman in his causal condition, in potency proximate to the production of the variegated and dependent world, as its 'substantial cause' (*upādāna kāraṇa*), i.e. the causal substrate from which the effect is produced; third, Rāmānuja speaks of Brahman in his effected condition, ontologically *as* the produced world. These last two states of Brahman Rāmānuja calls 'Brahman in his causal condition' (*brahma kāraṇāvastham*) and 'Brahman in his effected condition' (*brahma kāryāvastham*).[27]

For Rāmānuja the Brahman-reality is certainly not exhausted in its causal and effected conditions; he found it necessary to describe Brahman thus to do justice to those statements of the *Upaniṣads* which made Brahman the sole source and cause of all being. The idea looms large in the Vedānta that nothing can come into being or continue to exist independently of Brahman. Rāmānuja, like most of the classical Vedāntins, was deeply impressed by this idea. There could be no ontological 'creational' gap between Brahman and the finite order. The world in its origin and in its continuing being has Brahman alone for its existential support; it participates ontologically in Brahman, it is 'of Brahman'. Rāmānuja believed that this religious insight could be done justice to from the viewpoint of divine causality, as it were, by speaking of the world itself as the 'effected' Brahman, the result of Brahman himself in his causal state. In this way the ontological continuum between Brahman and the world (or its individual components) could be preserved.

Now this way of speaking, for all its welcome acknowledgement of the absoluteness of divine causality, has grave disadvantages. On the one hand, it compromises the substantival reality of the world, to the point of dissolving it away into Brahman: everything becomes Brahman in one form or another. On the other hand, it compromises the transcendent perfection of the supreme being itself by implying that this supreme being, as continuous existentially with its (dependent) effects, is subject to the various limitations of these effects.

To counteract this in part, Rāmānuja resorted to another way of speaking, 'from below', i.e. from the viewpoint of the world, which Śvetaketu represents. If the first mode of discourse, 'from above', emphasises unreservedly the non-difference between Brahman and the world, this second mode of discourse, 'from below', takes account of the non-identity between the two, although on the whole itself veering towards emphasising their identity. The terminology used here is derived from another relationship constituting the body–ensouler model, namely that between the 'mode' (*prakāra*) and the 'mode-possessor' (*prakārin*). Later we shall go into these concepts in some detail. For the present we note that by a 'mode' Rāmānuja means a being, substantival or non-substantival, such that it has no *raison d'être* of its own apart from, or realisation independent of, some other entity, namely the 'mode-possessor'. And the mode qualifies the mode-possessor in manifesting this relationship. If it is true that the epistemological and ontological inseparability of mode and mode-possessor accentuates their non-duality, it is no less true that the qualifying relation between them forces us to acknowledge their mutual distinction (since qualification is based on difference), the more so when the mode itself is a substantival entity. Rāmānuja applies the mode – mode-possessor relationship to the world and Brahman. The world in so far as it can neither exist nor be understood for the reality it is apart from Brahman is the latter's mode or *prakāra* (this can also be said of the world's individual substantival components); Brahman is the mode-possessor, the *prakārin*. Now, as we shall see, Rāmānuja uses both kinds of talk, i.e. talk of the causal and of the effected Brahman, and talk of the individual as mode of Brahman (the mode-possessor), in his exegesis of the *tat tvam asi* statement. This is because both kinds of talk are important for describing the relationship of identity-in-difference between Brahman and the world summed up by the body–ensouler model and seen by Rāmānuja to be encapsulated in the Upaniṣadic text. The former mode of discourse stresses the aspect of identity; the latter takes account of the difference.

We may now pass on to a further discussion in which we shall examine Rāmānuja's view on the theological scope of the denotation of words. Rāmānuja maintains that besides its macrocosmic, theological application (i.e. between Brahman and the world), the body–ensouler model has also a microcosmic, non-theological application which, as it were, 'patterns' the former. In this latter application, the *jīvātman* or individual self acts as the ensouler$_m$ and its empirical body as the body$_m$. That is, the individual *ātman* is to its body$_m$ what the ensouling supreme Self or Brahman is to the world-body$_m$ (or to the world's individual substantival components as bodies$_m$). This correspondence between the two levels has important repercussions in Rāmānuja's thinking for the denotation of words in its theological context. It is to this matter that we now turn.

In classical Vedāntic theory, the human person is an intimate association of the spiritual principle or *ātman* and a 'material' or prakṛtic[28] psycho-physical complement (which as a result of the union assumes the form of the living empirical human body, inclusive of its mental properties). Thus, strictly speaking, in Vedāntic theory the human body as we see it is part (the mind is the other part) of the result of the distinctive association between animating *ātman* and material complement. The Vedāntins differed as to whether there is but one (apparently) animating *ātman* (apparently) fragmented individually (thus the Śaṃkarites), or whether there are many (finite) animating *ātmans* (Rāmānuja and others). In fact, for the Vedāntins all living things imply the animating *ātman*. So far as Rāmānuja was concerned this meant that the word 'man', for instance, in its primary sense does not refer (via the *ākṛti* of man[29]) only to the (human) body (understood here in the enlarged sense of animate prakṛtic psycho-physical component) but also to the animating *ātman*. This makes good sense, affirmed Rāmānuja, because the body is the *prakāra* or mode of the *ātman*, the *prakārin* or mode-possessor. That is, without the *ātman* as its existential and intelligible support, without in fact the *ātman* being its ensouler$_m$ (exactly how we shall see later), the body cannot be 'realised' as a body, cannot be recognised for the thing it is. For this reason Rāmānuja held (to enlarge the principle), that whenever a mass of *prakṛti* is ensouled$_m$ by an *ātman*, by virtue of the mode–mode-possessor relation obtaining, the term ostensibly denoting the prakṛtic component (i.e. the body) 'comprehends' not only the body but also the ensouling$_m$ *ātman*.

He explains this feature of denotation as follows:

> Because the body is the mode of the ensouling self, and because words expressing the mode reach up to the mode-possessor also, we can properly say that words denoting the body reach up to the ensouling self. For, when an entity is apprehended as 'This is such', the mode is that part being apprehended as the 'such'. The mode rightly finds its terminus in the mode-possessor, since, as dependent on the latter entity, its being apprehended [for what it is] depends on that entity. Thus a word designating the mode reaches up to the mode-possessor as well.[30]

In other words, though the *ātman* in its pure state (that is, as disjoined from *prakṛti*) cannot be designated by such terms as 'flower', 'fish', 'man', 'god', and so on, in the embodied state it is designatable by such terms in their primary senses in so far as these senses 'comprehend' the whole entity referred to: individual *ātman* plus the prakṛtic complement or body.

Now this theory of denotation for Rāmānuja lays the foundation for a theological superstructure reaching up to Brahman himself. By virtue of the macrocosmic application of the body–ensouler relation in which the world (or its individual substantival components) is the body and

Brahman the ensouler, the world (or its individuals) may be considered the mode of Brahman, the mode-possessor. The consequence of this is that every (substance[31]) word finds its first denotative stopping-place in its natural referent and, since this referent is Brahman's mode, its final denotative stopping-place in Brahman himself, the mode-possessor. Furthermore, words are thus denotative in their primary senses. Just as in the natural order the denoting word comprehends the (hidden) ensouling$_m$ *ātman* (where there is one) as part of its basic or primary meaning, so in the meta-empirical order the word reaches up, still in its primary sense, to the supreme Self ensouling$_m$ and indwelling the finite entity. Rāmānuja says,

> Words expressing matter-*cum*-spirit, all of whose states are modes of the Lord, apply in their primary sense to the supreme Self when he is in the state of being qualified by these modes, just as the words 'god', 'man' and so on express the [embodied] individual self, just as, in fact, the words 'god', 'man', and so on apply in their primary sense to the individual self, the mode-possessor [determined] by the particular transformations of *prakṛti* as god, man, and so on, which exist as kinds of being only in so far as they are modes of the individual self. So also, because all conscious and non-conscious being is the mode of the supreme Self in that it is the latter's body, all words expressing [substantival entities within] such being apply in their primary sense to the supreme Self.[32]

We have here then, through this extended theory of the denotation of words, the basis for Rāmānuja's scriptural literalism. Because all words expressing kinds of being apply ultimately to Brahman as part of their literal meaning, the way is open for Rāmānuja to interpret a great many apparently non-literal scriptural texts in literalist vein. Let us take an example. Under *BrSū*, I.1.5 and 6, Rāmānuja considers a rival (Sāṃkhya) interpretation of *ChāndUp*, VI.2.3 and 4: 'It thought: "May I be many, may I bring forth". It emitted fire. That fire thought: "May I be many, may I bring forth". It emitted water . . . . That water thought: "May I be many, may I bring forth . . .".' The rival argues that it is the non-conscious, primal, causal, 'material' principle of the world (namely, the Pradhāna or Prakṛti) which, in the form of its "evolutes" of fire, water, and so on, is the subject of 'thought' in the passage; hence 'thought' here is to be understood figuratively. For fire and water cannot really think, and it is not uncommon in discourse to ascribed mental activity figuratively to non-conscious things, as when we say: 'The rice is on the look-out for rain' or 'The seed was gladdened by the rain'.

Rāmānuja rejects this interpretation and affirms that on the contrary all the instances of 'thought' in the text are to be understood literally. His rationale is as follows: no doubt fire and water in themselves, being non-conscious, cannot really think. But, since they are ensouled$_m$ by the supreme Self and exist for what they are in virtue of this – that is, are the supreme Self's modes – the words 'fire', 'water', and so on, are also denotative (ultimately) of the supreme Self. Now, from *ChāndUp*, VI.3.2 – 'Well, having entered these three deities, [i.e. fire, etc.] with this individual self, let Me proliferate name and form', which clearly states the intention of the supreme Self – we are apprised also of the intention of scripture concerning the texts under consideration, i.e. that it is the supreme Self as self$_m$ of fire and water, its modes, which decides to proliferate in the name of fire and water. The thinking ascribed to fire and water in the text, then, can and must be taken literally, since the words naming these entities do reach up denotatively ultimately to the supreme Self.[33]

A *tour-de-force*, one might think, and exegetically this may well be so. Nevertheless Rāmānuja believed that by this literalist approach he had scored exegetically over Śaṃkara and his followers within the Vedāntin camp. Certainly no one could accuse him of taking lightly the rule that a non-literal reading of scripture could be resorted to only after it was shown (or was obvious) that the purport of the text could not be literal. Later we shall take up what I consider to be the theological insight underlying this theory of denotation.

But to say that the word in its primary sense thus reached up to the supreme being did not mean that the trans-empirical surplus of meaning was not hidden except to the eyes of an informed faith. It was only scripture, more loving towards us than a thousand parents said Rāmānuja, which, when rightly understood, could procure for us this saving vision.

> Persons untutored in the Vedānta do not see that Brahman is the self of all individual selves and types of being, and they think that the terminus expressed by all [substance] words is only the various types of being [overtly expressed by these words]. But these are in fact only a part of what is expressed. Once they study the Vedānta statements they know that everything is ensouled by Brahman and that all words express Brahman as conditioned by various modes, in that everything is Brahman's effect and he is their inner controller. Well then, it may be objected, the ordinary application of words such as 'ox' and so on,

which express the various types of being, would be sublated. Not so, we reply. All words express the supreme Self as qualified by non-conscious being and individual selves. We know this from the text, 'Let Me proliferate name and form . . .' [*ChāndUp*, VI.3.2]. Worldly persons think, when using language, that with respect to what is expressed by a word, what is in fact only a part of the object expressed [i.e. the finite object] is the word's [denotative] terminus. This is because the principal part of what is [really] expressed – the supreme Self – is beyond the reach of perception [and the other empirical *pramāṇas*]. The truth is, study of the Vedānta *completes* the ordinary application of words.[34]

We can continue the discussion by asking if there is in the Sanskrit a syntactical construction best suited to fulfil the scriptural function of substance-words reaching up denotatively to the supreme being. Rāmānuja answers that it is in the form of correlative predication (CP) that such words do this. This is hardly surprising in view of the fact that there are numerous scriptural texts, some of them acknowledgedly crucial ones, in which substance qualifier terms are correlatively predicated of Brahman their referent. Consider the following examples: 'Among lights, *I* [Kṛṣṇa, the Lord] am the *radiant sun*' (*Gītā*, 10.21); 'Among all trees, *I* [Kṛṣṇa, the Lord] am the sacred *fig-tree*' (*Gītā*, 10.26, and elsewhere in this chapter); and indeed the *Chāndogya* refrain, '*That you* are.'[35] In order to maintain the literalist tenor of his exegesis, Rāmānuja must show how it is that the substance qualifier terms and referent terms of such statements apply (in a non-figurative way), in accordance with his definition of CP, to one and the same entity, their referent, Brahman. In clarifying this we shall be able to appreciate how Rāmānuja could assert the identity-in-difference peculiar to his theology and we shall also be ready to understand his interpretation of the *Chāndogya* text.

First we may ask, why should not statements such as these above be interpreted figuratively? Rāmānuja does not deny that correlatively predicated statements can be taken figuratively. He considers the examples, '*This Vāhika tribesman* is an *ox*.' Clearly 'ox' here is a metaphor. But it is a metaphor because there are positive grounds for not taking it literally: the referent cannot be the locus of the synthetic co-presence of humanity and oxhood. Again, the declaration is *clearly intended* to be figurative. But the correlatively predicated scriptural statements we are discussing are different. By complementing the rationale considered earlier (whereby substance words terminate denotatively in Brahman) by another line of thought, also comprehended in the body–ensouler model, Rāmānuja argues that it is in the (scriptural) correlatively predicated statement using of Brahman substance qualifier terms understood in literal vein that a measure of justice can be done to the identity-in-difference relationship obtaining between the absolute and the dependent orders of being. In the process he claims to have conformed to the exegetical rule that scripture should not be understood non-literally unless there are decisive reasons for doing so. Let us now examine how Rāmānuja sets about interpreting the type of statement being considered.

In a nutshell, for Rāmānuja correlatively predicated statements concerning Brahman in which substance qualifier terms are used accommodate both modes of discourse distinguished earlier: namely that 'from below', informed by the mode–mode-possessor relationship, and that 'from above', informed by the causal-Brahman–effected-Brahman relationship. Both modes of discourse affirm an identity-in-difference relationship between Brahman and the world (or individual substantival entities), and, as noted before, both modes of discourse emphasise, overall, the identity aspect. However, in so far as the mode–mode-possessor relationship is a qualifying one (the mode qualifying the mode-possessor) and qualification implies an underlying difference between qualificate and qualifier, the way of speaking informed by this relationship takes better account of the *difference* between Brahman and the world than the causal-Brahman–effected-Brahman mode of discourse. Hence, if one regards a statement in which substance qualifier terms are predicated correlatively of Brahman from the former point of view, the aspect of difference is given due weight; if one looks at the statement from the latter viewpoint, the aspect of identity is heightened.

Thus Rāmānuja can say in connection with the first aspect (and paraphrasing words of Kṛṣṇa the Lord to Arjuna his disciple),

> Just as the body, since it cannot be realised apart from the embodied self in virtue of being essentially nothing but the latter's [modal] qualifier, is to be described as thus related by correlative predication [in such statements as 'I am a man', 'I am fat', etc.], so know that the body and the embodied self, since they cannot be realised [for what they are] apart from Me in virtue of being essentially nothing but My qualifier, are to be described as thus related to *Me* by correlative predication . . . The *śrutis* themselves teach us [for instance in *BĀUp*, III.7.3] that the Lord ensouls the [composite of] embodied self and

> body – the latter in its form of aggregate of earth, and so on – in so far as it is their proper form and function to be nothing but the Lord's body . . . This condition of the Lord as self of all embodied selves through being their inner controller is the ground for [scripture's] describing this [relationship] by way of correlative predication.[36]

Here Rāmānuja is saying that substance qualifier words predicated correlatively of Brahman (who is the Lord) apply in a literal sense to their referent in so far as they denote entities ensouled$_m$ by Brahman by way of the mode ('qualifier' in the text) – mode-possessor relationship. That Rāmānuja has this relationship in mind is clear from his use of the phrase, 'since it cannot be realised apart from . . .'. An identity-in-difference is being affirmed in respect of one and the same entity – the referent, Brahman. Brahman can be said literally to *be* the entity predicated of him in so far as the latter is his mode, i.e. cannot be realised for what it is apart from him, and he is the mode-possessor, the entity's self$_m$. But the identity affirmed here is of a weak kind, not swamping by any means the difference between the Lord and the dependent entity *within* the unitary relationship. For all its dependence the entity in question has a substantival reality of its own (hence it is denotable by a substance word); it is separate. That is why it can qualify the Lord. This viewpoint, 'from below', allows Rāmānuja to maintain a realist stance ontologically in that it allows him to acknowledge the substantival reality of the first-order referent of the (substance) qualifier term ultimately predicated of Brahman. Note too that Rāmānuja claims by quoting scripture that this interpretation accords with the mind of scripture; he is not imposing a meaning on scripture from without.

We come now to the causal approach – that 'from above'. Here again an identity-in-difference between infinite and finite is affirmed, but with the accent on identity. When the Brahman-reality is distinguished into its causal and effected state, notwithstanding the *difference* between cause and effect, all can be affirmed to be Brahman (= identity) in one form or another. Rāmānuja maintains that an 'identity-statement' in the form of CP can best express this relationship.

> In the [*Chāndogya*] text [VI.3.2], 'Well, having entered these three deities with this individual self, let Me proliferate name and form', the expression 'three deities' refers to all non-conscious being. So from the statement that the Lord proliferates name and form by entering within non-conscious being and the individual self as their own self, we learn that all expressive [i.e. substance] words express the supreme

> Self as qualified by conscious and non-conscious being. This being so, correlative predication primarily applies when a word expresses an effect [of the supreme Self] in conjunction with a word expressing the supreme Self in its causal state . . . Because conscious and non-conscious being, in all their states, derive their reality from being the supreme Person's mode in so far as they are his body, the supreme Person himself, with them as his mode, is both cause and effect, and it is he who is expressed always by every word . . . .[37]

Here again the identity-in-difference is being affirmed, in accordance with the definition of CP, with respect to one and the same referent, Brahman. But the aspect of identity by virtue of the causal-Brahman –effected-Brahman distinction clearly predominates. And, observes Rāmānuja, it is in the correlatively predicated statement with the appropriate referent and qualifier terms that this aspect of identity (of the identity-in-difference relationship) is best expressed. We are ready now to consider Rāmānuja's exegesis of the *tat tvam asi* text, and we shall see that all the points discussed hitherto have a part to play. Perhaps the most comprehensive form of the exegesis occurs in the Summary. Rāmānuja writes,

> The 'you' which hitherto was known as but the [material] body's supporting agent in fact terminates in the supreme Self as its mode in so far as it is the body of the supreme Self. Hence the word 'you' declares your inner Controller qualified by you as his mode. From the text, 'Having entered with this individual self, let Me proliferate name and form', we learn that, since the ensouling self is itself ensouled by Brahman, Brahman is referred to by the names of the former. Thus it is Brahman who is expressed by the two words 'that' and 'you' applied by way of correlative predication. There the word 'that' declares him who is the cause of the world, the mine of every noble quality, blameless and without change, while 'you' declares that very Brahman qualified by the mode that is his body [i.e. Śvetaketu] in so far as he is the inner Controller of [Śvetaketu's] individual self. So one can say that the two words 'that' and 'you' are applied to one and the same Brahman in respect of a difference of grounds [in him] for the application.[38]

In the light of our previous discussions, there is no need, I think, to elaborate on this statement. It is enough to point out that in this interpretation the various factors treated of earlier come into play. The

Chāndogya text instantiates, with respect to Brahman, the definition of CP given earlier; identity-in-*difference* is proclaimed between infinite and finite being (Śvetaketu clearly representing the latter) from the viewpoint of the qualifying mode–mode-possessor relationship, and *identity*-in-difference from the causal-Brahman–effected-Brahman point of view. In deference to the identity form of the *Chāndogya* text, the exegesis allows the identity aspect, overall to predominate. Further, this interpretation is scripturally supported. Thus is classically illustrated the *viśiṣṭādvaita* ('the non-duality of qualified being(s)'), which, aptly, later lent its name to Rāmānuja's system.

We can see better now what Rāmānuja hopes to gain from such an interpretation and its underlying theory. For one, as already noted, he hopes to gain scriptural credibility: he expects to succeed in making 'literal' sense of, at the same time, the non-dualist and dualist texts of scripture. But further, through his body–ensouler model in its theological aspects of denotative theory and causality, he thinks he has scored over Śaṃkara and his followers by providing grounds for non-sublatable theistic discourse in which a literal purchase is accorded to our understanding of Brahman, and for lasting devotional worship to the transcendent Lord.

Before we summarise the content of this chapter, let us briefly examine Rāmānuja's critique of the Advaitic interpretation of the *Chāndogya* refrain. First, he makes the point that if the text intimated pure, non-differentiated being by absolutely identifying the universal Self (in 'that') and the inner Self (in 'you'), as the Advaitins maintain, its correlatively predicated form, which presumes differentiation in the referent, would be countermanded.[39] Second, any resort to oblique meanings (*lakṣaṇā*) in the interpretation of 'that' and 'you' (as later Śaṃkarites attempted to do[40]) is gratuitous and unwarranted in so far as an acceptable non-figurative interpretation of the terms (i.e. Rāmānuja's) is forthcoming, supported by the intention of scripture. Finally, the coherence of the *Upaniṣad* would be imperilled if the Advaitic exegesis were right, for the (absolutely) non-dualist understanding of 'That you are' intimating a non-differentiated Brahman would be in 'opposition to the [*Upaniṣad's*] introductory statement: "That [Brahman] thought, 'Let Me be *many*.'" '[41]

Let us conclude now by summarising this chapter. After having dealt in Chapter 1 with Rāmānuja's acceptance of the fact-assertiveness of language (especially scriptural language), here we have been concerned mainly with Rāmānuja's understanding of how language is equipped to yield factual information about the transcendent. We have seen that to this end he appeals to a structural correspondence between language and reality, as to both the word and the sentence. We have thus had to examine his notion of predication, especially divine predication with special reference to his position on correlative predication. In short, scriptural correlative predication presumes to reveal a differentiated Brahman-reality. In addition, in part I we discussed Rāmānuja's interpretation of a key scriptural correlatively predicated statement – the putative definition of *Tai*, II.1.1, as representing those texts purporting to give information about the sort of reality Brahman is. In the process we examined Rāmānuja's refutation of the Advaitic position on these matters. In part II we took up Rāmānuja's exegesis of a second scriptural correlatively predicated text: 'That you are' (*tat tvam asi*), representing those texts encapsulating the relationship between infinite and finite being. To this end we had to look briefly at the body – ensouler model in Rāmānuja's theology, especially in its ontological and predicational implications. We saw how Rāmānuja's exegesis of *tat tvam asi* illustrates the relation of identity-in-difference between Brahman and the world in a way characteristic of his theological perspective. Again, Rāmānuja's repudiation of the Advaitic interpretation was reviewed. Our discussions in this chapter have shown how Rāmānuja, while accommodating the figurative interpretation of scripture, can be said to have a literalist understanding of the texts.

So much then for a study of the meaning of meaning in Rāmānuja's theology. This has been essential for the right perspective on the importance and function of scripture in his thinking. Rāmānuja's whole thinking had, in one way or another, a scriptural orientation. And it was scripture's chief purpose to give veridical information about the finite (human) self and Brahman so that the desired union between the two, begun here in the stream of *saṃsāra* and consummated at the further shore, could be successfully effected. Rāmānuja held that this union could not be achieved without right understanding of the nature of the self and of Brahman. It is thus to a fuller examination of these two kinds of being in Rāmānuja's thought that we now turn.

3 The Essential Self

We saw in Chapter 2 that for Rāmānuja the finite (human) self cannot achieve salvation – which consists in union with Brahman, begun in this life and consummated in the hereafter – without first acquiring knowledge of its own and of Brahman's essential nature. Rāmānuja puts it thus:

> This is the object summed up in the apex of the collection of *śruti*, whose teaching is for the welfare of the whole world: the utterly delightful practice of contemplation, worship, and reverence at the supreme Person's gracious feet, brought about by one's duties of caste and station in life and preceded by the knowledge of the true nature of the individual self and of the supreme Self, and the fruit of acquiring this.[1]

In this chapter we shall concentrate on the central aspect of the individual self's or *jīvātman*'s[2] essential nature for Rāmānuja, i.e. the self as knower (*jñātṛ, jña*) for which we shall have to investigate the relationship between the *ātman* and consciousness.

At the outset we note that Rāmānuja was a realist about the plurality of finite selves in a way Śaṃkara was not; that is, Rāmānuja accepted that the distinction between individual selves endures into *mokṣa* or final liberation. The plurality of finite selves is neither provisional nor ultimately sublatable. In the course of this chapter we shall see how he sought to establish this by the use of reason. As may be expected, this is a pervasive and crucial tenet of his theistic, devotional theology and he lost no opportunity to give it scriptural backing.[3]

For Rāmānuja, the relation between the *ātman* and consciousness in its various ramifications may best be examined by a form of introspective self-awareness in which the knower catches itself at work, so to speak. For it is only in and through consciousness that the *ātman* can be present to itself, understand its essence and look into the grounds of its being. Though Rāmānuja's theoretical works abound in comment on and discussion of the nature of consciousness, his most sustained analyses are to be found in the Commentary. Accordingly, in the ensuing study it is mainly to this work that we shall direct our attention.

Rāmānuja's inquiries resulted in several descriptions of knowledge (*jñāna*) or consciousness (*caitanya*).[4] We can conveniently begin from there. Consider the following:

> [1] Consciousness is the illumining in the present moment, to its own substrate, by its own existence alone.
>
> [2] Or else, it is the establishing of its own object by its own existence alone.
>
> [3] A conscious act is the illumination of a particular object to its [the act's] own substrate by its [the act's] own existence alone.
>
> [4] The nature of consciouness is to make something into an object of the experience of its [consciousness's] own substrate through its [consciousness's] own being alone.[5]

The number and nuancing of these descriptions need not surprise us. Rāmānuja was trying to describe the nature of an experience so immediate and central to our lives as to defy articulation in ready-made terms. Nevertheless we see that for him consciousness is an 'illumining', a 'making present' here and now, of an object to a subject, by consciousness's own existence alone and not through the agency of something else. In examining these features we shall have occasion to analyse the complex relationship between the *ātman* and consciousness in Rāmānuja's thought.

Now what does it mean to say that consciousness is an 'illumination' by its own existence alone – that is, not through an external agency? Consider the following: 'That which has illumination for its essence is luminous, not as dependent on something else, but as a lamp. . . . In this way [i.e. as a lamp] the *ātman*, which is verily of the form of consciousness, has consciousness [also] for its quality. For to have consciousness for one's form is self-luminosity.'[6] Not only is this a somewhat paradoxical statement (consciousness is the 'form' of the *ātman* as well as its quality), but it is also central to Rāmānuja's understanding of the relation between the *ātman* and awareness. Clearly it hinges on the comparison drawn between the *ātman* and the lamp, and to appreciate the force of the analogy[7] we shall have to examine what Rāmānuja says about the nature of light and its relation to its source, the lamp. The most extended treatment occurs in the Commentary (under I.1.1[8]) though there are other allusions to the topic elsewhere in this work and in Rāmānuja's other writings. The key terms of the illustration are 'light' (*prabhā*), the possessor of light (*prabhāvat*), i.e. the flame, and (by extension) the lamp (*dīpa*) itself.

The lamp, i.e. the flame, is essentially luminous. Its luminosity is a luminosity that is self-originating and not dependent on another's. It lights itself up and in the process illumines other things. This is because, claims Rāmānuja, the one fire substance[9] exists in the form of both light and luminous matter, the flame. In fact, the stuff of the flame (*tejas*) may be spoken of as functioning both as substance and as quality. How is this? *Tejas* as light exists as a quality (*guṇa*) in so far as it has a substrate, the flame; yet *tejas* also exists as the flame itself, the substrate having the quality, and in this it acts like a substance. Rāmānuja points to a further unique feature of *tejas* as *light*. Light itself acts both as substance and as quality. It is quality because it has the flame as substrate, but it also possesses illumining-power and colour as its properties. Here it functions as a substance. In this it is different from other qualities, such as whiteness. The whiteness of a cloth, for instance, resides only in its substrate, while light is present not only in the flame but, by virtue of its illumining-power, in different parts of the room as well. In short, one and the same thing, *tejas*, acts as substance and property, depending on whether it is regarded as flame or light.

It is important to note that from this logically it does not follow that *tejas* has a dual nature such that it is both material (prakṛtic) and non-material, or neither material nor non-material. To say this would be to make a meaningless statement. Rāmānuja, like other Vedāntic thinkers, did not for an instant wish to repudiate the fact that *tejas* as a product of *prakṛti* was essentially non-conscious and material. What he was intimating, by his analysis of the lamp and its light, was that *tejas acts* in a unique way both as flame and as light, and that a *sui-generis* relationship of intimacy obtains between light and its substrate. Indeed, essentially they are of the same *tejas* stuff.[10] *Tejas* as the luminous substrate (the flame) manifests the features of a substance; *tejas* as the radiant light acts as a quality. Further, as light itself, in so far as it possesses colour, it functions as both substance and quality. *Tejas* illumines other objects in the act of self-illumination: 'Luminosity belongs to it because it illumines its own essential nature as well as other things.'[11] To say this is to say that it is essentially self-illumining. It is also to say that *tejas* expresses its own being in and through illumination (or light): that light is its self-expression.

The *ātman*, like the lamp – strictly speaking, the flame – is the substrate of consciousness while consciousness may be likened to light. Just as light and its substrate are the dual form of one *tejas* stuff, so also consciousness and its substrate (the *ātman* or knowing self) are essentially of the same stuff. The *ātman* is the permanent basis of its characteristic form of self-expression: acts of consciousness. These, as emergent from the *ātman*, share with it the same conscious nature, but, as numerically distinct from each other and the *ātman*, vary as to content and object. In fact this is what it means to be a knower (*jña, jñātṛ*), for 'it is essential to it to be the substrate of the quality of knowledge'.[12] It is not the case that the *ātman* is some sort of spiritual substance possessing a number of properties (such as eternity and unoriginatedness) among which is consciousness, and that all of these are related to it in exactly the same way. Rather, it is the nature of the *ātman* to produce conscious acts. Consciousness is *the* way of the *ātman's* self-expression; consequently it enjoys a *sui-generis* relationship with the *ātman*. As constituting the *ātman's* essence, it exists substantivally; as separate acts of consciousness characterising and flowing from the *ātman*, it acts attributively. This is what Rāmānuja is trying to articulate when he says that the *ātman* both is of the *form* of consciousness (*cidrūpa*) and has consciousness for its quality. In other words, the *ātman* as constituted of consciousness is at the same time a centre (the substrate) of conscious acts radiating out and terminating in their objects.

A number of distinctions stem from this which Rāmānuja is keen to establish. For one, he stresses that the *ātman* and consciousness cannot be identified without remainder. In the final analysis, this is what the Advaitin does, and in the process is dissolved not only the distinction between the conscious subject, the knowing-act and the object known, but also the plurality of individual selves, in an infinite, homogeneous, non-individualised expanse of Knowing (*jñaptimātra*): a position clearly calculated to strike a mortal blow at the root of theistic religion. Rāmānuja, in contrast, wanted very much to keep the mustard-tree of faith vigorously alive, and to do this it was necessary to show that the *ātman is* not consciousness, but that there are conscious selves. And to do *this* it was necessary to establish the distinction between the knowing subject and its – albeit unique – quality, consciousness.

The arguments Rāmānuja advances to show that awareness is not to be identified *simpliciter* with the individual *ātman*, that in fact consciousness in the form of conscious acts is the self's property, are simple and direct. First, he appeals to our experience of the recognition of objects in order to establish the permanence of the recognising subject in contrast to the transience of acts of recognition:

> Now the permanence of the producer [of conscious acts], and the origination, duration and cessation, as for pleasure and pain, of what is known as the conscious act, which is an attribute of its producer, are directly perceived. The permanence of the producer is established by recognition from [such judgements as] 'This is the very same thing previously known by me.'[13]

How could something be identified as the same over a period of time, i.e. be recognised, unless I, the knowing subject, had endured for that time? The fact of recognising an object implicitly but directly establishes the endurance of the recogniser, even though recognising-acts come and go.

The next argument shifts the focus of attention from the explicit term of the recognising-act as something external, i.e. the 'sameness' of the object recognised, to the internal, instantly apprehended sameness of the recognising-agent itself.

> From [such judgements as] '*I* know', '*I* did know', '*I* the knower have now lost [this] knowledge', the origination, [duration and cessation] of consciousness are directly established. Whence their [i.e. the knower's and consciousness's] identity? If it were accepted that selfhood derived from the momentary consciousness [of separate acts], recognition [of the form] 'On one day this was seen by me and on the next day *I* saw it again' could not take place, for it is not possible for something cognised by one to be recognised by another.[14]

We can see that these two arguments, besides establishing the distinction between the individual knower and its conscious acts, also implicitly establish the plurality of individual selves.

We have said that for Rāmānuja consciousness is the *ātman's* unique quality, so that, while seeking to distinguish the two in the manner described above, he was also at pains to stress the peculiar intimacy of their relationship. This he did by referring to consciousness as the determinative or defining property of the *ātman's* proper form (i.e. the *ātman's svarūpa – nirūpaṇa – dharma*). Wherever the *ātman* exists it exists as essentially conscious, and wherever there is consciousness there exists an *ātman* as its centre. Rāmānuja says that 'it is the *ātman's* proper form to be a knower',[15] i.e. a producer of conscious acts. This is what we meant when we said that the *ātman* cannot but express itself through acts of consciousness. Because consciousness is the determinative property of the *ātman*, Rāmānuja conceded that in certain circumstances it was permissible to speak as if identifying the two – that this was an acceptable shorthand. The scriptures, for example, whose aim is not philosophical precision, employ this device in such texts as *TaiUp*, II.5.1: 'Knowledge performs the sacrifice . . .'; and indeed the well-known statement of *TaiUp*, II.1.1: 'Brahman is reality, knowledge, infinite.' These texts, far from substantiating their Advaitic interpretation, make use of the linguistic shorthand mentioned above. Thus does Rāmānuja justify the linguistic form of texts in which knowledge and a self are apparently identified absolutely. He says explicitly,

> There is no fault in saying that the proper form itself of the *ātman*, the knower, is knowledge, because of [the *ātman's*] self-luminosity and because the knower's proper form is not definable except [in terms of] knowledge. For a word denoting a property defining the proper form declares, by virtue of that property, also the proper form of the property-possessor.[16]

Now, this affirms that the *ātman* has self-luminosity: in other words, the *ātman* in virtue of its conscious nature is self-luminous.[17] We can understand what Rāmānuja means by self-luminosity by examining his view on the subject and object of consciousness. In his descriptions of conscious experience an expression which looms large is 'to its own substrate'. Consciousness, these descriptions repeat, manifests its object 'to its own substrate'. Now we know that it is the *ātman qua* knower which is the substrate of consciousness for Rāmānuja. That is to say that Rāmānuja maintains that it is the *ātman* that is the real subject of consciousness. There is a crucial difference here from the Advaitic position. For (Śaṃkarite) Advaita one cannot say that the real subject of conscious experience is the individual *ātman*. Speaking from the transcendent point of view, the absolute Self must be identified with consciousness, *is* Consciousness, and the distinctions between individual knower, object known and act of knowing cease to apply. On the empirical level, where these distinctions do apply, what we experience as consciousness is not the real thing but a reflection, an imitation in the cognitive apparatus, of the real thing. The so-called conscious centre of the cognitive apparatus is not the true *ātman* but, like the cognitive apparatus itself, a non-conscious product of *prakṛti* called the 'internal organ' (*antaḥkaraṇa*), sometimes the 'ego' (*ahaṃkāra*, literally 'I-maker'). Rāmānuja repudiates this view: 'This cannot be the case because the ego, in the form of the internal organ, is, like the body, non-conscious, subject to *prakṛtic* modification, an object, outward, and for-the-sake-of-something-else, and because knowerhood has consciousness specifically for its essence [unlike the ego].'[18] Note the expressions 'outward' and 'for-the-sake-of-something-else' in Rāmānuja's description of the *prakṛtic* ego. This is in contrast to the 'inwardness'[19] and characteristic of being an end-in-itself of the *ātman qua* conscious. The implications of the latter feature we shall consider in a later chapter; the former we shall return to in connection with the *ātman's* self-luminosity.

If the *ātman* is the subject of awareness, what is the object of awareness? Though we can say that for Rāmānuja every act of awareness has subject and object, at this stage it is by no means clear what exactly the object is. It is in trying to understand his view on this that we shall come to grips with what he means by self-luminosity. First, we must make a distinction between what may be called *transitive* and *reflexive* acts of awareness. A transitive act of awareness is an act in which the explicit object of attention is something external to the knowing subject. Most of our cognitive acts are of this kind, ranging from everyday perception (of external sense-objects and internal mental states) to contemplation of the deity. Further, transitive conscious acts vary as to the degree of self-awareness involved. In some transitive acts, such as intent perception of an outside object, the self may be only minimally implicitly aware of itself. But in other transitive acts, such as the experience of memory, pleasure and pain ('transitive' because such acts, although introspective, are nevertheless, in Rāmānuja's reckoning, not to be simply identified with the *ātman*), the *ātman* is more explicitly self-aware.

A reflexive act of awareness is an act in which the chief object attended to is the knowing subject itself *qua knower*. The judgemental form of such an awareness is 'I know that I know.' Now, if by 'object of consciousness' is simply meant 'that which is known in an act of awareness', then, according to Rāmānuja's analysis, we shall have to distinguish further between an *implicit* object of consciousness and an *explicit* object of consciousness in all transitive conscious acts. What this distinction means will become clear in considering the following statement:

> The I-reality is evident in the I-awareness; the not-I is the object in the awareness of the 'not-I'. Hence to say that in [the conscious act] 'I know' the *evident* knower is the not-I is as nonsensical as saying that one's own mother is a barren woman. And this knower, the I-reality, is not luminous [or manifest] dependently on something else, for it is self-luminous. For self-luminosity is to have consciousness for one's essence.[20]

Here Rāmānuja is affirming, it is true, that every [transitive] conscious act is stretched between, so to speak, a subjective pole, the knower (the I), and an objective pole, the not-I. But what makes his statement momentous is that he is claiming more than this for the transitive act of awareness. He speaks of the 'evident knower' in it, of the knower's being self-luminous. He says in fact that in such acts the self is aware not only of the outside object, the not-I, made manifest to it by consciousness, but that it is also aware, *at the same time*, at least implicitly, *of itself*. This fact of consciousness cannot be proved, if by 'proof' is meant the conclusion of a syllogistic process. It is innate to the working of consciousness and is apprehendable directly – more or less implicitly in transitive acts, and more or less explicitly in reflexive acts.[21] Thus in the self's awareness of a jar, for instance, the explicit object of consciousness is the jar out there (the not–I), while, in one and the same act of cognition, the implicit object of consciousness is the knowing self. The *ātman* does not need to rely on a subsequent act of awareness to grasp itself as the knowing I.[22] In many, if not most, transitive cognitive acts it may thus implictly be conscious of itself only faintly, but this does not disturb the point being made.

The *ātman* by nature is conscious, and consciousness is essentially auto-transparent or self-luminous, making the *ātman* present to itself, catch itself as the 'I', in one and the same act of awareness. This is what Rāmānuja means by the 'inwardness' of the *ātman* as conscious in contrast to the products of *prakṛti* as 'outward'. Rāmānuja quotes the following with approval 'If the I-reality were not the *ātman*, the *ātman* could have no inwardness; for inward reality is distinguished from outward reality by means of I-cognition.'[23] This precisely is the nature of the *sui-generis* relationship between the *ātman* and consciousness: that it makes the experience of the *ātman*'s being present ('luminous') to itself possible.[24] To put it another way: consciousness lights itself up as the self-aware *ātman*. It may seem confusing to some to call the knowing subject at the same time an 'implicit object of consciousness' but the confusion is soon resolved if it is noted that by 'object of consciousness' is meant simply 'that which is known in an act of consciousness'. In so far as the *ātman* is aware of itself (at least implicitly) in every cognitive act, it is an 'object of consciousness', i.e. something known, no less than what may be the explicit object of awareness, the not-I or external object. A very important conclusion derives from the discussion so far: because the *ātman* is *essentially* conscious and therefore self-aware, it is impossible for this I-awareness to be sublated, as the Advaitins claim, in a higher or more immediate 'pure' awareness. Rāmānuja makes this clear: 'In truth, knowerhood is no illusion, for it is not sublated.'[25] There is no experience more direct to the knower than self-awareness.

In connection with the self–lamp analogy we can make a further observation. Light functions by manifesting objects. It can do this because being itself transparent it allows objects to be shown up. If light were not transparent it would itself become an object for illumination of some sort (*per impossibilem*) and the illumining-process would then collapse through infinite regress. Thus transparency is a necessary feature of luminosity (and is implied by self-luminosity). Consciousness too as 'luminous' – it manifests objects – is 'transparent'; it enables the object to be known-as-it-is in the knowledge-act. Knowledge, like light, can show up only what is there, and does not tend to distortion. This conviction lies at the basis (though there is much else) of Rāmānuja's theory of epistemological realism, in which error is not a positive distortion of reality or a superimposition of some object, but incomplete comprehension or partial knowledge. The person in error suffers from a false perspective. For example, when someone mistakes mother-of-pearl for silver, the silver is really there and perceived, but is mistakenly assumed to be all that is there. The mother-of-pearl, through a false perspective, cannot be seen for the silver.[26]

We shall be able to appreciate now why the following apparently influential description of Rāmānuja's position on consciousness and the self is, to say the least, grossly misleading. In an article entitled 'Rāmānuja's Theory of Knowledge'[27] Professor M. Hiriyanna tells us,

> Jñāna or knowledge is what eternally belongs to [the] self. To understand its exact nature, it is necessary to know a certain classification of ultimate entities which is peculiar to Rāmānuja's system. To the well-known distinction between 'spirit' and 'matter', respectively termed 'cetana' and 'jaḍa' in Sanskrit, it adds another which is neither, but is partly like the one and partly like the other. Jñāna is of this intermediate type. It is different from the jaḍa in that it can, unaided, manifest itself and external objects as well, neither of which is possible for the jaḍa. But what it thus manifests is never for itself but always for another. That is, it can only show but cannot know. In this latter respect, it is unlike the cetana, which knows though it is unable, according to the doctrine, to show anything but itself. . . . Jñāna . . . functions not for itself but for another – the self of which it is a unique adjunct.[28]

There is much to find fault with in this statement. It is not so much a question of pointing out that Rāmānuja himself uses *jaḍa* for 'matter' only when describing rival points of view, but of inquiring how *jñāna* can be an 'intermediate' type of being in the context of 'ultimate entities'. We have seen that for Rāmānuja *jñāna* is of the stuff of 'spirit' or the *ātman*. That is, both knowledge and the *ātman* are 'spiritual' in exactly the same sense. Thus knowledge is not some *tertium quid*, occupying a never-never land between spirit and matter in the manner of the 'unspeakable' (*anirvacanīya*) *māyā* of later Advaita. For Rāmānuja, who pours scorn on this notion, to hold this would have been unspeakable indeed! Nor could Rāmānuja, who has said that the ātman is of 'the form of consciousness' (*cidrūpa*), agree that knowledge is but an 'adjunct' (albeit unique) of the self.

We can conclude this chapter by a discussion of Rāmānuja's view on the relation between the *ātman*, consciousness and dreamless sleep (*suṣupti* in Sanskrit). Already in the *Upaniṣads, suṣupti* was recognised as a significant state of the individual, usually as presaging or symbolising the bliss of final liberation from the sorrow of *saṃsāra*. Rāmānuja (like other *ācārya* Vedāntins) gives *suṣupti* an interesting treatment, in the process clarifying distinctive features of his position on the conscious self, especially in contrast to the Advaitic view.

Both Rāmānuja and Śaṃkara are agreed that, though dreamless sleep is a state of the inactivity of the senses, consciousness yet persists. They disagree as to the manner in which consciousness manifests itself. Rāmānuja presents the Advaitic opponent as maintaining that in *suṣupti* one's I-awareness, the product of the ego, lapses and that only the non-differentiated, underlying Consciousness, to be identified with the absolute Ātman, remains. The conclusion of this is that individual consciousness in and through one's I-awareness is an illusion, a superimposition on absolute Consciousness, to be sublated in liberation permanently as it is in *suṣupti* temporarily.[29] As we have seen, Rāmānuja cannot accept this. Though he agrees with his opponent that the post-*suṣupti* experience is of the form 'I slept well, and was conscious of nothing, not even of *myself*', he rejects the non-dualist conclusion his opponent draws from this judgement. This judgement cannot be understood simplistically, he warns, for if taken at face-value it denies not only the experience of self-awareness during *suṣupti* but also the presence of so-called pure Consciousness itself – 'was conscious of *nothing*'! In fact, he affirms, analysis of the experience surrounding *suṣupti* shows that during this state consciousness does persist in the form of self-awareness and that *suṣupti* in some way betokens salvific bliss.

The chief argument Rāmānuja advances in favour of the first conclusion is similar to one noted earlier, i.e. from the fact of ineluctable first-person, post-*suṣupti* experiences of recognition we must deduce the continuance of self-awareness during *suṣupti*. 'The one who has woken from [dreamless] sleep judges thus with respect to something experienced before the time of such sleep, "This was done by me", "This was experienced by me", "It was I who said this."'[30] Only the same 'I' can make such post-*suṣupti* judgements. Now, since the *ātman* and its I-awareness are inseparable – that is, since the *ātman*, as we have seen, is essentially the auto-luminous substrate of consciousness – self-awareness must have persisted during *suṣupti*.[31] But you yourself have admitted, counters the opponent, that the judgement 'I was not conscious of myself' fairly sums up the dreamless state. If the self *is* self-aware throughout, what is being denied by the 'myself' here? In answer Rāmānuja makes an interesting distinction. He distinguishes two aspects to self-awareness: (1) the essential 'I' (which underlies all self-consciousness, persisting always), and (2) what may be called the empirical 'I' (extending and colouring, according to individual circumstances, the experience of the essential 'I', and temporarily dispensable).

> The object of the judgement 'I was not conscious of myself' must be distinguished. The object of the 'myself' part is the I-reality as specified by the generic characteristics [of caste, occupation, etc.] connected with it in the waking condition. The object of the 'I' part is the I-reality which is exclusively but indistinctly aware of itself as evident in the condition of [dreamless] sleep. That is, the experience in question here is of the sort: 'I was not conscious of myself *as* asleep in this place, or as this sort [of individual].'[32]

In the next chapter we shall examine in detail the way the distinctions mentioned above enter into Rāmānuja's notion of personal identity. Here let us make one or two observations about self-awareness in *suṣupti*.

From the above quotation it appears that for Rāmānuja dreamless sleep is a state of pure reflexive awareness, in which the *ātman* is aware only of itself as 'I'.[33] But it is important to note that for him this is far from being the ideal conscious state. In fact the self-consciousness of *suṣupti* is decried, and is described as indistinct and flickering.[34] In contrast Rāmānuja characteristically maintained that it is only through awareness as *relational*, in which the knowing subject is to be distinguished from the [external] object known, that the richness and depth of the ultimate relation of identity-in-difference distinctive of his theological interpretation of reality can begin to be grasped. In particular, the consciousness of enlightenment too, in which an 'I–Thou' union between the knowing subject, viz. the liberated individual and the object known, viz. the Lord himself, is established, is eminently relational. Rāmānuja had scant respect for the liberation of the Sāṃkhya, called 'aloneness' (*kaivalya*), in which the freed spirit remains for ever isolated in a pure, self-reflexive 'bliss'. His acceptance of the *ātman*'s inchoate self-awareness in *suṣupti* is the minimum requirement logically to counter the Advaitic stand in the matter, i.e. to establish the enduring identity of the individual *ātman* against the Advaitic view of a lapse of self-identity and a resurgence of non-differentiated Consciousness. And it is because this self-awareness is an instance of pure reflexivity, without any reference to an object outside itself, that it cannot be accounted for experientially in post-*suṣupti* relational consciousness.

However, for Rāmānuja there is a saving grace to *suṣupti*. Because in fact it comprises a non-relational awareness, it is free from sorrow and smacks of the bliss (*ānanda*) of liberation (*mokṣa*). The Vedāntins distinguished between bliss (*ānanda*) and pleasure (*sukha*, the saṃsāric correlate of pain or sorrow, *duḥkha*). Pleasure and pain are ego-centred, an integral feature of saṃsāric existence and the recompense (*karma* in its derived sense) for previous meritorious or unmeritorious self-interested action (*karma* in the primary sense). Bliss is of a different order. For Rāmānuja it is another aspect, the affective side, of consciousness itself. He affirms that bliss and knowledge or consciousness are co-terminous.

> Bliss is said to be the agreeable [aspect] of knowledge. . . . From the teaching of a distinction [between Brahman and bliss] in such texts as 'That is one bliss of Brahman' [cf. *TaiUp*, II.8.1], 'He who knows the bliss of Brahman . . .' [*TaiUp*, II.4.1] [we conclude that] Brahman is not bliss itself but one who experiences bliss. For to be a knower is to be one who experiences bliss.[35]

In other words, bliss is integral to conscious experience *qua* conscious. Amid the highs and lows, the pleasures and sorrows of mundane living, we may not be aware of the deep-seated bliss that is our birthright as conscious beings. It is only occasionally, in moments when we rise above the ego, or in the healing presence of a great soul (*mahātmā*), that we are taken beyond the surface turbulence of our selves to the calm, untroubled joy that wells up from the depths of the *ātman*.

For Rāmānuja the perfect state of this bliss is in *mokṣa*, when the *ātman* in the union of Brahman comes to the fullest realisation of its being. That is, the self's perfect bliss comes in the self's perfect realisation of union with its source and goal. The bliss of *suṣupti* then, in so far as it is contained in the flickering, purely reflexive self-awareness of the *ātman*, can no more than pressage the relational bliss of *mokṣa*. Yet it is not to be despised – it allows the self, oblivious as it is of the empirical condition in the dreamless state, a repose free from the angst of *saṃsāra*, by putting it, albeit unbeknowing, in touch with the source of bliss itself, Brahman. It is the inchoate bliss of *suṣupti* that accounts for the affirmation 'I slept well' when one arises, refreshed, to face the challenges of life again. In this connection Rāmānuja says, 'The dreamless sleeper, though still in *saṃsāra*, being disconnected from all his sense faculties, is rendered incapable of [empirical] knowledge and the feeling [of pleasure and pain]; having reached the supreme Self, the place of repose, he returns refreshed, to face worldly experience [once more].'[36]

In order to bring out the trans-mundane feature of *suṣupti*, we can contrast it with the sleep composed of dreams in Rāmānuja's reckoning. One of the chief purposes of dreams, according to Rāmānuja (and other Vedāntins), is to allow the dreaming individual to experience pleasure and pain by means of the objects of dream consciousness, in accordance with that individual's accumulated *karma* (in the derivative sense of the meta-empirical residue, in the form of 'merit' and 'demerit', of past moral action). In other words, dreams are morally cathartic (not to say anything of their psychological implications). In accordance with his extreme epistemological realism, Rāmānuja proposes a curious theory of dream objects. Such objects are 'illusory' only in so far as they have a provisional standing, lack public verifiability and are banished by waking consciousness; they are real in so far as they are actual objects of experience in the dream-state. In dreams, dream objects actually exist, though attenuatedly, in the manner described. They are, in Rāmānuja's description, 'a wondrous creation' by God himself, for the purposes of expending the dreaming individual's *karma*. Rāmānuja derives scriptural backing for his realist position (with its moral implications) on dream objects from such texts as BĀUp, IV.3.10,[37] which he applies to dream-states, interpreting these texts as affirming the actual production by the Lord of the dream objects. 'In the dreams of living beings', says Rāmānuja,

> the temporary objects as are in accordance with the merit and demerit [of these beings], and are to be experienced by this or that person alone, are produced by the Lord himself. . . . Such objects do not exist during the dream for the experience of any other person in that the Lord produces them for the experience of particular persons alone.[38] . . . When someone lying in his [bed-]chamber dreams that he goes off in the body to another place, there to be crowned king or have his head chopped off, these experiences, which are the fruits of merit or demerit, are made possible by the [Lord's] production of another [i.e. dream] body similar in configuration to the recumbent one.[39]

Extraordinary as this view is, we must conclude that for Rāmānuja dreams are of a piece with waking consciousness in that they are a medium for the expending of *karma* and a form of direct saṃsāric experience; *suṣupti*, in its obliviousness, is not. It may well be regarded as the reward for past meritorious action, but in itself it may be described as a form of suspended *saṃsāra* in which the *ātman* experiences an inchoate bliss presaging *mokṣa* by the shutting-out of the travails of empirical existence. And who will begrudge the blessed refreshment of dreamless sleep for such as we who must awake to face the burdens of life once more?

In this chapter we have discussed in some detail Rāmānuja's understanding of the relation between the *ātman* and its conscious experience, i.e. of the self as knower, without stressing the bodily implications and limitations of knowerhood. In the process we have examined the nature of consciousness for Rāmānuja, and of the conscious self in its (cognitively) transitive and (purely) self-reflexive states. In the next chapter we shall bring our investigation down to earth, as it were, by considering Rāmānuja's position on the self as (empirically) knowing, feeling and acting, the better to appreciate his distinction between the self's essentially conscious and contingent natures.

4 The Contingent Self

So far we have considered Rāmānuja's position on the *ātman* as knower (*jñātṛ*) in terms of its being intrinsically conscious. We have not gone into the question of the self as knower in relation to its prakṛtic embodiment. In this chapter we shall be concerned with this question together with Rāmānuja's view on the other two main Vedāntic descriptions of the self in its empirical conditon: as *kartṛ* ('doer') and as *bhoktṛ* ('enjoyer/sufferer', i.e. the 'experiencing' self). In other words, we shall be concerned with Rāmānuja's concept of personal agency with special reference to the saṃsāric state. In the discussion it will generally be more convenient to use the Sanskrit terms, *jñātṛ*, *kartṛ* and *bhoktṛ*, instead of possible English equivalents.

At this juncture we may inquire whether there was a particular descriptive term Rāmānuja used to express the *ātman*'s liability to (prakṛtic) embodiment. We think there was: *aṇu* (substantive and adjective, also as adjective *āṇava*: literally 'atom', 'minute particle'; 'atomic', 'minuscule'). But the question is not a simple one. The regular use of this protean word in Hindu philosophy was not matched by the clarity with which it was used; Rāmānuja's case is no exception. Thus we shall have to analyse carefully his use of this term if we wish to understand the nuances he gave to it. Such an analysis is rarely if ever attempted by scholars with respect to Hindu, and least of all Rāmānuja's, thought, so we shall be breaking new ground.

We note first that Vedāntic thinkers were constrained to take account of this term because scripture itself makes significant use of it. Thus in *BĀUp*, IV.3.20, we have 'Indeed, one has these channels called *hitā*; they are as *aṇu*- as a hair split a thousandfold'; *MuṇḍUp*, III.1.9, states, 'This *aṇu ātman* is to be known by thought' (cf. also *KaṭhUp*, I.2.20, etc.). These references intimate the ambiguity of the word. In the first reference, *aṇu* is applied to material, i.e. prakṛtic, being; in the second, to the spiritual *ātman*.

Coming now to Rāmānuja's use of the term, it is clear from the scriptural references just given that he cannot limit its meaning to the sense of 'minuscule physical quantity' applicable to prakṛtic referents (since only *prakṛti* is quantifiable). Indeed, on occasion he does predicate *aṇu* of prakṛtic entities.[1] But following scripture he also applies it to the individual *ātman*, the *jīva*, and it is in this that we are mainly interested here. With respect to the *ātman*, there seem to be three main senses in which Rāmānuja uses *aṇu*.

First, the term is used of the *jīva* in contrast to 'unlimited', i.e. 'great' (*bṛhat*), of Brahman. In Rāmānuja's commentary on *BrSū*, II.3.22, the opponent argues that the description of *BĀUp*, IV.4.22 – 'He is this *great* [*mahān*), unborn self' – refers to the *jīva*, which being great cannot also be atomic. Rāmānuja accepts the validity of this contrast, but denies its referent as suggested by the opponent. The Upaniṣadic description, in which 'great' occurs, applies to Brahman. Earlier in the Commentary, in explaining what 'great' means with respect to Brahman (or the Lord), this is what he says: 'In all cases the word *Brahman* refers to the quality of greatness. And where the greatness, with respect to both proper form and quality, is *unlimited and super-eminent*, there we have the primary object [of the word]. This is only the Lord of all.'[2] Thus, in contrast, the *jīva* as *aṇu* is existentially inherently limited and imperfect. This is the first meaning of the term, with regard to the individual *ātman*, to be isolated by us.

The second meaning can also be derived in terms of a contrast between the *jīva* and Brahman. In the Commentary under *BrSū*, II.3.20, atomicity is explicitly contrasted with omnipresence. The point is to show that it is Brahman who is omnipresent (*sarvagata*) or (all-) pervasive (*vibhu*), while the *jīva* is *aṇu*.[3] In connection with *BĀUp*, IV.4.2, which describes the self at death as 'going out by this light, either from the eye, or from the head, or from other parts of the body', Rāmānuja observes, 'This going out and so on could not occur if [the self] were all-pervasive.'[4] Thus we are to conclude that, in contrast to Brahman the all-pervasive, the *jīva* is in some sense wholly localisable in space and time, that at a particular moment in time in the saṃsāric condition it can be said to be 'here' rather than 'there'.

An interesting objection crops up here. What about those scriptural texts which seem to localise Brahman in, say, the space within the heart?[5] Rāmānuja answers that such texts, far from seeking to constrain Brahman in space and time (Brahman is essentially non-atomic in this sense, he says[6]), have the purpose of encouraging devout meditation on him. Brahman, by choosing to associate himself with a particular place or time, for some such reason as to invigorate our spirits out of profound compassion[7], becomes a convenient subject for contemplation. He is, not even contingently, localisable in the way the *jīva* is in the embodied or saṃsāric state. Such localisability of the individual *ātman* is manifest in the limitations of its causal efficacy and moral accountability arising from the distinctive association it has with its particular body. Under *BrSū*, II.3.36, Rāmānuja argues that the *jīvātman* cannot be all-pervasive (that is, by implication it is *aṇu*), for then it would have been equally related to all the prakṛtic bodies in existence. In that case, discerning individual responsibility for particular actions would be an impossibility: individual experiencing and the moral order as we know it would be unintelligible.

We can combine the two senses of *aṇu* we have identified so far in the following statement: *in the saṃsāric state, the individual* ātman *enters into a distinctive and limiting relationship of correspondence with the whole, and through the whole, with the individual parts, of a particular prakṛtic structure, through which it is enabled to experience the world.* Thus, not only can Rāmānuja say that *this* individual *ātman* is the animator and controller of *this* body, but also that the seat of each *jīvātman* is a particular part of its body, i.e. the heart.[8]

But there seems to be yet a third sense in which Rāmānuja would use *aṇu* of the spiritual *ātman* to contrast it with materiality. This is in the sense of 'subtlety', i.e. that characteristic which enables the *ātman* to be effectively present to something in itself mutable, to pervade or interpenetrate it, without itself being susceptible to essential change in any way. Under the influence of *ChāndUp*, VIII.1.1, he refers to Brahman as the 'small space' (*aṇu* could well have been used) within the heart – there to help meditation, yet, unlike the body (itself susceptible to change in old age and death), immutable in virtue of his 'ultra-subtlety' as the underlying, all-pervading, supreme cause of everything.[9] Rāmānuja clarifies this use of 'subtlety' under *Gītā*, 2.17, where he contrasts the *ātman*-reality's indestructibility by virtue of its unparalleled 'subtlety' as a pervading force, with the body's destructibility by virtue of its grossness as the pervaded. Here it is implied that the *ātman* is pervasive not *as* a substance, but through its property of consciousness which is all-encompassing.[10]

A final observation. So far we have considered the *ātman* as *aṇu* in its empirical condition; can the individual *ātman* be described as *aṇu* in any of the senses identified in liberation (*mokṣa*), i.e. when freed from the imposed connection with its body and the consequences thereof? Though Rāmānuja does not address this question explicitly, it would appear that *mutatis mutandis* he would still be prepared to describe the liberated *ātman* as *aṇu* in that it would continue to be limited existentially and enjoy its 'subtle' nature; this description would apply all the more if the freed *ātman* elected, for its own satisfaction, to act through or be embodied by a particular body (or bodies) constituted from a *sui-generis* (non-prakṛtic) substance (a possibility recognised by Rāmānuja, as we shall see later). In this event, the analogy with saṃsāric embodiment as a basis for the use of *aṇu* becomes clear.

Thus we have seen that, for Rāmānuja, to say that the individual *ātman* is *aṇu* implies that in the saṃsāric condition it is distinctively related to a particular quantum (or to particular quanta) of *prakṛti*. This means, as we shall go on to see, that in its embodied state the individual *ātman* acts as a knower of empirical objects, as a moral agent, and as the subject of pleasure and pain (for our purposes now, translations of *jñātṛ*, *kartṛ* and *bhoktṛ* respectively). Before we take up each description in turn, it will be useful to consider briefly the rival picture in terms of which Rāmānuja was keen to contrast his own position.

This picture represents the common ground between Advaitic and Sāṃkhya views of the self. Śaṃkara, for instance, the father of Advaita, maintained that the *pratyagātman*, or real, inner self – actually identifiable with Brahman or the Absolute Self – is pure, relationless consciousness, not susceptible of the distinctions of knowing subject and knowing-act. To think that the real self or *ātman* is the knowing 'I' extending in scope to the body, that it is in fact the I-centred focus of worldly experience, is of the essence of the saṃsāric condition. This indeed is a congenital illusion, the result of a reciprocal superimposition, on the one hand of the real consciousness of the inner *ātman* on the (inherently insentient) prakṛtic cognitive apparatus, which is *reflected* as I-awareness, and on the other hand, of the individuality of material embodiment on the non-individual, homogeneous consciousness that is the inner *ātman*. Śaṃkara says,

> The real *ātman*, [actually] ever liberated and neither a *kartṛ* nor a *bhoktṛ* in as much as it does not transmigrate, becomes a transmigrator [as it were] characerised as *kartṛ*, *bhoktṛ*, and so on, on account of the superimposition [upon it] of attributive adjuncts such as the discriminative faculty.[11]

Classical Sāṃkhya too, for all its differences from classical Advaita, described its, in the last resort, ineffable *puruṣa* or spiritual principle in similar language: 'In contrast to [*prakṛti*] we can be sure that the *puruṣa* is a witness, aloof, indifferent [to worldly experience], an observer and a non-*kartṛ*.'[12] Again, speaking of the mutual superimposition mentioned above:

> So, from the association of [*puruṣa* and *prakṛti*], the non-conscious subtle body [which acts as the substrate of empirical personality] becomes conscious as it were, and the dispassionate [*puruṣa*] becomes a *kartṛ* as it were, while in fact it is the *guṇas* [the constituents of *prakṛti*] which are the *kartṛ*.[13]

Thus in the Advaita–Sāṃkhya stance the spiritual principle could not properly or literally[14] be described as experiencing in the world through the body – if it did it could no longer be regarded as essentially immutable and homogeneous.

This is where Rāmānuja's philosophically realist bias put him in opposition. He made it a point to argue that the *ātman could* be said literally to act empirically under its three descriptions, i.e. to act really contingently thus, if not essentially. Let us examine this position.

(1) First, it is the *jīvātman* and not some pseudo-cogniser such as the Advaitic–Sāṃkhya non-conscious ego or *ahaṃkāra* that really is the knower in the empirical condition. We have seen in Chapter 3 how Rāmānuja was keen to establish that one's everyday relational conscious experience is the real thing and is not sublatable by some 'higher' non-individual awareness. But to say that the *jīvātman* is a knower (*jñātṛ*) of empirical objects is not to say that it is susceptible of essential change. Like the Advaitins and Sāṃkhyas, Rāmānuja was averse to saying that the individual *ātman* is essentially mutable. To admit this was to admit (all the orthodox Hindu schools objected to this) that the *ātman* is transient and destructible – the chief characteristics of *saṃsāra*, the realm of no permanent value. In contrast, the *ātman*, the authentic self, must be essentially changeless and enduring, so that it can fittingly symbolise and ground man's spiritual vision and goal amid the shifting sands of saṃsāric experience. Thus Rāmānuja argued that the knowledge of empirical objects implies that the *ātman* is only extrinsically subject to change: its intrinsic nature as a reflexive centre of (normally relational) conscious experience remains undisturbed. Again the analogy of the lamp and its light can helpfully be resorted to here.

Light in itself is potentially infinitely expansive, capable of showing up any object in its path. Light has two sorts of extrinsic limiters of form: the quantity of fire-substance available for burning and the material object light encounters as it radiates outwards. Thus the light of an oil lamp is small and weak compared to that of a blazing fire, while each object encountered 'gives [visible] shape' to the formless light rather as variously shaped jars 'give shape' to the formless space they circumscribe. Consciousness too radiates from its centre the conscious *ātman*, potentially unrestricted and capable of manifesting any object it encounters. Granted that in its substrate, the individual *ātman*, it is inherently limited as finite, consciousness is empirically subject, in its expression, to two sorts of extrinsic limiters: the essentially non-conscious prakṛtic component of the conscious individual (determining in its particularities the sort of conscious experience possible, i.e. human rather than brute, belonging to this individual rather than to that), and the particular object encountered, translated into the 'object of consciousness' *now* rather than *then*: in other words, into the transient cognitive act. In neither of these cases is the *ātman's* essence as the centre of conscious experience affected. Thus, while in the empirical condition it is the *jīvātman* that is really the knower, it undergoes change as a knower only extrinsically. It is with respect to the extrinsic limiters mentioned above that Rāmānuja comments, 'Though knowledge is unrestricted by itself, it is capable of contraction and expansion'[15]; contraction and expansion, that is, through its particular object and its particular body-dependent mode of experiencing.

(2) We come now to the *jīva* as *kartṛ* (literally, 'doer', 'producer'). A convenient way to understand Rāmānuja's use of this term is to consider different senses he gives to its correlate *karman* (literally, 'action', 'work'), since a *kartṛ* is the agent of *karman*. For Rāmānuja the standard (precise) meaning of *karman* is 'action which is of a meritorious or unmeritorious nature'.[16] In other words, *karman* in its standard sense is action that is self-centred, conscious and free: as such it is action for which one is morally responsible.

To say that such action is 'self-centred' means that it is not 'enlightened'. For the Vedāntins in general, 'enlightened' action is action performed not out of self-gratification, engendering its ordained saṃsāric fruit (*phala*) – indeed, enlightened action does not produce such fruit – but from a motive of either pure duty or selfless love for God, depending upon whether one's point of view is non-theistic or theistic. Self-centred action, on the other hand, is intended for the agent's own gratification and produces its due saṃsāric fruit. ('Action' – *karman* – must be taken here to cover the refraining from particular deeds.) Now we must distinguish between the 'fruit' (*sensu stricto*) of an action and the 'result'. The 'fruit' of an action is the pleasant or unpleasant saṃsāric consequence of that action, revealed on authority (usually scriptural authority). This consequence or fruit can well mature in a future existence. Thus the scripture-revealed fruit of the *agnihotra* sacrifice (in this instance we are talking of sacrificial action) is paradise (*svarga*).

Now it is not open to human insight to discern the fruit (of the performance or non-performance) of particular actions; no one can tell *a priori* or with certitude based on human intuition alone that the fruit of the *agnihotra* sacrifice is paradise, obtainable in a post-mortem existence. In other words, we must needs rely on scripture or scripture-derived authority for veridical information about the connection between an action and its fruit. Such fruit can be something 'objective' (for instance, a wife, progeny, wealth) or 'subjective', i.e. a particular sort of experience for the performer of the action (in each case fruit is pleasant or unpleasant). The 'result' of an action, on the other hand, is what naturally follows its performance, either subjectively (for instance, satisfaction on giving alms, remorse on inflicting cruelty) or objectively (for example, a kingdom or wealth consequent upon victory in battle), and as such open to discernment from everyday experience. Sometimes the result (so distinguished) of an action is loosely called its fruit in the texts; in any case, this is not an area dealt with clearly in Hindu ethics. The traditions are diverse and confused on this point.[17]

Action or *karman* in the standard sense, then, is self-centred in that it is performed for the agent's own gratification, engendering in due course its appropriate saṃsāric fruit. Such action is morally acceptable if it conforms, nevertheless, to the dictates of the agent's *dharma*, understood here as the code of obligations and practice circumscribing the agent's caste and stage in life. Such action is morally unacceptable if it goes against the performer's *dharma*. Dharmic action is 'meritorious' or not (it may be enlightened) depending on whether it is self-centred or not, on whether it 'merits' (pleasant) saṃsāric fruit or not. Adharmic action is always unmeritorious, earning for its agent unpleasant saṃsāric fruit.

Because *karman* or 'action' in the standard sense implies a self-centred mentality bound up with the necessary production of pleasant or unpleasant fruit for its agent – that is, because this action perpetuates its agent in the round of rebirth where it needs must experience its fruit – I shall refer to such action as '*saṃsāra*-immanent' ('SI' for short) action or *karman*. Enlightened action, on the other hand, as we have seen, has no regard for and does not produce fruit. For Rāmānuja it was not self-centred but other-centred, i.e. performed from the motive of the pure love for God. Such action eschews the saṃsāric mentality, does not build up for its agent the prospect of future lives in *saṃsāra*, but on the contrary works towards the dissolution of the agent's *karma* and its salvation out of rebirth. Accordingly I shall call such action '*saṃsāra*-transcendent' ('ST' for short) action or *karman*. ST action is exceedingly difficult to achieve (and gives rise to a valid though not standard sense of *karman*), yet Rāmānuja believes that it is possible, or at least increasingly possible in the life of the devotee, with the help of the Lord.

Now, in so far as saṃsāric embodiment is not essential to the individual *ātman*'s nature – that is, in so far as the *ātman* is required to be reborn in different bodily conditions only to expend its accumulated *karma* (i.e. the wages of self-centredness, realised in the experience of pleasant or unpleasant fruit) – neither SI nor ST action in the saṃsāric body is essential to the *ātman*. Thus for Rāmānuja, though the empirically embodied *ātman* is a real performer (*kartṛ*) of SI or ST action, it is not part of its essential nature to be so. He writes,

> [Knowledge's] proper form, contracted [in the first place] by [past] *karma* into the condition of the embodied self, exists [as further determined] in accordance with the variety of individual *karma*. It is conditioned once again by means of the senses [in everyday cognition]. And the feature of the rise and termination [of cognition] is a function of this flow of knowledge by means of the senses. Now, being a *kartṛ* has to do with the flow of knowledge, and this is not essential [to the *ātman*]. In other words, the *ātman* remains essentially unchanging in that [being a *kartṛ* is an extrinsic change] brought about by *karma*.[18]

We have said that *saṃsāra*-immanent action, besides being self-centred, is also conscious and free. Its being bound up with consciousness comes out in the above quotation; further, it is necessary to be conscious to be attentive to the fruit of one's deeds. Yet it is also free. This is why it is also moral in character. The opponent makes it a point to insist that such action must imply the freedom to choose in the agent when he observes in connection with the scriptural injunctions and prohibitions governing ritual action, 'only one capable of initiating or desisting from action by his own decision can be commanded to act'.[19] Rāmānuja's position seems to be faced with a problem here. On the one hand, he must preserve the agent's moral freedom to act (with respect to both SI and ST action); on the other hand, he is keen to affirm that the Lord is the agent's 'inner controller' (*antaryāmin*) as a function of his universal causality. The Lord is the cause behind all instances of causation in the world, free [moral] action notwithstanding.

An interesting answer to this dilemma is propounded. Rāmānuja says,

> The supreme Self has bestowed equitably on all conscious being all the equipment required for performing or desisting from action: for

> example, the capacity for the power of thought, for the power of willing, and so on. To bring this about he has become the support of these beings, and, having entered within them, exercises control as the consenter [to action], being established as their principal. The individual, conditioned by these powers endowed by the supreme Self, itself performs or desists from action. The supreme Self [merely] witnesses the doing and remains impartial. Thus all is in order.[20]

In other words, it is the individual agent which acts freely, while the Lord as the individual's existential support (*ādhāra*) allows this action to be realised, to take being. Elsewhere[21] Rāmānuja seeks to illuminate this 'co-operation' by an analogy.

When property is jointly and equally owned by two persons, the decision of one to transfer the whole property to a third party has no effect unless the other owner consents. Legally, this consent is a minimal act in that it just makes the transference of property possible; the consenter need not be regarded as initiating, determining or morally approving of the act of transference inspired by the first party. Similarly, says Rāmānuja, when the finite agent performs a [moral] action, the Lord as the agent's inner entitative support consents to bring the action into existence, but he neither determines nor necessarily morally approves of it. The indwelling Lord has regard to the 'act of will' (*prayatna udyoga*) of the agent and consents to its realisation.[22] This is a minimal form of consent, an 'ontological' consent, if you wish. The agent is morally responsible for the deed, not the Lord.

A little reflection will show, of course, that this is hardly a resolution of our dilemma concerning the Lord's universal causality and the possibility of finite free action. For is the agent's 'act of will' in the first place dependent upon the consent of the Lord or not? If it is, how is the agent really free to initiate action? If it is not, the Lord is not universal cause. There is the added problem of the Lord's 'consenting' to bring an evil action of a finite agent into being: must he not be responsible for it in some way? Yet Rāmānuja is adamant that the Lord is in no way responsible for finite agency, let alone for moral evil. For these reasons, it seems to me, Rāmānuja has sought to do no more than provide an illuminating analogy, by way of partial explanation, for the 'co-operation' between the Lord and the individual *ātman* in the performance of free action. In a later chapter, when discussing Rāmānuja's theological method, we shall see why it was not to his purpose to attempt to resolve logically the dilemma under consideration. For the time being we leave this topic with the affirmation that Rāmānuja, like so many theistic theologians of the East and West, was keen to maintain at the same time the universal causality of his God and the moral autonomy of the finite agent.

From the preceding discussion it should be clear that in performing SI action the individual is conscious and free but self-centred in that such action tends to produce (pleasant or unpleasant) saṃsāric fruit that needs must be experienced in the future; we may say that SI action is 'fruit-intended'. In performing ST action, on the other hand, the individual is no less conscious and free but acts other-centredly without any desire for worldly fruit. ST action is not fruit-intended and does not produce (saṃsāric) fruit. In other words, it is the *intention* (*saṃkalpa*) of a morally acceptable (i.e. dharmic) action that determines its SI or ST nature. Outwardly a deed may look the same, yet in the one case, when fruit-intended, it binds its performer to the saṃsāric condition; in the other, when not fruit-intended, its agent is on the way to experiencing the only 'fruit' that really matters – salvific bliss. Rāmānuja says with passionate clarity,

> Behold this great difference: that, with respect to the same action, by the difference of intention alone, there are some agents who, partaking of even a little of its [worldly] fruit, become fallen in nature, while there are others – these do not return [to saṃsāra] – who share only of that fruit which is the attainment of the supreme Person: unlimited and pre-eminent bliss.[23]

Rāmānuja's was neither a legalistic nor a mechanistic ethic; like the other Vedāntic teachers he held that it was the nature and purity of the intention that determined the moral worth of an action.

On occasion Rāmānuja, taking his cue from scripture, predicates *kartṛ* of the Lord himself, either in his transcendent or in his avatāric form. For example. Rāmānuja sees *BĀUp*, IV.3.10 – 'Then he produces ponds, pools of lotuses and rivers. For it is he who is the maker [*kartā*]' – as referring to the Lord as agent.[24] Of course in such cases *kartṛ/karman* is to be understood in the ST sense. Now and then Rāmānuja fixes on specialised senses of this correlated pair.[25]

It will complete the discussion and further understanding if we finally consider senses in which Rāmānuja is prepared to accept that the *jīvātman* can be said to be a 'non-doer' (*akartṛ*). It seems to me that Rāmānuja distinguishes two such senses. The first must be understood in the context of a soul totally devoted to the Lord and performing actions in his name alone. Thus in interpreting Kṛṣṇa's words to Arjuna in *Gītā*, 2.47 ('Action alone is your responsibility, never its fruits; let not your motive be the fruit of action, nor your attachment to non-action') our theologian paraphrases,

> Where scriptural action is concerned [Arjuna], whether [this is to be performed] regularly, occasionally or as desired, and connected as it is to some particular fruit, your responsibility, as one always motivated by purity and yearning for liberation, must be for the action alone, never for the fruit known to be connected to the action. Because [action] with fruit [in view] binds [one to *saṃsāra*] and [action] without fruit [in view] performed as worship to Me is the reason for liberation, have no motive either for [fruit-bearing] action or its fruit. You, as one always motivated by purity and yearning for liberation, must regard yourself as a non-doer with respect to action enjoined on you [by your *dharma*].[26]

In other words, the devoted soul is being counselled to 'cast all its actions upon the Lord'. Such a soul, as a matter of fact, is still really the doer (*kartṛ*) of its actions, but in so far as they are *saṃsāra*-transcendent, performed solely as worship to the Lord and without any desire for the fruit they would otherwise most certainly have produced, they may be regarded as inspired by and under the total control of the Lord. In this case the devotee has not surrendered one whit of his moral freedom, but as one who has acquired a 'holy will' – we may borrow the Kantian expression with perfect propriety here – spontaneously and in total harmony with the wishes of the Lord, the devotee may cry in the spirit of a Paul, 'I act: now not I. The Lord acts in me.' This is one sense in which the *jīva* may regard itself as a 'non-doer'.

There is another. This is the meaning required to make sense of such texts as *Gītā*, 3.27: 'In all cases, actions are done by the *guṇas* of *prakṛti*: the *ātman* deluded by the ego thinks, "I am a doer."' Rāmānuja interprets this as follows: 'The *ātman*, deluded by the ego, thinks that it is a doer of those actions performed in fact by *prakṛti*'s *guṇas* – *sattva*, [*rajas* and *tamas*] – in accordance with their respective natures.' Enlarging on this under v. 29 he says,

> this is the position regarding the *guṇas*' being a doer: that this being-a-doer does not belong to the *ātman*'s proper form; in fact, it arises through connection with the *guṇas*. In other words, that being-a-doer is *guṇa*-produced is known by discriminating what happens from [the *ātman*'s] conjunction with and disjunction from [*prakṛti*].[27]

That is, since embodied action is essentially a function of *prakṛti* in its *guṇas*, the *jīva* can say that it is not (essentially) a doer (*kartṛ*).

(3) We may pass quickly over the *jīvātman* as *bhoktṛ*, i.e. as experiencing pleasure and pain, in Rāmānuja's thought. This is because he regards *kartṛ* and *bhoktṛ* as coextensive. In other words, *mutatis mutandis*, the standard senses given to *kartṛ* have parallels with respect to *bhoktṛ*. Rāmānuja observes,

> Scriptural texts such as 'Let him who desires paradise sacrifice' and 'He who yearns for liberation should worship Brahman' connect being a *kartṛ* with being a *bhoktṛ*, whether the fruit [in view] be paradise or liberation. For a conscious being [i.e. the *ātman*] cannot be responsible for the agency of something non-conscious [i.e. *prakṛti*]. . . . Hence the scriptures have point only if a conscious being experiences [pleasure and pain] in virtue of its being a *kartṛ* itself'.[28]

Whether the deed in question be SI or ST in nature, only the doer himself of the deed can experience its 'fruit' (*sensu lato*).

We may fittingly conclude this chapter with a discussion on a topic much attended to in philosophical circles in the West, but rarely dealt with by commentators in Hindu philosophy: personal identity. In connection with Rāmānuja's philosophical theology this topic has not yet received adequate treatment. Now the question of personal identity in Rāmānuja's system does seem to present problems. This can be appreciated by juxtaposing the two following statements. First:

> The individual *ātman*'s proper form, bereft of its various [non-essential] differentiations in the form of particular prakṛtic modifications as god, man and so on, has for its properties solely knowledge and bliss. When [the individual *ātman*'s] *karma*-produced differentiations of being a god, and so on, are [eventually] done away with, this much we can say: that the distinction of its proper form cannot be expressed in words and is known to [the *ātman*] alone; that it has knowledge for its proper form. We must say the same for all [individual] *ātmans*.[29]

The second statement is quoted with approval by Rāmānuja:

> If the I-reality were not the *ātman*, the *ātman* could have no inwardness; for inward reality is distinguished from outward reality

> by means of I-cognition. He who seeks liberation applies himself to the scriptures with the thought, 'May *I* reign (in the end), enjoying eternal bliss, with all sorrows gone.' If he thought that liberation consisted in the destruction of the I-realty, he would slink away at the mere whiff of any talk about liberation.[30]

Clearly this is intended as a criticism of the Advaitic view of liberation, but in the process it seems to affirm the continuance of personal identity after death (assuming, as Rāmānuja does, that it is the *ātman* which is the seat of personal identity). The first statement, however, suggests that the proper forms of all *ātmans* are identical qualitatively and distinct only numerically. Can the two statements be reconciled in terms of Rāmānuja's thought?

We can begin with a few clarifications. In the West there has been much philosophical debate about the nature of the person or self, and on occasion, 'self' and 'person' have been distinguished. For our purposes however, it will do to treat the question of personal identity as coinciding with that of self-identity. Further, let us accept the prevailing minimal requirement for selfhood: that the self should be a centre of conscious and volitional experience. In the light of our study so far we can say then that for Rāmānuja, who accepts the plurality of *jīvātmans*, the *jīvātman* is a self or person in the minimal sense, and further, as noted above, that it is the seat of one's personal identity. Finally we note that we may seek to determine, philosophically, two kinds of personal identity. The first may be called first-person personal identity, for which sufficient epistemological grounds or criteria are sought to determine one's own personal identity over a span of time, i.e. to answer the question, 'On what grounds can one say that the person one experiences oneself to be at time t_1 is the very same person as the person one experiences oneself to be at time t_2?' The second may be called third-person personal identity, for which sufficient epistemological grounds or criteria are sought to determine the personal identity of another over a period of time, i.e. to answer such questions as 'On what grounds can I say that from t_1 to t_2 this person is Devadatta not Yajñadatta?' Our inquiry will take into account Rāmānuja's view on both kinds of personal identity (especially the first).

Now the question of personal identity may be discussed with respect to two conditions of the individual self: (1) in the embodied state, and (2) in the disembodied state: specifically in the liberated state or *mokṣa*.

(1) At the outset, we recall from the last chapter that according to

Rāmānuja it is essential to the *jīva* to be a knower, and that it is essential to knowerhood to be reflexively self-aware implicitly or explicitly in every cognitive act. In other words, the *jīvātman* as conscious is self-luminous in the form of an 'I'. Further, this I-awareness, even if not attended to (in a transitive cognitive act), as a continuous experience is intuitively and ineluctably known to its experiencer by means of the same I. Such self-awareness *as an experience* is incommunicable. It establishes the distinctive individual personal identity of every conscious agent, and in its experiencing sets up an uncollapsable distinction between its own 'I' and other I-awarenesses. This means that such I-awareness cannot be sublated or dissolved by or in a form of 'higher' unitive consciousness as the Advaitins claim. Here we have the epistemological basis, in its most general form, of Rāmānuja's position on personal identity. Here too we have the basis for reconciling the two statements quoted earlier. While the first, after affirming that all *jīvātmans* are identical in this, that their essential characteristic is consciousness (and bliss), adverts to the incommunicability of each *jīva*'s experience of personal identity *as* experience, the second goes on to clarify this experience of personal identity as (self-reflexive) I-awareness (hence the contrast between the conscious *ātman* as 'inward' and material being as 'outward'), an experience which of its nature is self-distinguishing for each *jīvātman*. But to say that the *jīva* is always aware of itself as the same I is not to say that it is always aware of the same determinations of this I, nor indeed that its I-consciousness cannot be a composite consciousness. Let us examine these statements with respect to the *jīva* in the embodied state.

We have seen that, according to Vedāntic philosophical anthropology, the human individual is a composite of spirit, i.e. the *ātman* as a centre of conscious experience, and matter, i.e. the prakṛtic psycho-physical complement. This intimate (but nevertheless distinguishable and, in the final analysis, separable) union of spirit and matter gives rise, certainly for Vedāntins of Rāmānuja's way of thinking, to a composite I-awareness. That is, this I-awareness is constituted of what we may call 'basic self-identity' and what may be termed 'empirical self-identity'. The *jīva* is aware of its basic self-identity maintains Rāmānuja when it is aware of itself formally as 'I', through different states of existence. This formal I-awareness remains the same whether the *jīva* be embodied or disembodied, whether it be embodied in this way or that. But Rāmānuja also held that in the saṃsāric embodied state the *jīva*'s I-awareness is informed, shot through as it were, by determinations which are a function of its particular psycho-physical complement; for instance, human rather than praeter-human (i.e. *deva-*) consciousness, awareness of being male rather than female, excitable rather than placid, Brahmin rather than Vaiśya, fat rather than thin, and so on.[31] These psycho-physical features, stemming from the *jīva*'s prakṛtic component, give rise to the *jīva*'s 'empirical self-identity'.

Now, in the saṃsāric condition the *jīva* is congenitally ignorant, in so far as it is unenlightened, of the composite nature of this I-awareness, and indeed that it is not part of the essential I to have the characteristics of the present empirical I. In other words, though the *jīva* can say, 'I am *really* human, male, Brahmin, excitable, fat', and so on, it cannot say that it is *essentially* these things. For we have seen that it is not essential to the *jīvātman* to be embodied prakṛtically, determined by the psycho-physical characteristics this entails. Though the *jīva*'s empirical characteristics 'belong' to the perduring basic I, are underlain by it, and indeed are identified by it as belonging to this *jīva* over a period of time rather than to that, they are but contingent to the basic I. The contingency of the psycho-physical determinations is all the more apparent in the context of the Hindu belief in rebirth. Each of the physical embodiments the *jīvātman* undergoes in its saṃsāric journey engenders an empirical identity-set 'belonging' to the same I for the duration of that embodiment and 'colouring' the *jīva*'s I-awareness for the period. Enlightenment consists, among other things, in discriminating the hitherto undiscriminate composite I-awareness, in *realising* the distinction between one's basic self-identity and one's empirical identity in spite of the fact, so long as embodiment persists, that the same I-focus continues to be determined simultaneously by essential and contingent empirical characteristics. Such enlightened awareness of oneself gives rise to a non-egoistic ethic, i.e. an ethic that does not centre round, reinforce and perpetuate one's empirical self-identity.

In the light of all this, on what grounds can one say that the person one experiences oneself to be at time t_1 is the very same person as the person one experiences oneself to be at time t_2, if t_1 and t_2 are within the same embodiment? Rāmānuja would answer, as we have seen in Chapter 3, 'on the grounds of "recognition" of the same I perduring from t_1 to t_2 in and through its empirical determinations (however variable these may be)'. This 'recognition' is an intuitive, self-authenticating experience. Though Rāmānuja does not go into the question of the possibility of 'false' memory-experiences producing unauthentic I-recognition, he would answer no doubt that 'false' memory-experiences affect the recognition of one's empirical self-identity and not of one's basic self-identity. As to the question of determining the personal identity of another, here one would have to *decide* upon agreed criteria for doing this (for instance, trustworthy testimony of the person concerned and other appropriate persons).

With respect to the grounds for determining first-person personal identity when t_1 and t_2 do not qualify the *jīvātman* in the same embodiment, a peculiar problem arises in that the I-awareness at t_1 is outside the purview of the *jīva*'s recognition-experience at t_2 as a result of extrinsic limiting factors, such as the erasing of the memory-continuum between t_1 and t_2 by the 'trauma of death'. In this case, though in fact the *jīva*'s basic I-awareness at t_1, coloured by and distinguishing as it does the *jīva*'s set of empirical characteristics at t_1, is identical with the *jīva*'s basic I-awareness at t_2, coloured by and distinguishing the set of empirical characteristics at t_2, the *jīva* is not aware of this sameness. At this stage a question arises. Though the individual *ātman* undergoes fresh embodiment at each rebirth, shedding in the process for all practical purposes any memory of its previous empirical identity, is there no sense in which, when liberation has been attained, the empirical identity of each embodiment can be said to have made a lasting impression on the self-awareness the soul carries into its final state? In other words, when the liberated *ātman* attains salvific communion with its Lord after its saṃsāric journey of many births, of many lives each with its joys and sorrows, loves and hates, and complement of human relationships, does it lose all connection with the memory of these as completely as it does with the corruptible bodies that were their field of experience? This is an important question, for its answer reflects Rāmānuja's view on the importance of human living and its social relationships. This leads us to a consideration of personal identity in *mokṣa*.[32]

(2) In this state the individual *ātman* has achieved self-fulfilment. For Rāmānuja this means that the *ātman* is no longer subject to extrinsic limiting factors, that its individual consciousness by participating in the all-knowingness of the Lord expands to its fullest extent, and that the *ātman*, in the company of the blessed, exists in loving and blissful communion with the Focus of that company – the Lord himself. In other words, in *mokṣa*, the *ātman* carries over from the saṃsāric condition a self-consciousness individuated by the same basic I-awareness of that condition. Commenting on *BĀUp*, I.4.10 ('Seeing this, the seer Vāmadeva realised, "*I* was Manu and the Sun too"'), Rāmānuja makes clear that *mokṣa* entails an individuating I-awareness for the liberated *ātman*: 'We know this from Vāmadeva's and others' – all their ignorance

having been purified in intuitive communion with Brahman's very self – experiencing their *ātmans* as an "I".'[33] In other words, the liberated *ātman* continues as an identifiable person; its identity is not swallowed up or submerged in some homogeneous and amorphous Consciousness as Advaita claims.

But what is the content of this mokṣaic I-awareness? Is it a blank, formal I-awareness, qualitatively identical but only numerically different for the liberated *ātmans*, in each case continuous with the basic I-awareness of the saṃsāric condition, but purged of every trace of the empirical colouring of that condition? In *mokṣa* is the whole saṃsāric experience 'blacked out'? Rāmānuja, as in other cases, has not gone into this issue, but the evidence exists to formulate an answer on his behalf.

To begin with, in *mokṣa* the *ātman*'s awareness is expanded not contracted. The *ātman* shares in the all-knowingness of the Lord. Surely this means, if the ātmanic I of *saṃsāra* continues, duly enlightened, as the ātmanic I of *mokṣa*, that the liberated *ātman* cannot be ignorant of the experiences of which it was really (if only contingently) the subject during its saṃsāric pilgrimage. Thus mokṣaic personal identity must incorporate, in some way, the empirical identity-sets of the saṃsāric condition. Since the liberated *ātman* is wholly blissful, however, in contrast to its unenlightened saṃsāric experience as sorrowful, this incorporation takes place *sub specie aeternitatis*, as it were, by which all that the *ātman* has undergone and done in the past – the good and the bad, the triumphs and the failures, the joys and the woes – are summated and transmuted in a final healing vision of fulfilment, where, to quote the Christian mystic Julian of Norwich 'All shall be well and all shall be well, and all manner of thing shall be well'. Thus, for Rāmānuja, one's saṃsāric journey is not to be explained away as the experience of some pseudo-self engaging in a mundane transaction that never really was, as in Advaita; rather, it is reflected in an enlarged and enriched mokṣaic identity which gives to it a lasting worth.

This concludes our treatment of the nature of the individual self, in the saṃsāric and liberated states. We must now embark, in the next chapter, on a study of Rāmānuja's view of the supreme being, Brahman, for we have seen that for Rāmānuja the knowledge of Brahman's nature no less than the knowledge of the nature of the self is a prerequisite for salvation.

5 Brahman

Rāmānuja's use of *svarūpa* (literally, 'proper form') in describing Brahman's nature is not fixed. Sometimes he seems to use this word in a strict sense, sometimes in a broad sense.[1] From a logical point of view this flexibility may be lamented, but theologically it accords well with Rāmānuja's characteristic of making Brahman the focus of different perspectives. We have seem earlier that on occasion Rāmānuja theologises 'from above' – that is, by focusing on Brahman's comprehensiveness; here the Brahman-reality is made to comprehend the whole of being so that justice may be done to the immanentist religious (and scriptural) insight that Brahman is the source, ground and terminus of all reality (in a perspective where the notion of creation 'out of nothing' seemed unintelligible). On occasion, however, Rāmānuja theologises 'from below' – from the viewpoint of finite being – to preserve the Lord's purity and transcendence and to account for our experience of both imperfection and (relative) moral and existential autonomy in the world. The concept of Brahman's *svarūpa* then, i.e. of that form proper to Brahman *qua* Brahman, must remain flexible enough to be susceptible to these shifts of perspective. Nevertheless, as I have noted above, we can detect a strict use of *svarūpa* for Brahman in Rāmānuja's thought, at least in the sense of Brahman's quiddity or essential nature, i.e. Brahman *per se* or in himself, in his innermost core. For the present let us concern ourselves with Brahman's *svarūpa* in this sense; later we shall consider the broader senses.

In Chapter 2 we examined Rāmānuja's understanding of what he acknowledged to be a definition of Brahman, i.e. a description of Brahman's proper form (*sensu stricto*). The definition, contained in *TaiUp*, II.1.1, is that Brahman is 'reality, knowledge, infinite'. We shall not repeat the exegesis except to point out that elsewhere[2] Rāmānuja expands these definitional characteristics so that there seem to be five in all: reality (*satya*), knowledge (*jñāna*), bliss (*ānanda*), purity (*amalatva*) and infinitude (*anantatva*). By this the adequacy of the *Taittirīya* definition is not substantially impaired in that both 'bliss' and 'purity' may be seen as drawing out and clarifying the original content of the definition. We have seen that Rāmānuja maintains[3] that, while 'bliss' is not synonymous with 'knowledge', it is coterminous with it such that bliss is the agreeable aspect of knowledge. 'Purity' amplifies 'infinitude'. If 'infinitude' means 'the absence of limitation due to place, time and being', 'purity' denotes the quality and intensity of Brahman's perfections and their freedom from taint or blemish of any kind (i.e. from any sort of limitation such as necessary contact with materiality, the power of *karma*, and so on). Coupled with that of 'infinitude', the concept of 'purity' emphasises the uncompromising transcendence of Brahman's *svarūpa* over finite being.

It is worth pointing out here that our earlier observation[4] about the *sui-generis* relation between the *jīvātman*'s *svarūpa* and its definitional qualities applies, *mutatis mutandis*, to the relation between Brahman's *svarūpa* (*sensu stricto*) and its essential qualities. Also, as for the *jīvātman*, for Brahman or the supreme Self (*paramātman*) too, knowledge (in its infinity and absolute purity) may be said to be *the* defining characteristic, in so far as it affirms the supreme Person that Brahman essentially is. In Rāmānuja's theology the personhood at the core of Brahman's being stands in marked contrast to the 'impersonal' or hyper-personal nature of the Advaitic Absolute.

But to say that the supreme being has certain defining qualities or characteristics is not to say that Rāmānuja denied other qualities of it. On the contrary, it is typical of Rāmānuja's divine descriptions to attribute to Brahman a host of supereminent perfections. Our theologian makes it a point to say that Brahman is characterised by a twofold aspect: a positive and a negative. The positive describes what Brahman is by attributing to him all sorts of perfections; the negative says what Brahman is not by removing from him all imperfections.

> Everywhere, in *śruti* and in *smṛti*, the highest Brahman is referred to as having a twofold characteristic. That is [at one and the same time] he is possessed of the marks of being free from every defect and of being a mine of illustrious qualities. For example [in *ChāndUp*, VIII.1.5, we have]: 'He is free from evil, old age, death, sorrow, hunger, thirst, with wishes come true and intentions realised'; and [in *Viṣṇu Purāṇa*, VI.5.84–5, we have] 'He consists of all illustrious qualities, supporting the emission of being with but a trace of his power; he is no other than a mass of qualities such as lustre, strength, sovereignty, great wisdom, valour and power. Higher than all else is he, in whom, Lord of high and low, there is no blemish'.[5]

The point of Brahman's having the *ubhayaliṅga*, i.e. the twofold (positive and negative) mark is to emphasise (not only against non-dualist views of the Absolute but as the focus of true theistic devotion) Brahman's variegated perfection and its transcendent purity.

If the defining qualities indicate what Brahman is in himself (i.e. necessarily, in respect of 'proper form' in the strict sense), the host of non-defining qualities affirms his variegated perfection and superiority in contrast to finite being. We shall not here go into the question of describing and analysing the non-defining qualities. With an important exception that we shall take up in due course, these qualities make up the usual catalogue which theists ascribe to their God; besides, others have considered this matter.[6] Instead, after stressing that it is central to Rāmānuja's theology to affirm the *relatedness* of his God to finite being, let us examine a crucial aspect of this relatedness: the Lord's originative causality. It is my contention that this is one of the distinctive areas of Rāmānuja's theology, a feature of his unique theological method (which we shall consider in detail in Chapter 7). In analysing the Lord's originative causality – an analysis which typically has frequent recourse to scripture and claims to interpret it – Rāmānuja the theist seeks to preserve the delicate balance between the counterweights of divine transcendence and immanence.

In his writings Śaṃkara refers to Upaniṣadic *mahāvākyas* or 'great utterances', and it has been claimed that it is on the basis of his interpretation of (selected) *mahāvākyas* as pivots of Upaniṣadic meaning that he has constructed his system.[7] I think there can be no doubt that, for all practical purposes, Rāmānuja too has his hermeneutic *mahāvākyas*. One such is the utterance 'Being only, my dear, was this in the beginning, one only without a second. It thought, "May I be many, may I bring forth".'[8] The implications of this statement reverberate throughout Rāmānuja's theology and reflect the different uses to which he puts the text.[9] One such is as the basis for arriving at an understanding of Brahman's originative causality. 'By the statement, "Being only, my dear, was this in the beginning, one only"', he says 'is proclaimed that Brahman, in so far as he wishes to create, is the substantial cause [of the world]. It occurs to one that there must naturally be another cause to *produce* the effect [as in worldly experience]. The expression "without a second" rejects this [notion].'[10] So Brahman is at the same time the 'substantial cause' (*upādāna-kāraṇa*) and the 'efficient cause' (*nimitta-kāraṇa*) of the world. Let us examine what Rāmānuja means by this.

The *Upaniṣads* and other Hindu scriptures contain many statements which by implication ill accord with the traditional Christian picture of creation as the production of being, by God's power, out of nothingness. In Vedānta specifically, such a picture of originative causality made little or no sense. Rāmānuja in particular took seriously the many scriptural images and utterances which seemed naturally to imply that finite being emerges from or issues out of Brahman, its permanent ground or substratum and the fund into which it is reabsorbed in a dissolution. Philosophically–theologically this meant that the 'creational gap', i.e. the ontological chasm between infinite and finite being, represented by the *ex nihilo* of the *creatio* doctrine was eschewed, and that instead an existential 'umbilical cord', i.e. a continuous existential relation between the originative cause (Brahman) and the finite order was posited. The concept of the substantial cause served this requirement. The substantial cause (*upādāna-kāraṇa*)[11] is that out of which the effect is produced such that the latter derives its being from the former. This can be understood relatively, in which case the specific nature of the relative substantial cause enters into consideration – for example, the (material) clay is the relative substantial cause of the (material) clay pot, its effect, keeping the latter in existence by being what it is – or it can be understood absolutely, in which case Brahman is known to be the ultimate originative source, the mainstay and the terminus of finite being *qua* being. Rāmānuja and the other Vedāntins were quick to argue that we cannot deduce, by a process of strict reasoning, that Brahman is the ultimate reality out of which the world is produced.[12] On the contrary, we can derive this information from scripture alone, from such key passages as *ChāndUp*, VI.1.1ff.

The concept of substantial cause presupposed what was known as *satkāryavāda*, the doctrine that the effect (*kārya*) pre-exists (*sat*) in the cause. Substantial causation, then, is the effect's being educed and being existentially conserved out of the effect's underlying cause. It is important to note, however, that substantial causation is *not* simply the being made manifest of what was hidden – the arising or being uncovered, as it were, of a ready-made effect. To use (Christian) Scholastic terminology, quite appropriately here, I think, substantial causation was regarded both in the Sāṃkhya tradition (which seems to be the original home of the *satkārya* theory) and in Vedānta (which took over the notion and 'theologised' it for its own purposes) as the actualisation of the effect existing in 'proximate potency' in the cause.

The substantial cause could or could not undergo what was regarded as essential change in the exercise of its causality. In the example clay–pot, the substantial cause (the clay) undergoes only accidental change in the production of the effect (the pot). But in the examples milk–curds and seed–tree (both well-known examples in Sāṃkhya and Vedāntic theory) the substantial cause (milk, seed) undergoes what may well be regarded as an essential change in the production of the effect (curds, tree). In any case, the main point of substantial causation is this: at each stage, between cause and effect an entitative continuum is regarded as existing such that there is a continuous flow of being, as it were, in one direction only – from the substantial cause to its effect. Whether the substantial cause undergoes what is thought to be an essential or an accidental change, the effect is in some sense both identical to and different from the cause. It is identical in that it derives from the being of the cause; it is not something absolutely other. It is different (even in the case of the substantial cause's accidental change) in that it is not the cause; it has a form that is either accidentally or essentially different from that of the cause. In other words, the *satkārya* theory and its attendant notion of substantial causation pays philosophical tribute to the belief, so characteristic of Sāṃkhya thought and of much of Vedāntic theology, in identity-in-difference between the originative cause and its effect(s).

We have seen that it is characteristic of Rāmānuja's theology to subject the Brahman-reality to different points of view. One such perspective takes account of Brahman as substantial cause. From 'above', from the viewpoint of Brahman that is, Brahman as substantial cause is regarded as the existential source and substrate of the world. In this way of speaking, which partakes of what we may call in general the 'inherence' mode of discourse[13] – so as to preserve the ontological continuum between Brahman as (substantial) cause and the world as his effect, Rāmānuja speaks of Brahman in his 'causal condition' and in his 'effected condition' respectively.[14] The rationale for this way of speaking is given in the following statement: 'The effect is not a substance different [from its cause], but the cause itself passed into a different condition.'[15] In the process the identity aspect of the identity-in-difference relation is stressed (and we have examined the use to which Rāmānuja puts this feature of his theology in the 'That you are' exegesis).

The theological gains of the inherence mode of discourse in respect of the stress laid on the identity aspect between the substantial cause and its effect(s) are, as we have indicated before, the apparent conformity with the appropriate scriptural texts and the articulation of that almost universal theistic experience that it is God *in* whom we live and move and have our being. Generally, in Vedānta, we come entitatively from Brahman and to him we must return. This immanentist insight is distinctively Vedāntic, and Rāmānuja articulates it by what we may call his 'participative' theology within the inherence mode of discourse.[16] But we know that now a problem arises. It is all very well to be so convinced of the immanence of Brahman, of the existential continuity between him and the world, that we are prepared to speak of finite being itself as 'Brahman *qua* effect'. But finite being is limited being and limited being is imperfect being. Does not participative theology imply that the supreme being, Brahman, shares in the limitations and imperfections of finite being, perhaps by being part perfect and part imperfect? Rāmānuja himself mocks this picture of Brahman; it is, he says, like picturing Devadatta with one hand adorned with sandal-paste, rings and bracelets and the other beaten with a hammer and thrust into the fire of doomsday![17] If participative theology were all that was on offer it could well end up as the view Rāmānuja mocks. But to counteract the objection it raises he supplies correctives. One lies within the inherence mode of discourse. We shall now consider it.

This corrective is what we may call Rāmānuja's 'partitive' theology, which is expressed in terms of a 'part–part-possessor' polarity. It helps Rāmānuja preserve Brahman's transcendent perfection over against finite, limited being, still within the inherence mode of discourse. Consider the following extract, which has a number of already familiar ideas:

> Brahman always has conscious and non-conscious being as his modes [*prakāra*][18] in that such being is his body. Sometimes his body consists of conscious and non-conscious being in an extremely subtle state incapable of being designated as separate from him. Brahman is then in the causal condition. But sometimes his body consists of gross conscious and non-conscious being separated out into name and form. Then he is in the effected condition. Now, where the passage into the effected condition is concerned, the non-conscious part, bereft in the causal condition of word [designation], undergoes change of an essential kind in so far as words now attach to it in that it becomes the objects of experience [*bhogya*]. The conscious part, so that *it* may become the [embodied] experiencers [*bhoktṛ*] of particular karmic fruits, undergoes a change in the form of expansion of knowledge in accordance with [the individual requirements of] the experiencing-condition. Finally, with respect to that part which is [Brahman] the Controller, qualified by both [kinds of] mode [i.e. the non-conscious and the conscious], a change also occurs in the form of [Brahman's] being doubly qualified by the aforementioned condi-

tions. Thus a like change takes place in the two modes as well as in the mode-possessor inasmuch as there is a passing into another condition from the [original] causal one.[19]

Here Rāmānuja speaks of a tripartite Brahman (clearly within the inherence mode of discourse): there is the part of (potentially and actually) non-conscious being (*acidaṃśa*), the part of (potentially and actually) conscious being (*cidaṃśa*), and the part of Brahman as Controller of the other two, which represents a change, even from this point of view, in a minimal, accidental sense. In fact, under the aspect of this third part, which is a 'part' only in a formal sense (with respect to the whole Brahman-reality), Brahman is really the *part-possessor* (*aṃśin*) in relation to the other two parts in that he is their Controller (hence in the text Rāmānuja semantically balances the modal parts – which he identifies with the body$_m$ of Brahman – against the mode-possessor or *prakārin*). In other words, we have here, in terms of 'partitive' theology, a part–part-possessor (*aṃśa–aṃśin*) polarity. Let us see what Rāmānuja makes of this.

In the Commentary, under *BrSū*, II.3.45, he observes that the relationship between part and part-possessor is of a piece with the relationship between qualifier (*viśeṣaṇa*) and subject qualified (*viśeṣya*). And he exemplifies the latter relationship as that which obtains between radiance and the sun, generic characteristics and their subject, the body and the embodied self. In other words, there are two features to this relationship especially relevant for our purposes: (1) that the part cannot exist as the sort of thing it is independently of the part-possessor, because it may be regarded as an aspect of the latter, inhering in it; and (2) that, notwithstanding this existential dependence, the nature of the part is different from that of the part-possessor. As to (1), when speaking of the 'part' it is clear that Rāmānuja is not talking of quantitative parts (i.e. khaṇḍa as opposed to aṃśa). Not only do the above examples testify to this, but so does his definition of *aṃśa*: 'Being a part [*aṃśa*, of something] is being one aspect of that thing.'[20] For instance, one's particular body cannot exist independently of the *ātman*, for it may be regarded as a feature of, if not an expression of, the *ātman*. At death, in the absence of the *ātman*, the body is no longer a body in the proper sense; for a time it retains the shape and outward appearance of a true body, but in reality it is simply an aggregate of different substances no longer organically united for a common, higher end, and hence in the process of dissolution. A quantitative part, on the other hand (for example, a piece of cake) cannot exist as the sort of thing it is independently of the part-possessor (the whole cake) only in a formal sense (since it is a part of the whole); but as a part it can exist by itself, retaining its original nature (as cake). Note that Rāmānuja's definition of *aṃśa*, by implying the language of existential inherence, indicates that we are still in the inherence mode of discourse.

But (2) adverts to the aspect of difference (rather than of identity) within this mode of discourse. This is the point of making the part–part-possessor relationship of a piece with the qualifier–subject-qualified relationship. The qualifier, says Rāmānuja, cannot fulfil its function unless it has a nature different from that of the subject qualified. Thus, in the examples cited earlier, the sun is substantival, the radiance qualitative; the embodied self is spiritual, the body itself material; the subject qualified by the generic characteristic is particular, while the generic characteristic is universal. Similarly, the part (*aṃśa*) as qualifier of the *aṃśin* or part-possessor (the subject qualified), though continuing to derive its being from the *aṃśin* and to be regarded as a qualifying feature of it, has a nature different from it. In making this point, in talking of the part as *qualifying* the part-possessor, Rāmānuja is saying that the part–part-possessor relationship (as described by him) brings out the *difference*-in-identity of the relation's terms.

When the *aṃśa–aṃśin* relationship is applied to Brahman the Controller as part-possessor and to finite being as his part(s), this differentiating function allows Rāmānuja, by pointing to the difference of nature between the part(s) and part-possessor, to affirm Brahman's transcendent perfection over against the limitations of finite being – still within the inherence mode of discourse (in that the *aṃśa* inheres in the *aṃśin*). In our last long quotation he helps this contrast along by referring to the conscious and non-conscious parts as Brahman's body$_m$ and to the mode-possessor (or subject qualified, i.e. the part-possessor) aspect as the Controller of the other two. The contrast is made clearer in the Summary, where he uses *ŚveUp*, I.12 ('Having known the experiencer, the object of experience and the Mover – all this which has been declared is the threefold Brahman') as the occasion for his 'partitive' description of Brahman. Though he does not use partitive language explicitly, the tripartite division described here corresponds exactly to that of the earlier passage, with this difference: that the natural distinctions between the three aspects are more clearly demarcated. The first division stands for the order of object of experience (*bhogya*), in nature non-conscious and the abode of change; the second for the order of individual *ātman as* experiencer (*bhoktṛ*), essentially knowledge and bliss but subject to saṃāric embodiment and capable of attaining salvation; while the third division corresponds to Brahman as inner Controller or Mover (*preritṛ*) of the other two and the abode, essentially, of a 'flood' of unmeasured (noble) qualities.[21] Thus, in the Essence of the Vedānta, Rāmānuja can say, emphasising the distinction between the (order of) *jīvātman* as *amśa* and Brahman as *aṃśin* (a natural distinction all the sharper between the order of non-conscious being as *aṃśa* and Brahman as *aṃśin*), 'When the *jīva* is viewed as a part [*aṃśa*], its nature as a part is not the same as that of the supreme Self, the part-possessor [*aṃśin*]; for in all cases there is a distinction between the qualifier and the subject qualified as to the natural capacity of [their respective] proper forms.'[22] Thus within the inherence mode of (theological) discourse, notwithstanding its overall emphasis on the identity aspect between Brahman and the world, Rāmānuja seeks to balance to some extent 'participative' language by 'partitive' language. Divine transcendence is not submerged by divine immanence (in the broad sense of Brahman being 'one' with the world through a sharing of being in which the world participates).

Though partitive theology helps, the central and crucial[23] corrective to the theological dangers inherent in participative language is Rāmānuja's analysis of the Lord as efficient cause of the world. The efficient cause (*nimitta-kāraṇa*) is that cause by which the production of the effect is actuated. For example, in mundane experience, the potter is the efficient cause of the pot he is making. Further, in mundane experience the substantial cause and the efficient cause (as 'internal' and 'external' causes respectively of the effect) are not the same thing (hence Rāmānuja's previously quoted observation that 'It occurs to one that there must naturally be another cause to produce the effect'). However, in the case of the production of the world, Rāmānuja identifies Brahman as simultaneously the substantial and the efficient cause: this establishes the uniqueness and absoluteness of Brahman's creative[24] act. We shall see now that by characterising Brahman's efficient causality as presupposing thought and as totally unnecessitated, Rāmānuja affirms the unimpaired sovereignty and transcendence of Brahman.

As to the conscious nature of the producing of the world, the relevant scriptural texts, Rāmānuja observes, refer to this creative act as connected with thought (by the use of the root *īkṣ* – 'to think, reflect'). For example, *ChāndUp*, VI.2.3, says, 'It *thought*, "May I be many, may I bring forth" '. The Sāṃkhya opponent argues that such texts in fact refer to the non-conscious *prakṛti* or *pradhāna*[25] as originative agent, the word 'thought' being used only metaphorically. Not so, answers Rāmānuja. We must follow the exegetical ruling to seek to interpret scripture literally and scripture tends to connect 'thought' in these creational texts to 'being' (*sat*) understood as the universal, underlying existential cause of everything. Such a being cannot be the non-conscious *prakṛti* but only the 'all-knowing, all-powerful, supreme Person'. Creation (*sṛṣṭi*), therefore, is thought-dependent.[26] We may add here another consideration which presupposes that Brahman's creation of the world, for Rāmānuja, has a cognitive component. This is the belief that Brahman produces the world – following a dissolution – after considering the particular sort of world it is to be on the basis of its future inhabitants' pending *karma*.[27] (In this connection the Lord's 'remembering' of the Vedas to be promulgated[28] is part of the 'plan of creation'.) No one but Brahman has the requisite knowledge and power in this regard.

The second characteristic of Brahman's originative efficient causality for Rāmānuja is its unnecessitatedness. Now unnecessitatedness can be intrinsic or extrinsic. To begin with, Rāmānuja maintains that the Lord's creative action is intrinsically unnecessitated. In other words, the production of the world depends on the will (*saṃkalpa*) of the Lord, which is physically free to create or not. This is an important consideration, for the notion of divine substantial causality might imply that Brahman is by nature constrained to be the substrate of the world (just as the seed is by nature constrained to be the substrate of the shoot). For Rāmānuja nothing could be further from the truth. Let us see how this is so.

We can begin with an observation which Rāmānuja does not explicitly make but which no doubt was implicit in his perception of the matter. The creational utterances ascribed to Brahman in scripture are in the so-called optative or potential mood: for instance, 'May I be many, may I bring forth' (or, 'Let Me be many, let Me bring forth').[29] We have seen in Chapter 1 that for the exegetes of the Earlier and Later (i.e. Vedāntic) School of Interpretation this is the mood *par excellence* of the sacred injunction which Rāmānuja (in an earlier discussion[30]) has agreed presupposes physical freedom in the finite agent to comply or disobey. He would no doubt argue that by parity of reasoning the use of the optative for the creational utterances in scripture imply in the supreme being the physical freedom to produce the world or not.

This physical freedom is in no way intrinsically subject to some such power as *karma*. Now, *karma* may be regarded as a freedom-constraining force, both intrinsically and extrinsically. In the case of the embodied self, for instance, the *jīva's karma* from birth to birth determines the composite of which the *jīva* is a part, intrinsically, by determining that composite's body, dispositions and other empirical capacities. Thus, the *jīva*'s freedom to be and to act is, in and through the composite, intrinsically severely limited. *Karma* may be regarded as extrinsically freedom-constraining in so far as any ātmanic composite is limited in its options for acting and living by the *karma* of the collective which determines the sort of world the composite is to inhabit. Now, neither the Lord's creative action in particular nor his nature in general is subject to *karma*, intrinsically or extrinsically, in any of the ways described above. However, the Lord may be said, in Rāmānuja's reckoning, to be extrinsically constrained by *karma* in so far as he chooses freely to create each new world after first having considered the unmatured *karma* of the previous worlds. This is a self-imposed, moral restraint – as such enabling *karma* in our world to be regarded as an aspect of the Lord's justice in his dealings with us – and does not affect in any way the point of the total divine natural transcendence over *karma*'s sway.

It is this total natural transcendence over *karma* of the Lord – a transcendence which makes it possible for the Lord to use *karma* creationally and creatively at the threshold of each world-production – that Rāmānjua refers to, among other things, in the following extract:

> [In *ChāndUp*, VIII.1.5] 'free from evil' means 'free from *karma*'; that is, 'bereft of any trace of subjection to *karma*'. Now only the *jīvas* are subject to *karma* in virtue of being the experiencers of pleasure and pain consequent on their *karma*. Whence being 'free from evil' [or *karma*] is a characteristic of the supreme Self, as distinct from the *jīva*. And from this follow other characteristics peculiar to the supreme Self and contingent upon his proper form: (a) being Lord of the world and of his wishes and (b) being the inner self of all [finite] being, which arises from his having a will for the real.[31]

It is in explaining the 'having a will for the real' (*satyasaṃkalpa*) and its counterpart, 'having a desire for the real' (*satyakāma*) (cf. *ChāndUp*, VIII.1.5), which are predicated of the Lord, that Rāmānuja is able to emphasise the utter sovereignty of the Lord's originative efficient causality. This is done in the Summary (para. 132).

The 'real' (*satya*) of the expression 'having a desire for the real' (*satyakāma*), says Rāmānuja, refers to the 'true reality' (*satyatā*) – that is, to the essential and eternal immutability – of that category of finite being called the *nityas* or *sūris*. These, which correspond to the genus of angelic being of traditional Christian (especially Scholastic) philosophical theology, are heavenly spirits who from all eternity have enjoyed the divine presence and have never been subject to the thrall of *saṃsāra*.

Nevertheless, as finite beings, they depend existentially on the Lord, their sole delight being subservience to him.[32] And as such Rāmānuja describes them as 'the means for the experience of [the Lords's] personal enjoyment' (*svabhogyabhogopakaraṇa*). But the *satya* of *satyakāma* is also said to refer to the existential 'durability' (i.e. *sthiratva*) of all material entities and composites of spirit and matter, which in virtue of their materiality are the seat of essential change. Such beings Rāmānuja calls 'the means of [the Lord's] "play"' (*līlopakaraṇa*). Both categories of being (the heavenly *sūris* and the manifest beings of this world) are dependent on the Lord's will (*saṃkalpa*) for their existence.

This becomes clear from Rāmānuja's exegesis of 'having a will for the real' (*satyasaṃkalpa*). This expression signifies that manifest beings in countless numbers come anew into existence at each world-production by the mere will (*saṃkalpamātreṇa*) of the Lord. Rāmānuja then gives a more comprehensive exegesis of the expression. He says that *satyasaṃkalpa* signifies that the proper forms, the continuance, the activities and the distinctions of conscious and non-conscious beings, of permanent and transient entities, all depend on the will (*saṃkalpa*) of the Lord. Elsewhere Rāmānuja says that scriptural creation texts declare that Brahman, by reason of the causal agency of his will (*svasaṃkalpād*), is conditioned by various modes which essentially are the different mutable and immutable entities.[33] Thus Rāmānuja shows that the creative act does not presuppose thought only, but implies also the sovereignty of the divine will.[34] Further, the creative act has two 'moments', as it were: an originative one, in which being is bestowed, and a conservational one, in which bestowed being is given continuance (*sthiti*; cf. the comprehensive sense of *satyasaṃkalpa*).

There is another feature of Brahman's originative causality in Rāmānuja's thought which we may take up now. This concerns the *immediacy* of the divine agency. In Chapter 1 we came across evidence that Rāmānuja seemed to accept the traditional mythological accounts of creation which intimate that after the supreme being gives the impetus to create, so to speak, by producing Brahmā (the demiurge) and other primevals, he then sits back and lets Brahmā and company get on with the job though he remains as the substantial cause of the produced world *in toto*. Theologically speaking (whatever may be said of its mythic value) this account imperils the universality and absoluteness of the divine creative act, and from the theological point of view Rāmānuja rejects this account. God's creative act is universal and immediate. Earlier we saw that in interpreting *satyasaṃkalpa* Rāmānuja maintained the immediacy and universality of the Lord's creative efficient causality.

We shall now adduce a reference or two to show that these characteristics are intended to apply to Brahman's originative causal agency in general and to his substantial causality in particular. In the Commentary, under II.3.10, the question is explicitly asked whether remote effects have their origination from the causal agent immediately preceding each of them, or whether in fact they arise from Brahman *qua* conditioned as their antecedent causes. The answer is given subsequently in more than one statement: for instance, 'It is the supreme Person himself, as embodied by the antecedent [causal] entities, who is the cause of all effects . . .',[35] and 'Brahman is the immediate originative support of everything.'[36]

It will be opportune to consider here Rāmānuja's position on one of the most maligned doctrines of Vedāntic theology in the Western understanding: the doctrine that God creates the world for his 'sport' or 'play' (to translate the Sanskrit *līlā*). This has given rise to the Western (in point of fact Christian) objection that God has been irresponsible and uncaring in creating the world, that the world and especially its personal inhabitants have no intrinsic purpose to their existence. In fact Rāmānuja explicitly considers the question of the divine motive for the production of the world; in explaining his view we shall be able to clarify his understanding of *līlā*.

The matter is taken up in the Commentary under II.1.32–3. The opponent argues that, though it is in the Lord's power to produce the world, the Lord cannot be the creator of the world. His argument is as follows. All thought-dependent activity, such as creation, is invested with a motive (prayojana). This motive may be of two kinds: one's own benefit or that of another. Now the Lord, being totally self-fulfulled, does not create for his own benefit. To consider the second alternative: creating for the benefit of others. One, such as God, who has every wish realised acts for the sake of another only out of benevolence. And an all-powerful benevolent being, i.e. 'one possessed of compassionate love [*karuṇā*] does not emit a world such as this, replete with endless misery of various kinds, such as birth, old age, death and hell. On the contrary, he who creates out of compassionate love would create a world solely unto happiness. Brahman therefore, since he lacks any motive, cannot be the world's cause.'[37]

Rāmānuja answers, perhaps surprisingly, with an illustration. Brahman, who is perfect, totally fulfilled, creates from the motive of sport (*līlā*) in the manner of some unrivalled world-emperor, who, wanting for nothing, plays a ball-game purely for sport. But this illustration is revealing. In effect Rāmānuja is saying that thought-dependent activity need not be performed for the purpose of gain. The opponent on the contrary implies that thoughtful action, from the viewpoint of its agent, is always gainful. By adducing the illustration of the world-emperor with nothing to gain engaging in a game of balls for pure 'sport', Rāmānuja is in fact distinguishing between two kinds of sport: 'competitive' and 'non-competitive'. 'Competitive' sport is sport not in the sense intended by Rāmānuja in the illustration. Such sport, by its non-spontaneous and calculating nature, through its inherent motive to worst others, is self-centred and grasping. To resort to a moral distinction drawn earlier, it is squarely *saṃsāra*-immanent activity. In the Hindu context, 'competitive' sport is of the stuff of tournaments, tests of skill, indices of fate (cf., for instance, the dicing-game in the second book, the Book of the Assembly Hall, of the *Mahābhārata*), and so on. 'Non-competitive' sport, on the other hand, 'sport' in the intended sense, is of itself not consciously gainful or self-interested. It is essentially spontaneous, an expression of *joie de vivre*, a brief invigorating release from the normal wheeling and dealing of everyday life. As such, in itself, it tends to fall outside the purview of SI action. When 'sport' (*līlā*) in this sense is applied to Brahman's creative activity it signifies that this activity is unselfish, non-delusory, i.e. enlightened, and totally 'spontaneous', i.e. unnecessitated in any sense that implies imperfection in its agent. There is a further connotation to *līlā* in the intended sense: that such activity is unfrustrated and unfrustrating. This meaning has its English counterpart in such expressions as 'It was child's play' used to describe some deed performed without difficulty. Brahman's creative action is also 'child's play' (*līlā*) for him: a totally unimpeded production and conservation of being.

With respect to the world's production so far as others (i.e. the world's personal inhabitants especially) are concerned, the objection is made that the creator of a sorrow-laden world such as ours cannot be a benevolent being, and, therefore, is not the Lord. Rāmānuja meets this objection on the grounds that it is under the (self-imposed) regulative influence of primal world-*karma* ripening into the sort of world we live in, that the Lord creates. Such *karma* is the product of the world's conscious beings themselves, not of the Lord. Such being then, directly and collectively, and not Brahman, is responsible for the nature of our sorrow-laden world. Of course, this answer does not go far enough. For it may be asked why the Lord willed the creative (cyclic) process in the first place (even though, in Hindu belief, there is no beginning to it). This is a question Rāmānuja, and every other Vedāntic theologian for that matter, never asks. For the Vedāntin, the cyclic, beginningless production of the world is an unquestioned datum for life and thought. But Rāmānuja would answer the charge against the benevolence of his creator God not only by reference to primal *karma*, but also by pointing to the Lord's *avatāras* into this world for the protection of the righteous and the confounding of evil-doers, and by stressing that the Lord indwells this world and each person individually as Controller and Guide (*antaryāmin*) unto fulfilment. In other words, the grace of the Lord is active in this world in different ways, notwithstanding the ultimate mystery of the divine originative causality. Later we shall take up this matter again in another context.

We can bring this chapter to a close by discussing a distinctive feature of Rāmānuja's theology in respect of Brahman. This feature may, at first sight, appear unattractive to Christians, but it will repay further scrutiny. This concerns Rāmānuja's affirmation that the Lord possesses a 'supernal form' (*divya rūpa*), unique to him, anthropomorphic and male in appearance (having physical properties), yet constituted of a special substance which is neither prakṛtic nor the result of karma[38], and the focus of the heavenly abode. The *locus classicus* for the description of the supernal form is paragraph 134 of the Summary.[39] Before we go on to other considerations, the first question we must ask is why Rāmānuja accepts the existence of such a celestial form in the first place. Among the various reasons which come to mind, the first is scriptural.

Both *śruti* and *smṛti* appear to speak of a supernal divine form. *ChāndUp*, I.6.6–7 says, 'Now this golden person who is seen within the sun . . . and has eyes like a lotus, has risen above all evil'; *ŚveUp*, III.8, speaks of 'the great person of the colour of the sun, beyond the darkness'. Again, *smṛti* texts too refer to such a form (cf. for example, *ViPu*, VI.7.79f.). If these texts are to be taken seriously and, if possible at face value, as Rāmānuja would recommend, it is not unreasonable to conclude that Brahman, the supreme Person, has a celestial (anthropomorphic) form.

Secondly, the acceptance of the supernal form would make intelligible and reconcile apparently conflicting scriptural texts, in the literalist way desired. Take *ChāndUp*, III.14.2: 'He who is the Self of space . . . to whom belong all smells, all tastes.' Take again *KaṭhUp*, I.3.15: 'without taste . . . without smell'. According to Rāmānuja both these *śrutis* refer to the Lord; yet they seem to contradict each other, the former predicating taste and smell of the Lord, the latter denying such experience of him. The contradiction can be removed, he would aver, with the exegetical advantage of understanding both texts at face-value (*mukhyatayā*), if the first were taken to refer to the Lord experiencing in his supernal form, and the second were understood to deny all *prakṛtic* smells and tastes of him. The *Chāndogya* text can be taken to refer literally to 'all sorts of *non-prakṛtic*, exclusive, flawless, unexcelled, illustrious smells and tastes which are objects of [the Lord's] enjoyment'.[40] Only the non-prakṛtic divine form could have the corresponding sense-organs capable of experiencing such supernal pleasures! We shall make some general theological observations about the celestial form later, yet here we may say that the idea of a divine experiencing in a heavenly (or 'spiritual') body is not as far-fetched as might first appear. After all, does not a high Christology require such experiencing of the risen Lord in his resurrected body (not to mention the dead when raised on the last day) ? Certainly some New Testament texts (for example, the resurrection narratives) have been understood as lending support to this idea.

Thirdly, Rāmānuja accepts the supernal form because, he contends, such notable authorities as Bādarāyaṇa, Taṅka and Dramiḍa accept its existence. Surely they have read scripture aright! Finally, the fourth and by no means the least reason is that the supernal form, as an object of meditation, plays a central role in the development of the aspirant's salvific devotional relationship with the Lord in this life, and is the focus of bliss in the next. As we shall see more fully in the next chapter, Rāmānuja maintains that it is, at the very least, greatly conducive to advanced spiritual progress for one to fasten with the mind's eye on the Lord's celestial form as the *śubhāśraya* (i.e. the secure and appropriate resting-place) of devout meditation.

In accepting the supernal form Rāmānuja implies that more than one careful distinction obtains between it and other aspects of the divine reality. We may consider these distinctions briefly; in the process we shall gain an idea of what he means by Brahman's proper form (*svarūpa*) in the broad sense.

In the first place, the supernal form must not be confused with Brahman's proper form understood in the strict sense. Rāmānuja speaks of the former as a body of some sort, owning a physical disposition of parts, localisable and localised (i.e. in the heavenly abode), and composed of a non-prakṛtic substance about whose specific nature he wisely says nothing.[41] We have seen that Brahman's quiddity, however (i.e. his proper form *sensu stricto*), is essentially spiritual, defined by the five characteristics mentioned earlier and in the way described earlier, and is not localisable in the manner of the supernal form. However, Rāmānuja does give the impression that the supernal form is a necessary if personal expression of the Lord. To this end he refers, on occasion, to the supernal form as an aspect of Brahman's proper form, but here 'proper form' must be undestood in the broad sense, in the sense of a 'form' or expression of being uniquely related to Brahman (Brahman being the dominant term of the relationship) and peculiar to him.[42]

Then again, the supernal form, although closely related to the Lord's avatāric forms (as we shall now see), is logically closer to the divine quidditative centre than the latter. It is Rāmānuja's view that a divine avatāric form is a particular manifestation or expression of the supernal form itself, both being non-prakṛtic in nature (i.e. in effect non-dependent on personal *karma*). Rāmānuja says, 'The most compassionate Blessed One [*bhagavān*], by his own desire and out of love for the devotee, makes this innate [supernal] form take on godly, human and other configurations, in accordance with the devotee's understanding.'[43] Thus, though an avatāric form 'is fashioned from' the supernal form (without yet 'exhausting' it), it is contingent, while the supernal form is innate. The avatāric form is contingent upon the production of the world, upon the will of the Lord to manifest, upon the age or period (*yuga*) of the world's development, and upon the understanding of the devotee(s), among other things. The supernal form is contingent in none of these ways.

Finally, we may make some general observations on the concept of the supernal form in Rāmānuja's theology. It will be convenient to start with a quotation from that learned and pioneering work by Fr P. Johanns SJ, *To Christ through the Vedānta*. After describing the characteristics of the supernal form he writes,

> We shall not insist on this conception. Although it does not seem to contradict it, the existence of this body [i.e. the supernal form] is not required by the System. It is only introduced to adapt the conception of God to traditional mythological aberrations. The 'God' to whom this body belongs is not the God whom all nations adore, but the popular Vishnu, a creation of anthropomorphism. Its mention in the Bhasya only implies that Rāmānuja, unlike most non-Christian Philosophers, has not consented to divorce his philosophy from his religion.[44]

There are a number of points here worthy of consideration; we can take up only a few. When Johanns lays stress on Rāmānuja's system as a philosophy, in respect of the supernal form, he is misguided. Rāmānuja's work is primarily a theology; no doubt in many respects, as we have seen, it is philosophical too, but its overall thrust and purpose is theological.[45] In a theological system such as Rāmānuja's the conception of the supernal form fits in well. We have reviewed the particular reasons for his acceptance of this entity, but in general it may be said that theologically the notion of the supernal form emphasises the accessibility of the Lord to the human seeker. This feature of divine accessibility is central to Rāmānuja's system, which is *theological* in the strongest sense of this term. And a crucial aspect of the Lord's accessibility is his supernal form. It bestows a lasting intrinsic value to the human form. In an ultimate sense it represents the 'human face' of God. It is the object and support of devout meditation in this world and the focus of everlasting bliss in the next. These ideas touch upon the charge Johanns makes of the supernal form's 'anthropomorphism', a charge a Christian at any rate needs to make with caution.

Johanns the phenomenologist if not Johanns the theologian would no doubt appreciate that from Rāmānuja's point of view the supernal form is not 'anthropomorphist' if by this term is meant 'pertaining to a human paradigm in some way'. That is, so far as Rāmānuja is concerned, he does not theologise on the supernal form, or conceive of it, starting from the human model; on the contrary, his starting-point is the revelation of scripture which logically precedes human paradigms and experience. For Rāmānuja scripture (not human speculation) gives evidence of the supernal form, and if this form is anthropomorphic this is a theological datum which we must accept; it does not make the supernal form 'anthropomorphist'. To adjudge this form 'anthropomorphist' as Johanns implies ('It is only introduced to adapt the conception of God to traditional mythological aberrations') is to evaluate theologically. It is not to make a phenomenological statement: in this instance, to show whether the supernal form is appropriate or valid from within the framework of Rāmānuja's theology itself.

One last consideration. Does not the charge stick at least in this that by reason of its particularity the supernal form lacks universal appeal, or at any rate, is not such appeal thereby significantly impaired? Is not the supernal form's theological appeal weakened not only for non-Hindus, but also for non-Vaiṣṇavaites, not least for women, since the heavenly form is described as male! Apart from the general observations made earlier in respect of the Lord's accessibility to man through the supernal form, we may well have to agree that Rāmānuja's description of this manifestation does lessen its universal appeal. But there is a mitigating consideration where this form's apparent maleness is concerned, a consideration which in the first instance devolves round the distinction between 'maleness' and 'masculinity'. If we subject Rāmānuja's description to scrutiny we shall see that the supernal form, in being deliberately and sensitively made to conform to the Hindu aesthetic ideal of man, tends towards androgyny. In other words it tends to harmonise male and female characteristics. On the one hand, it is described as 'having muscular, rounded and long arms' and as being 'broad-chested'; on the other, it is said to have 'large eyes, spotless as the petals of a lotus', to be 'lovely browed' 'with cheeks radiant and tender' and 'delicate as the smile of a flower'. Again, though armed with conch, disc, club and sword, the celestial form is also adorned with ornaments which include earrings, necklace(s), bracelet(s) and anklet(s). In more egalitarian vein it has the qualities of 'radiance, beauty, charm and youth'.[46] Thus, through its androgynous character, the supernal form becomes a transparent symbol of the *imago dei* that the man is, rather than a tribute to male chauvinism.

This concludes our treatment of the nature of the supreme being in Rāmānuja's theology. In the course of this chapter we have studied Rāmānuja's God under different aspects: in his proper form strictly and broadly considered, as creator and sustainer of finite being, in his participative and partitive relationships, in his transcendence and in his immanence – in short, in his distinctive relationship of identity-in-difference with the world. In the process we have gained some appreciation of what Rāmānuja means when he insists that without a personal understanding of Brahman's 'proper form' we cannot achieve salvation.

In the next chapter we shall treat of the way to and the goal of salvation in Rāmānuja's thought. In the final chapter we shall seek to draw together the strands of all that has gone before, by a consideration of Rāmānuja's theological method.

6 The Way and Journey's End

In this chapter we shall be concerned with Rāmānuja's understanding of the way to liberation and of the nature of this final state. In respect of the liberating relationship between the human individual and the Lord there seem to be two movements to Rāmānuja's thought: one is 'from above', from the Lord's side; this concerns the divine initiative in the salvific process, which initiative may be referred to as 'election'. The other is 'from below', from the point of view of the individual's response to the divine initiative. We may call this response *yoga*. Let us consider each activity in turn.

ELECTION

In connection with this idea an important text for Rāmānuja is *KaṭhUp* I.2.23: 'This Self is not to be obtained by discussion, nor by the intellect nor by much scriptural instruction; him whom this [Self] chooses, by him is it to be obtained, and to him this Self reveals its form.' Commenting on this text early in his exposition of *BrSū*, I.1.1, Rāmānuja writes,

> Having first said that there is no way to attain the Self only by the hearing of scripture, reflecting and meditating upon it, the text goes on to say that 'him whom this Self *chooses*, by him is it to be obtained'. Now only a beloved becomes 'chosen' – to be one's 'beloved' is to be exceedingly dear to that one. The Lord himself has said [cf. *Gītā*, 10.10 and 7.17] that he strives to bring it about that his beloved attains the Self. . . . In other words, only one who experiences a direct calling-to-mind[1] [of the Lord] – an experience itself excessively dear to the experiencer on account of the excessive dearness of the object called to mind – becomes the highest Self's chosen one. Further, we can go on to say that the highest Self is obtained by such a one. This kind of steady keeping-in-mind [of the Lord] is designated by the word 'devotion' [*bhakti*].[2]

About *bhakti* so-called, which we shall go on to examine in due course, Rāmānuja says again, 'it arises, through the grace of the supreme Person, with the unfailing performance of one's regular, occasional and optional religious works done as worship to the supreme Person'.[3]

Now, other considerations apart, both these quotations seem to make the point that it is only someone who has reached a certain stage of the spiritual life – the devotionally and theologically informed stage of the 'beloved' in point of fact – who becomes the recipient of divine salvific grace. No doubt, in Rāmānuja's theology this is true so far as it goes. In other words, once the devotee has become the beloved, enjoys more or less continuous imageful contemplative (but not inactive) union with the Lord and offers up all his actions as expressions of divine worship, his spiritual ascent becomes ever more sure, unitive and grace-laden. But, we may ask, what about the aspirant whose intention is right but whose steps falter or who is at the beginning of the spiritual life; or, for that matter, what about those who are ordinary if spiritually inept and uninformed folk of the world? Would Rāmānuja in no way speak of such as recipients of the divine salvific initiative? We can answer, 'Yes, he would.' If the beloved can be said to be 'elected' by the Lord in the strong sense of this term, there is a weak sense in which we may call all mankind 'elected' or at least the object of the Lord's saving outreach. Let us dwell on this topic for a while.

Our first consideration must be the setting in which the human individual is placed, i.e. this saṃsāric world.[4] We recall that this world is fashioned consequent upon the Lord's consideration of the previous worlds' inhabitants' pending *karma*, and that each individual's situation and position in this world is a result of that individual's particular *karma*. Nevertheless we have seen that Rāmānuja is keen to maintain that within the bounds of *karma* so described, each individual is equipped by the Lord to lead a righteous life and is morally free to do so. The appropriate righteous life either in this birth or in a subsequent one – for in this context the doctrine of rebirth must be kept in mind – culminates in liberation (*mokṣa*) or salvation, the final state of never-ending blissful communion with the Lord. As salvific aids the Lord bestows upon man, among other things, the life-giving message of the scriptures containing directions for discerning meritorious and unmeritorious actions and for performing salvific ones. The Lord himself indwells man as his inner controller and support, desirous of guiding him to his true and final end. In other words, in so far as our world contains the real possibility for – indeed, may even be said to be geared towards – our eventual liberation, as its inhabitants we may be regarded as the recipients of a general divine salvific initiative. This we can discern from the following extract:

> Now it is [scripture] which declares what is meritorious and unmeritorious action, of the form either of worship to the Lord or the contrary, i.e. action which is either pleasing or displeasing to the supreme Person and which produces its fruit of pleasure or of pain. . . . And the Blessed One, the supreme Person, . . . having laid down the two kinds of action [in scripture], the righteous and the unrighteous, bestows upon all embodied selves, equitably, the requisite sensuous embodiment to perform such works and the power to control their bodies; then, providing the scriptures, which make known his commands, he enters these [selves] as their ensouling Self to accomplish [scripture's] end, and as the One who permits [all actions] he remains as the Controller. The embodied selves, for their part, endowed with their powers by the Lord, possessed of bodies and senses bestowed by him, and with him as their support, themselves, in accordance with their own wishes, engage in meritorious and unmeritorious actions. Thence [the Lord], regarding the performer of meritorious actions as one who conforms with his commands, blesses with virtue, wealth, desired objects or liberation. But to the transgressor of his commands he ordains the contrary. Thus the objection of the defect of arbitrariness [in the Lord's dealings with us] finds no scope.[5]

In other words, *karma*, both general and particular, may be regarded as the expression of the Lord's justice; it is the stabilising parameter within which human freedom, the justifying or condemning role of the scriptures and the guiding action of the Lord may be exercised. As such it makes possible the divine general salvific outreach to all mankind.

But an objection presents itself. Is not Rāmānuja confining his comments in this regard to Hindus, specifically to the members of his own sect, the Śrī Vaiṣṇavas? How else are we to understand his references to the teaching-function of the (Hindu) scriptures and (presumably) to their correct interpretation? In this context we cannot speak then of God's salvific will for *all* mankind. Now I do not think that Rāmānuja would tolerate this objection. No doubt he accords pride of place, in the economy of salvation, to the Śrī Vaiṣṇavas. This is only to be expected in the atmosphere of cultural and sectarian chauvinism of his age (and no less a feature of our own religious times, for that matter). But there is more than enough evidence to show that his theological vision was universal in aspect. He speaks time and again of the Lord as the inner controller of all embodied selves and of the whole world as the Lord's body$_m$. There are recorded episodes in his life in which he showed a burning concern for the salvation of people outside the Śrī Vaiṣṇava pale.[6] Again, the notion of general *karma* as regulative, in the divine mind, for the production of a new world needs must take account of the moral actions of all unliberated selves. All human individuals, therefore, according to their particular circumstances, must enter the purview of the Lord's general saving-concern: all human individuals must be, in the long run, candidates for salvation. We say 'in the long run' because it was open to Rāmānuja to argue, granted his acceptance of the doctrine of rebirth, that the righteous Hindu or non-Hindu unbeliever could receive in this life enough saving grace to be born in the next as a Śrī Vaiṣṇava eligible for salvation. We shall see in the next section that, within the constrictions of his time and place, Rāmānuja may well have subscribed to this view. However, I believe that if Rāmānuja were to have theologised today, in an age when theologians are becoming open to genuine inter-religious dialogue, the breadth and grandeur of his vision would have prompted him to accommodate all human beings in the divine plan of salvation in the present life without outsiders having to take the circuitous route of being born as Śrī Vaiṣṇavas eligible for salvation in their next birth.

Now, though it will not be to our purpose to discuss Rāmānuja's theology of the divine *avatāra* (i.e. 'descent') at length, here let us consider his view about the Lord's descent into human affairs as an expression of the Lord's overall concern for the welfare and salvation of man. In general Rāmānuja seems to acknowledge three reasons for the divine *avatāra* into *saṃsāra*: (1) to restore religious law and order and to confound their opponents (cf. *Gītā*, 4. 7–8, and Rāmānuja's commentary on these verses); (2) to act as an appropriate refuge and mainstay for his devotees; and (3) to complete and sum up, as the exemplar and type, a particular lineage or order of being.[7] It is important to point out that the *avatāra* is a free action of the deity.[8] Further, it is an essential part of the teaching that there has not been only one divine descent but that many, repeated descents are the order of the day. This is brought out in the following quotation, in which also the second reason for the *avatāra*, mentioned above, is given prominence: 'The highest Person, without abandoning his own [divine] nature, and by his own desire, is generated in many ways, taking on characteristics, qualities, configurations and natures similar to those of the gods, [men] and so on, so as to be an appropriate refuge.'[9] By 'in many ways' Rāmānuja is presumably referring to the animal no less than to the anthropomorphic *avatāras*, but the point being made is that all the *avatāras*, not excluding the animal, are for the benefit of unliberated rational creatures among which human beings occupy a central place. Again to quote Rāmānuja:

> The highest Brahman, the supreme Person, Nārāyaṇa . . . without abandoning his own essence, has descended repeatedly in the various worlds and has been worshipped by them, bestowing the fruit desired therein[10] –virtue, wealth, desired objects and liberation. On the pretext of removing the burden [of evil] from our world, he has descended as a fitting refuge even for such as ourselves [in order to alleviate the sufferings of *saṃsāra*] . . . .'[11]

No doubt Rāmānuja believed that the chief beneficiaries of the Lord's avatāric intervention in this world were virtuous Śrī Vaiṣṇavas[12], but he did not confine the *avatāra*'s saving presence to these. In so far as the Lord comes to restore the religion of the Vedas[13] he has a much wider concern, and in so far as he is open to all persons of good will[14] he evinces a universal outreach. In the next section we shall take up a point we can but note here: that the divine *avatāra* is made not only to help man towards some 'other-worldly' salvation but also to take account of legitimate, if lesser, worldly, desires, such as 'wealth' and 'desired objects'. Thus the divine *avatāra* is a tribute to the Lord's compassionate accessibility.

But this accessibility is seemingly imperilled from another point of view. It is true that the anthropomorphic *avatāras* for example, especially the Kṛṣṇāvatāra, which by common consent is the most salvific for man and theologically the most profound, are neither tricks nor illusions for Rāmānuja.[15] They are real; but, we may ask, are they 'the real thing'? Compared to the Incarnation in traditional Christian teaching, according to which the Son took real flesh in the humanity of Jesus, the answer is 'No'. The avatāric bodies, as phenomenalisations of the supernal form, are non-prakṛtic in nature. Put another way, this means that, unlike the bodies of human beings in *saṃsāra*, divine avatāric bodies are not the unavoidable karmic result of egocentric action. They may look and behave and feel like saṃsāric bodies but they are not real enfleshments in the manner of such bodies. From the Christian point of view, at least, such a view may well be thought to distance the *avatāra* from man, theologically and perhaps devotionally. In other words, so far as his human form was concerned, Kṛṣṇa was not a man like us in all things save sin, considerations about the type of life he lived and his death apart. So far as Rāmānuja was concerned, however, by distancing the *avatāra* from the human predicament in the manner described, he felt freer theologically to make the out-of-the way *avatāra* nature a transparent disguise for the transcendent Reality within, and as such, to his mind, the fitting focus of devotion. As if to accentuate these observations on the apartness (and its import) of the divine *avatāra*, Rāmānuja thinks it quite normal to make Arjuna implore Kṛṣṇa, after the latter's stupendous theophany in the eleventh chapter of the *Gītā*, to resume his four-armed form, complete with crown, mace and discus.[16] In Rāmānuja's thought the divine *avatāra* (in contrast to the Incarnation) does not merge into the shadow of finite being, for all that it is a potent means of the Lord's loving and saving outreach to man in his 'fallen' (i.e. saṃsāric) condition.[17]

YOGA

In this section we shall inquire into the qualifications and response required on the part of the devotee, according to Rāmānuja, to achieve salvation. Thus, though Rāmānuja uses the word *yoga* in a variety of senses, as we shall see, we are using the term, as the heading of this section, in the broad sense of (the aspirant's) 'fitness' for liberation. We can begin with some general considerations, broached earlier, in connection with the requisite qualifications for *mokṣa*. Clearly, at the very least Rāmānuja implies that the one ideally qualified (i.e. the *adhikārin*) for embarking on the path to salvation in the present life is a pious Śrī Vaiṣṇava male, belonging to one of the twice-born castes, and duly initiated by the proper teacher into reflection upon the Vedas and into the performance of the ordained sacrifices. All this is implied in the following statement:

> We know that sacred study, which is repeating what the teacher recites, and has for its fruit the comprehension of that immortal collection [the Vedas], belongs to him who is capable of the [ordained] particular vows and duties and who has been duly initiated [into caste life] by a teacher sprung from a good family, established in sound conduct, possessed of the [requisite] qualities of the self and knowledgeable in the Vedas.[18]

In other words, those apparently excluded from the salvific experience in their present lives are women (Śrī Vaiṣṇava or otherwise), Śūdras (those belonging to the fourth and lowest stratum of the caste-system and not to be numbered among the twice-born) and outcastes (whether Hindu or not). Now there seems to be no doubt at all that Rāmānuja thought it quite possible that individuals from among the excluded categories mentioned above could live virtuous lives. For example, while arguing under *BrSū*, I.3.33f.[19] for the ineligibility of Śūdras to attain liberation *qua* Śūdras, on the grounds of the Śūdras' exclusion from studying and meditating upon the Vedas, performing the attendant sacrifices and so on (an argument which clearly extends to the other two categories[20]), Rāmānuja explicitly allows for piety and spiritual wisdom in a Śūdra. It is significant, however, that this piety and wisdom are explained in terms of righteous actions in previous lives. But it is this very explanation which implies that members of the excluded categories, by the means of a virtuous life, may so qualify themselves by birth in the next or a future life as to be directly eligible for embarking on the path to salvation.

To a Christian this idea of categories of people *a priori* excluded from salvation in their present life may appear abhorrent. I do not wish to express sympathy for the Hindu view, but the Christian would do well to note the frame of reference for the Hindu's (in our case, the Vedāntin's) understanding of the economy of salvation. This is a frame of reference to which an unquestioned belief in the doctrine of rebirth is integral. An individual's present existence is not necessarily decisive (as it is in traditional Christian teaching) for determining that individual's ultimate state; on the contrary, one's present life, if liberation is not attained in it, is a phase in a potential process of 'soul-making' which comprehends the physical rebirth (or rebirths) to come. In other words, for the Hindu one's salvific options are open beyond this life. In terms of time and space the Hindu is used to a much wider perspective for understanding personal growth and its fulfilment, in and through the doctrine of rebirth, than the traditional-minded Christian. I do not claim that the Hindu view in this respect is either logically or theologically problem-free or that it is superior to the Christian view, but I do maintain that, understood in perspective, it does not so obviously face the charge of 'salvational exclusivism' raised earlier. Further, I venture to repeat the point that, had Rāmānuja theologised today, all the indications are that he would have reinterpreted his doctrine of rebirth so as to eliminate or minimise the theological implications of its sexism and cultural chauvinism, possibly with a view to fostering dialogue with a Christian reinterpretation of the classical doctrine of purgatory.[21]

Having looked into the matter of the general qualifications requisite for salvation in Rāmānuja's thought, we may inquire now into the question of the response, on the part of the devotee, to the Lord's saving-action. Is any disciplined response required at all? – we may ask in the first place? Is not the Lord's election in a response of faith enough to save? In fact a debate on this very issue broke out in the Śrī Vaiṣṇava sect two to three centuries after Rāmānuja's death, and played an important role in splitting his followers doctrinally into two camps. It was claimed by one group (the Northern or Vaḍagalai School), on the authority of Rāmānuja of course, that there was but one way to salvation and that this consisted in a relationship of loving co-operation between God and the soul, the one bestowing elective and efficacious salvific grace, the other responding with a life of single-minded and disciplined devotion. The image for this relationship was the co-operation between mother and baby monkey where the latter's safety was concerned, the one actively transporting out of harm's way, the other actively clinging on for dear life. The Southern or Tengalai School, on the other hand, while not repudiating the 'way of co-operation' described above, taught, no less on Rāmānuja's authority, an alternative route to salvation. The regulative image here was that of a new-born kitten, carried without effort on its part to safety in the mouth of its mother. In the same way the devotee, by pleading inability to practise the disciplined way of active co-operation with the Lord, had but to yield passively to the divine saving-action to be transported out of the saṃsāric condition. What had Rāmānuja himself to say about this alternative route of self-surrender (*prapatti* in the specialised sense)? Indeed, can his position be decided clearly enough to lay the debate to rest? After we have dealt with the uncontested 'co-operative' path to salvation, mainly now from the side of the devotee, we shall return to the question of Rāmānuja's position on the putative alternative way.

It is usually said that Rāmānuja sought to harmonise the spiritual disciplines of action, knowledge and devotion (i.e. *karma-*, *jñāna-* and *bhakti-yoga* respectively) in his understanding of this 'yogic' path to liberation. This may well turn out to be a rather simplistic statement in the light of our analysis of what is meant by *yoga* here. It will be useful to start by adverting to a distinction Rāmānuja makes concerning three kinds of votaries of the Lord. In point of fact this distinction appears originally in Rāmānuja's *ācārya* predecessor Yāmuna's Summary of the Meaning of the Gītā (*Gītārthasaṃgraha*). In this work, brief but seminal for Rāmānuja's own interpretation of the *Gītā*, Yāmuna says with reference to the aim of Chapter 8 of the Gīta, 'In the eighth chapter is stated the division of those seeking [the Lord], [1] for the sake of power,

[2] for the true nature of the imperishable [state], and [3] for refuge in the Blessed [Lord himself]; also, what they should know and have recourse to [in order to achieve these ends]".[22] Rāmānuja accepts this division and refers to it in his commentary on *Gītā*, 7.28. Those who worship the Lord in order to be granted 'great power' in this and in post-mortem worlds, he calls the 'power-seekers' (*aiśvaryārthins*); those votaries who seek 'liberation from old age and death in order to contemplate the proper form of the self disjoined from *prakṛti*' he calls the 'cravers for liberation' (*mumukṣus*) or 'solipsists' (*kaivalyārthins*); and those who desire nothing more than 'attaining the Lord' in love and communion he calls the 'knowers' (*jñānins*), the truly wise in matters of ultimate good.[23] Let us comment on the goal and the way, of each type of devotee.

(1) The first group, the power-seekers, are not condemned out of hand. They are a type of all those who worship the Lord for gainful ends, for success in any field of worldly activity. The Lord does not reject such people; he is accessible to them in so far as they call upon him and seek to follow his dictates, and he will answer their prayers in the way he sees fit. The power-seekers who are votaries of the Lord are not to be grouped with those wanton men and women who, throwing all religious restraints and ideals to the winds, worship only themselves in their lust for power. Such people will sooner or later feel the wrath of the Lord through the fruition of their bad *karma*. On the contrary, most of us, Rāmānuja no doubt would say, Śrī Vaiṣṇava or non-Śrī Vaiṣṇava, who seek to know and follow the Lord, with an eye to self-serving goals (for instance, worldly success, protection from various kinds of danger and harm, even a pleasant after-life) would at some time or other, if not for most of our lives, fall into the camp of the power-seekers in the acceptable sense. Such power-seekers build up meritorious *saṃsāra*-immanent *karma* for themselves and remain in the unliberated state after death. Nevertheless the Lord does not abandon them; the prospect of liberation is always open in so far as they co-operate with the Lord, ideally in the ordained Vedic manner, to root out egoism from their lives.

(2) The second group, the so-called solipsists or cravers for liberation, are more difficult to come to terms with in Rāmānuja's thought. He is ambivalent in his treatment of them. To begin with, he seems to think their goal, a permanent *saṃsāra*-transcendent state in which the liberated *ātman* reposes solipsistically in its intrinsic consciousness and bliss (hence kaivalyā*rthin*, literally 'seeker after "aloneness"', after the ideal of liberation of the Sāṃkhya–Yoga tradition), a permissible one to

strive for. It seems that the members of this group acknowledge the Lord (and his dictates) rather in the manner of the followers of the classical Yoga school, i.e. as a prime focus of meditation, as an exemplary *yogin*, and possibly as a helper along the arduous path of ego-renouncing mental and physical discipline they have chosen – no more. For them the Lord is not the supreme and beloved personal goal and fulfilment of their being in this and the post-worldly existence, as he is in the theistic context which justified Rāmānuja's own activity as a thinker.

As mentioned before, then, Rāmānuja seems to think the solipsist's goal of *ātmā*-vision (*ātmāvalokana*) a permissible one (from its seeker's point of view). He even refers to it as a 'liberation' (*mokṣa*). No doubt it can be regarded as a liberation in that it implies a detachment from an egoistic immersion in materiality (*prakṛti*). In any case Rāmānuja refers to the solipsist's or *mumukṣu*'s goal as a liberation, under prompting from the *Gītā*. Under *Gītā*, 5.28, for instance (which refers to the disciplined sage intent on 'liberation', *mokṣa*, with desire, fear and anger removed, as indeed liberated), he comments, 'the sage who, desire, fear and anger gone . . . has liberation for his sole aim, ever practising *ātmā*-vision, is liberated indeed; that is, he is liberated on the way as if he had reached his goal'.[24] But this statement is significant in that it does not actually ratify the goal *as intended.* In other words, though Rāmānuja seems to concede that the solipsist's goal is permissible, he is not clear here and elsewhere if it is attainable as desired by its aspirant – that is, as a permanent solipsistic state. Clearly, from the theological point of view – the point of view in which Rāmānuja is in his element – the solipsist's goal is woefully lacking. No doubt Rāmānuja requires an intuitive *ātmā*-vision even of the model votary of the Lord, the *jñānin* or knower. We recall that he says often enough that an essential prerequisite of ultimate communion with the Lord is self-knowledge. We shall see that in its final stages this self-knowledge implies an intuitive realisation of the nature of the *ātman*. But to all appearances the *ātmā*-vision desired by the *jñānin* is quite different from the *ātmā*-vision desired by the solipsist. The *ātmā*-vision desired by the *jñānin* is one which penetrates to the rootedness of the finite *ātman* in its ultimate source and goal, the Lord himself. This is an important part of what is meant by referring to the model votary as a 'knower', and constitutes the highest realisation advocated by the *Bhagavadgītā*. The *ātmā*-vision desired by the solipsist seems to be of a different order. There is no talk of intuiting the *ātman* as rooted in the Lord and as finding its fulfilment in divine communion.

Now it is not entirely clear if Rāmānuja is prepared doctrinally to allow the solipsist, if he achieves his end, i.e. the limited liberation of what we may call 'first-level' *ātmā*-vision, to remain permanently in this self-enclosed, non-theistic, natural state of *saṃsāra*-transcendent consciousness and bliss, or if he requires first-level *ātmā*-vision, by the transforming impetus of the Lord's grace, to culminate (perhaps after death) in the *jñānin*'s 'second-level' *ātmā*-vision. Here the *ātman*'s essentially God-rooted nature is intuited. In the latter event it would seem to follow that like the *jñānin* the *kaivalyārthin* too would eventually enjoy lasting communion with the Lord. The indications are that Rāmānuja espouses the second alternative, especially in view of his tenet that the finite *ātman* is ensouled by the Lord, the supreme Self. It is hard to see how any 'liberating' (and hence veridical) intuition of the *ātman* (including the *ātma*-vision of the 'solipsist' when attained) can fail to comprise, sooner or later, the awareness that, as ensouling Self of the finite *ātman*, the Lord is the latter's ultimate source and goal. And this awareness would seem to demand fruition, on Rāmānuja's terms, in divine communion. In his *Śrī Bhāṣya* commentary on IV.3.14, Rāmānuja makes a somewhat cryptic statement about what happens to enlightened souls immediately after death: '[The psychopomp] leads [on to Brahman] both those who meditate on the highest Brahman [as a means to liberation] and those who meditate on the self [*ātman*], which disjoined from *prakṛti* is of the Brahman nature'.[25] In other words, two kinds of enlightened souls are led on to Brahman, those whose direct means to liberation is meditation on Brahman himself and those who (finally) attain salvation through contemplation of the *ātman*-nature (which participates in Brahman). The question is, are the first group the *jñānins* and the second group the *kaivalyārthins* or 'solipsists'? Probably.

There are (again indirect) comments in the *Gītābhāṣya* which lead one to suppose that the successful *kaivalyārthin* after death does not remain in a theological limbo. Under *Gītā*, 8.23, Rāmānuja refers to a part of *ChāndUp*, IV.15.5: 'He [a psychopomp] leads them [souls] to Brahman; this is the path of the gods, the *brahma*-path'. (In fact, it would appear that Rāmānuja had this text in mind in his comments in the *Śrī Bhāṣya* under IV.3.14, referred to above.) Now *Gītā*, 8.24, bears a marked similarity to this text in that it also speaks of the knowers of *brahman* (*brahma-vid*) upon death going to *brahman*. No doubt this is why Rāmānuja refers to the *Chāndogya* text under 8.24 when he says,

> From the [*Chāndogya* text's] reference to the attainment of *brahman* both the knower of the true nature of the self [the *kaivalyārthin*] and the devotee of the supreme Person [the *jñānin*] are to know that their

self-stuff, disjoined from non-conscious [*prakṛti*], is essentially accessory to Brahman by virtue of being ensouled by him [*or*: by virtue of being of the Brahman-nature]'.[26] Is it not legitimate to assume, then, that, since both types of votary are to end up with the same realisation, they must also (eventually) experience the same goal: communion with the Lord? For his part, Rāmānuja, perhaps surprisingly, is not forthcoming on this point, and we can do no more than attempt to extrapolate a view – as we have done above – from opaque references he provides. It seems in fact that Rāmānuja implies that the *ātmā*-vision of the *kaivalyārthin* – when attained – merges, after death, into the *ātmā*-vision of the *jñānin*.

If our assumption is correct – that is, if both the *kaivalyārthin* and the *jñānin* end up in the same state – it seems that Rāmānuja permits two separate paths to salvation, one 'by default', as it were, and one by recommendation. The path 'by default' is the path of the *kaivalyārthin* or so-called solipsist, who is a solipsist only by misguided intention, and who will eventually be rewarded for his ego-renouncing pains by the Lord with divine communion in the liberated state. The path by recommendation is the path embarked upon straightaway, with fuller understanding, by the aspirant who will become a *jñānin* or 'knower'. A path which is in effect the path of informed devotion. It is a case, where Rāmānuja's view of the salvific way is concerned, of all roads leading, if not to Rome, then to Vaikuṇṭha – the Lord's abode.

Again, with respect to the *kaivalyārthin*'s path itself, Rāmānuja seems to have countenanced two different 'lanes': the lane of the discipline of knowledge (*jñāna-yoga*) and the lane of the discipline of works (*karma-yoga*). According to the first the *yogin* strives for his version of *ātmā*-vision by hearing and reflecting upon scriptural teaching and then by contemplatively internalising this teaching by, so far as this is possible, a life of total withdrawal from all action relating to caste and stage of life and to daily needs.[27] Under influence of the *Gītā*, Rāmānuja is quick to point out that it is much harder to make headway along this lane than it is by the way of works, and that the risk of failure is great. Even for the contemplative-minded *kaivalyārthin* the way of works is to be recommended, and for a number of reasons. First, human nature is more disposed to act than to abstain from action (though, in this event, action is to be undertaken without selfish desire for the saṃsāric fruits of such action). Secondly, one's debt to society (a statutory obligation imposed on all twice-born males, according to the traditional Hindu dharmic code[28]) is the more readily paid by the example of a life of disinterested action than by one of the renunciation of action. Those disinclined in the first place to follow any discipline to root out egoism would be more likely to be attracted to such a discipline by the first kind of life than by the second kind. Finally, the way of selfless action is the way of the Lord himself, who works ceaselessly, with no thought of personal gain, for the moral and social stability and order of the world.[29]

Since we have spoken above of *yoga* and of '*ātmā*-vision', it may not be going too far afield to clear up here a doubt relating to *yoga* as *ātmā*-vision. Two Rāmānuja scholars, J. A. B. van Buitenen and R. C. Lester, express puzzlement (which they acknowledge derives from an observation by S. N. Dasgupta[30]) that in his commentary on *Gītā*, 15.15, Rāmānuja lumps *yoga* with what he regards as *pramāṇas* or original and authoritative sources of knowledge, i.e. sense perception, inference and testimony. Van Buitenen observes, 'yoga- in the sense of "intuitive presentation" is not a separate pramāṇa . . . but, being memory (smṛti-), is implied by perception; that here yoga- is included among the pramāṇas is certainly, as Dasgupta points out, an anomaly'.[31] The charge is ill founded and rests on a misunderstanding, it seems to me, regarding (a) what Rāmānuja means by *yoga* here, and (b) his use of the term '*pramāṇa*' in this context.

(a) Now, by *yoga* in the passage under consideration Rāmānuja means '*ātmā*-vision', a sense by no means uncommon in his *Gītābhāṣya*. Thus under 6.1 Rāmānuja says, 'Here the rules will be declared for the practice of *yoga* as *ātmā*-vision which is the goal of *jñāna*- and *karma-yoga*'.[32] Under 6.3 we have, '*karma-yoga* is said to be the cause, for one desiring liberation, of attaining *yoga*, i.e. *ātmā*-vision',[33] and so on. In other words, *yoga* here is being used to refer to an intuitive experience, an unmediated knowledge (*parokṣajñāna*) of the *ātman*. It is surprising that it has been taken, by both van Buitenen and Lester, to refer to a species of memory knowledge (*smṛti*). On the contrary, taking his cue from the *Gītā*, under 15.15 Rāmānuja is set on distinguishing *yoga*, together with sense perception, inference and testimony, from memory knowledge. Kṛṣṇa, in 15.15, says, 'I am fixed in the heart of all. From Me come memory, knowledge and the removal [of qualms]. It is I who am to be known by all the Vedas; I, who know the Vedas and consummate them'. Commenting on the second sentence Rāmānuja says, '[Here] "memory" [*smṛti*] is knowledge arising solely from an impression [produced] by [previous] direct experience, and having for its content something [directly] experienced previously. "Knowledge" [*jñāna*] is certitude about things arising from the senses, inference, testimony and *yoga* . . . .'[34] Since Rāmānuja is here placing *yoga* in a category of knowledge which he distinguishes from memory, he cannot be using *yoga* to refer to a species of memory knowledge. Here *yoga* means '*ātmā*-vision', an intuitive knowledge of the self not based on an impression (*saṃskāra*) arising from some previous knowledge.[35]

(b) As such, why is *yoga* mentioned with the three *pramāṇas*? Not because *yoga* itself is reckoned to be a *pramāṇa* in the ordinary technical sense of this term but because Rāmānuja wishes to include a form of self-certifying, non-representative cognition (of much significance for the *Gītā*) with other forms of such cognition (i.e. sense perception, inference, testimony).

(3) Finally we come to the third kind of votary, the *jñānin* or 'true' knower. For Rāmānuja the *jñānin* is the model devotee, for he seeks the Lord for himself on the basis of a single-minded commitment growing continuously in knowledge and love. The way of the *jñānin* and the interplay between *karma-*, *jñāna-* and *bhakti-yoga* in his life is well expressed in the following rather lengthy extract from Rāmānuja's interpretation of Aṅgiras's teaching to Śaunaka given in the *Muṇḍaka Upaniṣad:*

> Two knowledges, a direct and an indirect one, both having Brahman for their object, must be resorted to by one desirous of attaining Brahman. The indirect knowledge is that based on the scriptures. The direct knowledge is that based on *yoga*. Of the two, the [direct] means for attaining Brahman is the direct knowledge, and this takes on the nature of *bhakti*. We have this specified in [the *MuṇḍUp* text] 'him whom this [Self] chooses, by him is it to be obtained'. Now the means for [attaining] this knowledge is the knowledge based on the scriptures and possessed of the sevenfold discipline of [ritual] purity, [detachment from desire, the practice of contemplating Brahman, performance of sacrifices, virtue, resolute cheerfulness in adversity, and calmness]. This we know from the *śruti* [i.e. *BĀUp*, IV.4.22]: 'This the Brahmins seek to know by recitation of the Vedas, sacrifice, gifts, austerity and fasting.' . . . When the text starts off with 'The lower [knowledge] being the *Ṛg Veda*, the *Yajur Veda* and so on' – the law-books being implied at the end – the indirect knowledge, which is

> based on the scriptures and which is the cause [of the origination] of the presentational experience of Brahman [i.e. the direct knowledge] is meant. This is because the Vedas, together with the six auxiliaries, the epics, the *purāṇas*, the law-books and the systematic inquiry into these, are the cause of the origination of the knowledge of Brahman. But by 'Now the higher [knowledge] is that by which that Imperishable is known' the knowledge which takes on the nature of *bhakti*, also called 'meditation' (*upāsana*), and characterised by presentational experience of Brahman, is meant.[36]

This extract describes the means the eligible (ideally, the Śrī Vaiṣṇavite) model devotee must take on the path to salvation. It is important to note that according to Rāmānuja this path can be embarked upon in the householder's stage of life.[37] One does not have to become a *saṃnyāsin*, i.e. a renouncer of the world and its human relationships, to be eligible for the supreme experience (as Śaṃkara maintained). We are told that the devotee must acquire two knowledges, the 'indirect' and the 'direct' (which correspond to the *śruti*'s 'lower' and 'higher' wisdoms). The indirect knowledge (which brings about the origination of the direct knowledge, about which more presently) is based on a systematic inquiry into the sacred texts, both *śruti* and *smṛti*. It comprises imbibing the right understanding of the scriptures at the feet of a *guru*, and a series of meditations on Brahman. As such it may be regarded as a discipline of knowledge (a *jñāna-yoga*). But Rāmānuja is quite clear that hand-in-hand with this intellectual and contemplative understanding must go a discipline of works (a *karma-yoga*). The works here consist in the performance of the ordained and permissible rituals and sacrifices, and the acquisition of virtue. In other words, the aspirant's progress is characterised by the combination of (the disciplines of) knowledge and works (*jñāna-karmasamuccaya*). But the intention informing this path is quite different from that of the power-seeker or the so-called solipsist. In the case of the *jñānin* the intention is to do everything for the love of the Lord. This makes the combination of knowledge and works, even from the preliminary stages, where much may yet remain to be done to wean the self from its attachment to worldly affairs and desires, a discipline of love (*bhakti-yoga*). Rāmānuja implies that, compared to the love of the next stage, of that informing the direct knowledge, this is a 'lower' *bhakti*: there is still much ego in evidence in one's love for the Lord.

Nevertheless, the aspirant has embarked on a way of life which through its complementarity of knowledge and action continually deepens his understanding of his own and of Brahman's nature as well as of the relationship between Brahman and the world, on the one hand, and purifies the single-minded love he has for the Lord, on the other. In the process, the devotee becomes a totally integrated soul – perfectly in tune with himself and with his God. His accumulated *karma* is progressively annulled, no fresh deposit being acquired, and he reaches the state Rāmānuja calls *yoga* proper. This is a state of intuitive realisation of the *ātman* (*ātmāvalokana*) in its rootedness in the Lord – its source and final goal. It goes far deeper than the *kaivalyārthin*'s goal, which we have called first-level *ātmā*-vision: a solipsistic experience of the *ātman*'s intrinsic consciousness and bliss. By contrast, in experiencing his *ātmā*-vision, the *jñānin* takes 'sole delight in being entirely the Lord's accessory'.[38] At this stage what may be regarded as the higher *bhakti* of the soul – total and selfless devotion to the Lord – takes over. In his turn, in an ever-deepening relationship of intimacy, the Lord is attracted to shower abundant graces on his chosen one. The sign of this election is a more or less uninterrupted mental representation, in the devotee, of the divine supernal form. This representation seems to be a fusion of, on the one hand, a 'revelation' of sorts through the Lord's grace, and, on the other, the product of the devotee's imageful contemplation of the scriptural descriptions of the divine supernal form.

We can now say a little more about this 'higher' knowledge or direct representational experience of the Lord. As noted before, it is based on and informed by second-level *ātmā*-vision, in which not only the *ātman*'s true nature as dissociated from *prakṛti*, but also the *ātman*'s true existential relationship with the Lord, is intuited. By this stage the devotee, relieved of the heavy psychological and moral burden of past *karma* and innocent of the accumulation of fresh *saṃsāra*-immanent *karma*, performs all actions from single-minded love for the Lord. The concomitant representational experience he enjoys of the Lord is itself, as Rāmānuja is wont to say, delightful on account of the object represented,[39] and continues to strengthen the union between the Lord and his votary. Of this experience Rāmānuja observes,

> We know that the knowledge intended to be enjoined as the [direct] means to release is a [worshipful] contemplation [*upâsana*] because there are [scriptural] initial and concluding statements which do not differentiate between 'knowing' and '[worshipfully] contemplating'. For example, [in *ChāndUp*, III.18.1] we have 'Let him [worshipfully] contemplate [*upāsīta*] the mind as Brahman'; and [in *ChāndUp*, III.18.3] 'He who knows [*veda*] thus, shines and glows with glory, fame,

> and the radiance of Brahman.' . . . Now this meditation [*dhyāna*] is of the form of a stream of unbroken calling-to-mind [= *smṛti*], like the flow of oil; that is, it is a steady calling-to-mind. . . . This calling-to-mind is tantamount to seeing. . . . it is like seeing because of the predominance of imaging [*bhāvanā*] in it. . . . This kind of steady keeping-in-mind [*anusmṛti*] is designated by the word *bhakti*.[40]

Thus *bhakti* so-called – the 'higher' *bhakti* or *bhakti par excellence* – is, epistemically, a steady imaging of the divine (supernal) form, so clear and vivid as to be presentational in character. For all this, it is not a direct vision of the Lord;[41] this is reserved, on a limited scale, for such special occasions in this life as the theophany described in chapter 11 of the *Gītā*, for which Arjuna was given a 'divine' eye, and, in its fullness, for the state of eternal communion with the Lord in liberation. Nevertheless, the representational experience of which we speak is to be prized most highly: it is the mark of a chosen soul in the way and for the reasons described earlier, and the token of the devotee's nearness to final salvation. As such this experience directly eases into the presentational experience of *mokṣa* upon the death of a body for which all maturing *karma* has been expended. It is worth noting here that the higher *bhakti*, the direct means to salvation, is described in terms of various constitutive knowledges, notwithstanding the ineffable delight involved (in this respect the designation of the Lord's model votary as a 'knower', *jñānin*, is significant). In thus describing the path to liberation in terms of ignorance giving way to knowledge, in preference to any other choice of terms, Rāmānuja shows himself to be distinctively Hindu.

It may not be out of place here to take up one or two matters relating to the question of the means of salvation. Thus, we have said little or nothing about the role of Śrī, the divine consort, in Rāmānuja's theology. This is because there is little or nothing to say. No doubt it is significant that Rāmānuja's sect was called the *Śrī*-Vaiṣṇavas (to distinguish his followers from other kinds of Vaiṣṇavas?), and no doubt Śrī merits an important mention in both contested and uncontested works of Rāmānuja, but there is precious little theologising about her. Perhaps the most powerful tribute to Śrī occurs in the best-known hymn attributed to our theologian, the *Śaraṇāgatigadya* (its authorship of late being the subject of dispute), but even here there is no doctrinal treatment of Śrī. It seems Rāmānuja was reluctant to take up an issue which because of its sectarian character would gravely undermine both the universality of his theological appeal and the seriousness of his claim that his theology was validated by commonly accepted scriptural authority. This does not mean, of course, that Śrī played a small part either in his own and in his sect's theological outlook or in Śrī-Vaiṣṇavite personal devotion.[42]

Then there is the question of whether Rāmānuja advocated *prapatti*, understood in its later sense of total surrender to the Lord, as a separate path to salvation independent of the discipline of knowledge-*cum*-works described above. Some of Rāmānuja's followers and some modern interpreters claim that he did. For my part, I can find no solid evidence for it. Indeed, I do not think there can be the slightest doubt that for Rāmānuja the only path to salvation was a God-centred integration of knowledge and works in the life of the devotee – there was no alternative to that. No doubt the term *pra-pad* (from which *prapatti* is derived) finds expression in various linguistic forms in the contested and uncontested writings. Thus, much is made of this usage in the celebrated commentary under *Gītā*, 18.66, and in the hymns. But in every instance, I submit, the usage cannot be shown to have the technical implications of the later doctrine, nor can we seriously countenance the view that Rāmānuja taught one thing in the theoretical works, and recommended an alternative, with much ambiguity and without doctrinal elaboration, in the devotional hymns.

At this point it may be as well to comment on the authenticity of the authorship of the *Gadyatraya*, the three devotional prose hymns traditionally attributed to Rāmānuja. We noted in Chapter 1 that the two main schools into which the Śrī Vaiṣṇava sect divided some time after Rāmānuja's death both accept Rāmānuja's authorship of the hymns. But of late this authorship has been challenged, some maintaining that none of the hymns can be attributed to Rāmānuja, others arguing that one or other of the hymns is not by him.[43] It seems to me that in this matter of determining authorship the hymns must be regarded collectively, for they have in common not only a particular style and tone, but also a number of distinctive expressions. Further, I do not think that the case can be resolved with certainty one way or the other: to begin with, too much of the underlying theology of the hymns remains unsaid. But, in so far as one can back a hunch on the basis of a study of the style and content of the hymns in the perspective of Rāmānuja's unchallenged works, I veer towards those who doubt rather than those who accept the traditional view of authorship. Without going too much into detail and without repeating points already made, I offer the following observations which seem to me important for any resolution of the debate.

For one, for hymns meant to be primarily devotional in nature, one may question, at the very least, their Sanskritic expression, in view of the fact that the Śrī Vaiṣṇava sect itself was Tamil-based and oriented, and that the average devotee would have been more at home praying in the vernacular. Further, surely this was Rāmānuja's chance, as *ācārya* of his sect, to contribute towards and to continue the rich tradition of devotional Tamil literature in the sect's possession. To all this it could be answered that there may well have been non-Tamil followers in the sect (Rāmānuja is recorded to have travelled about in India, to as far north as Kashmir), and in deference to them, and to foster the solidarity of the worshipping community, Rāmānuja composed hymns in the religious *lingua franca* of the day (the situation being analogous, rather, to the use of Latin in the Roman Catholic Church till recently). This may well have been the situation – but one cannot be sure.

Furthermore, even the hint in the hymns (especially in the *Śaraṇāgatigadya* and in the *Śrīraṅgagadya*) that there might be an alternative route to salvation centring round the devoted utterance of the 'sacred *mantra*' (whether in terms of the doctrine of *prapatti* or not) is thoroughly at variance with Rāmānuja's analysis of the salvific discipline in his theoretical works, as noted earlier. True, the fervour of an expressed devotion tends to cut intellectual corners, but it is quite another thing to embark upon what may well be a change of direction. In reply it could be said that in the theoretical works, written for public dissemination, Rāmānuja expounds the 'ordinary' way to salvation, in accordance with commonly accepted, orthodox scriptural sources and norms of behaviour, while in the hymns, the exclusive property of the sect, an alternative, 'extraordinary' way to salvation is given – a (surer?) 'short-cut' for the members of the sect alone. This sounds too much like theological special pleading to me, and I remain unconvinced.

Then again, I find it strange, to say the least, that Rāmānuja should have peppered his hymns with new terminology and new emphases only to leave us in the dark as to their true significance (even the two main schools of his sect dispute their meaning). For example, the suggestive compound *parabhakti-parajñāna-paramabhakti* crops up often in the *Śaraṇāgatigadya* (and does not appear in the theoretical works), but is left unexplained. (Is it to be translated, 'the higher devotion – the higher knowledge – the highest devotion', or indeed, 'devotion to the higher one [i.e. the *ātman*] – knowledge of the higher one – devotion to the highest [Self]', or what; and then what does it mean?) And rather more seems to be packed into the use of the term *kaiṃkarya* ('servitude') throughout the hymns, to describe the soul's longed-for relationship with its Lord, than Rāmānuja's developed thought might warrant. One could express more doubts in connection with this whole matter, but, like the ones already expressed, they would be in the end no more than doubts; I could not settle the debate in my mind on their basis. And perhaps there we should leave it, with the final observation that in expression the hymns are beautiful, and are worthy of Rāmānuja.

We can conclude this chapter with a brief comment on the post-mortem state of salvation, bearing in mind that something on this state has been said towards the end of Chapter 4. There it was argued that for Rāmānuja communion of the liberated soul with Brahman involves not only seeing and knowing Brahman as he really is but also an expanded awareness of personal identity, comprising and summing up the multiple identities experienced by the soul along its saṃsāric pilgrimage. In salvation the Face of Truth is finally unveiled, and the liberated *ātman* comes into its own, experiencing the Lord in its centre and its centre in the Lord. Now, communion liberation may be, but is it *communal*, one may ask? That is, is it an essential feature of mokṣaic bliss to enjoy the fellowship of the saved? Certainly Rāmānuja implies that it is, by his frequent allusions to the company (*parikara*, *parijana*) of the blessed, which the soul looks forward to joining to sing the praises of the Lord in liberation. Further, concern for the community at large and partaking of the fellowship of the worshipping community are both essential aspects of the discipline of the spiritual path, being included in the various virtues and duties to be cultivated. But I think it true to say that a theology of the community is not developed either in Rāmānuja's soteriology or in his discussions of the last things. Such a theology is implied and needs to be drawn out and even extrapolated, as we have attempted to do on occasion. And salvation, for all its communal features (and there is no doubt that Rāmānuja would have found it abhorrent to contemplate the salvific process as some 'flight of the alone to the alone') is still stressed as an individual, personal thing.

In *mokṣa*, by acknowledging its rightful place as an accessory (*śeṣa*) of the Lord, its Principal (*śeṣin*) – we shall have more to say about these concepts in the final chapter – the *ātman* paradoxically participates in the Lord's sovereignty (*svatantratā*)[44], knowledge and bliss. The idea of divine participation (*sādharmya*) is typically Vedāntic, and we have seen what Rāmānuja makes of it through his theology of identity-in-difference. He can say that in *mokṣa* the soul bathes in the originative, life-giving refulgence of Brahman: Brahman is that 'singular light which obscures all [other] shinings and which is the cause and support of all [other] shinings'.[45] Well may he quote the profound statement of the *Upaniṣads*: 'There the sun shines not, nor the moon and stars; nor do these lightnings shine, not to speak of fire. But when He shines everything shines after him; in His refulgence all this shines'.[46]

The last chapter especially will bring out how positive a view Rāmānuja takes of the concept of matter in general, even though at times he is ambivalent on matter's prakṛtic (as opposed to non-prakṛtic) expression. It is worth pointing out here, however, that Rāmānuja allows for the liberated *ātman* to assume at will, in furtherance of its power and enjoyment, non-prakṛtic, apparently anthropomorphic, bodies. Rāmānuja thus pays significant tribute to the human form and its *modus operandi*.[47] Further, there is a remarkable statement in the Commentary, certainly not out of step with his theology, and applicable primarily to the liberated soul, in which Rāmānuja affirms that the very world which is a source of so much sorrow to a *karma*-ridden individual becomes a source of unalloyed delight to the morally and cognitively purified soul.

> For embodied selves under the sway of *karma*, the world in its entirety in so far as it is experienced as [completely] different from Brahman becomes sorrowful or pleasurable-within-limits, in accordance with the selves' individual *karma*. Now it is experiencing the world as [completely] different from Brahman that renders experience in the world sorrowful or pleasurable-within-limits. It is the experiencing of the [false] difference that brings this about, and *karma* is the cause of this experience. Thus when one is freed from *karma* in its form of ignorance, this same world, through its being [rightly] experienced as a manifestation and attribute of Brahman *qua* qualified, becomes nothing but pleasurable.[48]

Rāmānuja is not saying that the liberated soul ceases to perceive the evil and suffering of the world, which indeed continue; on the contrary, he is saying not only that the liberated soul continues to keep in touch with the world,[49] but also that, experiencing the world for what it is essentially – an expression of Brahman in the relation of identity-in-difference Rāmānuja has sought to articulate – the liberated soul has overcome the world; it is no longer under the world's karmic sway. The world can no longer become the arena to embroil it in a web of egoistic and misguided relationships. Instead the liberated soul experiences the world in its divine rootedness and as the means for the expression, through the outworkings of the karmic law, the *avatāra* and so on, of the Lord's justice and mercy. This realisation becomes the source of unalloyed pleasure. Paradoxically, what was before but the instrument of *saṃsāra* has now become a part of the experience of liberation; *saṃsāra* has become *mokṣa*, for Brahman is in all and all is in Brahman. In *mokṣa* the soul has come home.

7 The One and the Many: Observations on Rāmānuja's Theological Method

In this, the last chapter of the book, we shall be concerned primarily with drawing the strands together, so far as this is possible, of Rāmānuja's multi-faceted theology. To do this we shall have to consider, in some detail, Rāmānuja's theological method. We have seen that it is characteristic of Rāmānuja's theology to be concerned with the *relationship* between Braham and the world/individual and that he expresses this relationship as a distinctive identity-in-difference (*viśiṣṭādvaita*). Further, as the book progressed we noted, on various occasions, that it is characteristic of Rāmānuja's mode of theologising to view Brahman's relationship with the world/individual simultaneously from more than one standpoint. Now, we may ask, is there a central theme or model[1] in terms of which Rāmānuja understands this pivotal theological relationship in his characteristic multi-perspectival way? Earlier it was intimated that there is such a theme: the ensouler–body (*śarīra–śarīrin*) or self–body (*ātmā–śarīra*) model. In this chapter it will be our main task to examine how the ensouler–body model can be seen to function, methodologically, to draw together the various strands of Rāmānuja's thought. It should be noted at the outset that here we are concerned to examine Rāmānuja's *theological* method, i.e. the ensouler–body model in its body-of-God application.[2] Above all, Rāmānuja was a theologian (no doubt in different ways, the philosophical included) and the model in question was intended to have primarily a theological application. Thus, as we shall see, the more purely philosophical aspects of Rāmānuja's thought – such as his position on the self as conscious and as embodied, discussed earlier to give sense and depth to his 'theology' of the self – enter into the model's theological comprehension only indirectly. Further, I must point out that neither in Rāmānuja's own writings, at least explicitly, nor anywhere else have I come upon such a treatment of Rāmānuja's theological method as is proposed here.[3] Thus it may be said that my treatment in this respect is innovative. But I submit that it is only by articulating (and extrapolating where necessary) the ensouler – body model that Rāmānuja's many sided and complex theology can be properly rendered coherent and intelligible, so as to be seen in its best light as a *system* proper. And there can be no doubt that Rāmānuja intended his theology to be systematic. In other words, we can say that the aim is to make explicit what is only implicit in Rāmānuja's way of theologising.

It is as well here to take note of the sources influencing Rāmānuja to speak of the world/individual as Brahman's 'body'. Though Rāmānuja was an original thinker, he did not pluck this idea out of thin air; besides, in keeping with the theological expectations of the time, as we have seen, he had to show that it was rooted in scripture. Thus Rāmānuja's main source for the body-of-God theme was scripture, especially given the frquency with which he quotes from it, the seventh section of the third chapter of the *Bṛhadāraṇyaka Upaniṣad*. There it is said, for example, 'He who dwells in all beings, who is within all beings, whom all beings do not know, of whom all beings are the *body* [*śarīra*], who controls all beings from within, he is your Self, the inner Controller, the immortal One . . .'.[4] There are many other such statements. But Rāmānuja seems also to have had a theoretical and sectarian source, to which he never explicitly refers, possibly because of its sectarian and only germinal character. Though we cannot go into this matter here, it seems likely that Rāmānuja's *ācārya* predecessor Yāmuna entertained the idea, without developing it at all, that finite being(s) and Brahman were related as 'body' to self.[5] In any case, to Rāmānuja belongs the credit for making much of the body-of-God theme, and we shall see how it can be worked out, in terms of his own premises, to embrace all the significant aspects of his theology. Now, in order to understand the ensouler – body relationship and its function in Rāmānuja's theology, we shall first have to examine what he meant by 'body' in this context. To this we now turn.

It is especially in the Commentary (mainly under II.1.8 – 9) that Rāmānuja is at pains to clarify the relevant senses of 'body' (*śarīra*). The discussion is conducted in the traditional way, through the cut and thrust of a debate between adversaries (with one of whom the author is in sympathy) till the author's own view is finally established (the *siddhānta*). Now, surely, argues the opponent, we cannot speak of any worldly object as Brahman's body, for is not a body 'the locus of the senses which are the means for experiencing the pleasure and pain that are the fruit of [one's] *karma*, [a locus] which supports and yet depends upon the five modifications of breath and which is a special aggregate of the elements earth and so on'?[6] Surely Brahman, transcending *karma* and the exigencies of prakṛtic materiality as he does, cannot be supposed to have such a body! Rāmānuja answers by rejecting the opponent's definition of 'body' as too narrow. We must make use of a sense of 'body', he says, which takes into account all the literal uses of the term. Thus the opponent's definition covers only that kind of body which is the result of *karma*. It does not apply to the avatāric bodies of the Lord and to the bodies the released selves assume at will, neither kind of which is prakṛtic in nature or the result of personal *karma*. If we understand the reference to 'body' in the quotation from the *Bṛhadāraṇyaka Upaniṣad* literally (as we are expected to do in the first instance) the opponent's definition of 'body' comes amiss for obvious reasons, as well. Again, continues Rāmānuja, drawing upon accepted understandings of plant life and the workings of the karmic law, that definition does not extend to the bodies of such immovables as plants, which though possessed of breath do not have breath in the five modifications of the vital air (as the definition demands), nor does it extend to the bodies of folkloric figures such as Ahalyā, whose bodies being of wood and stone were the result of *karma* no doubt but were hardly the abode of sense-organs. 'Thus', says Rāmānuja, concluding with his own definition of 'body', 'any substance of a conscious being which can be entirely controlled and supported by that being for the latter's own purposes, and whose proper form is solely to be the accessory of that being, is the "body" of that being'.[7]

The following points are worth noting. In the definition Rāmānuja claims to have exposed the basic *literal* sense of 'body', one shorn of any *accidental* surplus of meaning and hence covering all the referents mentioned above. In this he thinks he has scored over the opponent, whose definition is tied to only one sort of referent. More important, by his definition Rāmānuja has cleared the way, as we shall see, for interpreting the *Bṛhadāraṇyaka* quotation (and others like it) *literally*, with all the exegetical advantages this implies. It is worth pointing out here that nowhere does Rāmānuja say that the world or any of its substantival components is *like* (Sanskrit, *-vat* or *iva*) Brahman's body. He affirms on the basis of a literal understanding of scripture that they *are* so, though not in any *obvious* literal sense. Another consideration is that 'body' in the sense isolated is to be predicated only of a substance related in the appropriate manner only to a conscious entity, to the *ātman* in fact. This is why the model in question can be described as an 'ensouler–body' model or a 'self-body' model, 'ensouler' having the same purport as 'self' here. Finally, the definition of 'body' prescinds from whether its referent is spiritual or material; any substance, spiritual or material, related to a self in the required way can be said to be, for Rāmānuja, the 'body' of that self. This makes it possible for him to affirm that not only material substances but also spiritual substances, i.e. finite *ātmans*, are the 'body' of the infinite, supreme Self or Ātman.

We may inquire now into the meaning of 'world' (*jagat*; cf., for instance, *ShBh*, II.1.9) in the expression 'the world is Brahman's body_m' (where, as distinguished before[8], body_m is body in its specialised sense). Rāmānuja has not addressed this question explicitly, but the meaning he gives to 'world' here is clear enough. To begin with, 'world' must not be understood in the sense of a *system* of some sort, whether open or closed. In general, whereas 'system' connotes 'an organised inter-relation of discrete parts', for Rāmānuja 'world' means simply 'the aggregate of finite conscious and non-conscious beings' (*cidacidvastujāta*), especially in their empirically manifest (*prapañca*) form. In other words, 'world' here becomes no more than a collective term, a convenient shorthand for all finite individual substantival (conscious and non-conscious) entities and aggregates of such entities, and we note that Rāmānuja is as prone to refer separately to such individuals/aggregates as Brahman's body_m as he is to the 'world'. This understanding of 'world' renders Rāmānuja's body-of-God view immune from the sort of objections levelled by A. Farrer, for example, against the *anima-mundi* doctrine of the ancient Western world, a doctrine Farrer assumes is based on regarding the world as some kind of system, open or closed, and the relationship between the ensouling Spirit and the world as an organic one.[9] There is nothing 'organic' in the usual sense about the relationship Rāmānuja perceives between Brahman and the world as his body_m, and it is quite misleading, to say the least, when modern commentators describe this relationship thus.[10]

So far we have approached Rāmānuja's self–body model with a view to clarifying its terms. It will now be helpful to give an explicit statement describing the self–body model in terms of the relations it comprises. Rāmānuja says,

> This relationship between *ātman* [self] and body [comprises] the relation between support and thing supported such that the latter is incapable of being realised apart from the former, the relation between controller and thing controlled, and the relation between

> principal and accessory. The *ātman* – from *āpnoti* ['it obtains'] – is that which in every respect is the support, controller and principal of that which is the thing supported/controlled and the accessory, i.e. the 'body' or form which exists as a mode [of the mode-possessor, the *ātman*], incapable of being realised apart [from the latter]. Now this is the relation between the [finite] individual *ātman* and its own [material] body. And, because the supreme Self is also 'embodied' [in the special sense] by everything, it is expressed by every [type-naming] word.[11]

Note that here Rāmānuja implies that the self–body model is instantiated on two levels, so to speak: the microcosmic, between the finite *ātman* and its material body[12]; and the macrocosmic, between Brahman and the world/its individual substantival entities. Though our interest lies chiefly in the second, i.e. the theological, level, we shall see that the first-level instantiation of the model has an important part to play in our appreciation of Rāmānuja's theological method. We can now go on to examine the three component relationships of the self–body model as described by Rāmānuja above, in terms of which, microcosmically and macrocosmically applied, he understands the interplay between the One and the many. Let us consider each relationship in turn.

(1) *The support – thing-supported* (ādhāra–ādheya) *relationship*. The above passage informs us that the operative expression describing this relationship is 'incapable of being realised apart from' (*pṛthak-siddhy-anarha* in the Sanskrit, or PSA for short). That is, in the context of the self–body model, the thing supported is related to its support in such a way that the former is 'incapable of being realised apart from' the latter. Now, Rāmānuja does not explain the PSA expression explicitly with reference to the support–thing-supported relationship. But, as the passage under consideration shows us, he uses the PSA expression again to describe the sort of relationship obtaining between the mode-possessor (*prakārin*) and its mode (*prakāra*), saying that the body$_m$ is the mode (of its mode-possessor, the *ātman*). And, as we shall see presently, he does indicate what he means by the PSA relationship between mode and mode-possessor. Thus we can get a good idea of what is meant by the PSA relation between support and thing supported by considering what is meant by it in the mode–mode-possessor context. In this context there seem to be two aspects to Rāmānuja's understanding of the PSA expression: (a) ontological; (b) epistemological.

(a) We can start with the following statement in the Summary:

In the case of things such as generic characteristics, because they are the mode of an entity in that they express the generic configuration [of that entity] – here the mode [i.e. the generic characteristic] and the mode-possessor [i.e. the individual entity] are different kinds of being – the mode is incapable of being realised apart from [the mode-possessor] and indeed of being rendered intelligible apart from [the latter]. . . .[13]

Rāmānuja is here considering the ontological dependence of such things as generic or class characteristics (which he calls the modes of the individual entities instantiating them) on the latter entities. For him a class-characteristic (or *jāti*, such as 'cowness'), like the Cheshire cat's grin, cannot exist *in abstracto*, as it were; it is realised in and through the individual (cows). *Mutatis mutandis*, the same observation applies for properties (or *guṇas*) such as 'white', 'brown' and so on. Modes such as properties and class-characteristics, which for Rāmānuja have a tenuous reality-status, essentially have a borrowed being: they exist as the things they are by inhering in their ontological supports. In other words, from the point of view of their being they 'are incapable of being realised apart from' their ontological supports. Thus, the first sense given to the PSA expression by Rāmānuja points to this kind of ontological dependence, a dependence which Rāmānuja implies obtains between the support and the thing supported in the context of the self–body model.

Where the support is the finite *ātman* and the thing supported its material body, the ontological (modal) dependence of latter on former is not absolute. It is true, of course, as Rāmānuja points out, that the body cannot subsist as an organic entity independently of the existential support of its *ātman*; that at death, i.e. at the separation of body and *ātman*, the body ceases to be a body in the proper sense and disintegrates.[14] Nevertheless, the finite *ātman* is not the bestower of being to its body in the absolute sense: it has no intrinsic power to originate its prakṛtic body (which is thrust upon it by the outworking of *karma*) or to stave off biological death permanently. However, in the case of Brahman as ontological support and the world/its individual substantival entities as thing supported, Brahman is, absolutely speaking, the bestower and mainstay of being. Finite being totally depends on Brahman's existential support. Does not our understanding of this dependence, we may ask, if carried to its logical conclusion, prevent us from affirming the substantival reality of the world (or of its individual components)? Now we know that, in contrast to the Advaitins, Rāmānuja is keen to affirm the substantival reality of the world. Later we shall see, when dealing specifically with his theological method, how Rāmānuja seeks to reconcile talk about the total derivativeness of the world's being from Brahman with talk about the world's substantival reality.

(b) The passage considered under (a), besides making an ontological point, makes an epistemological one as well. This it does in its last phrase, where it is said that the mode depends on the mode-possessor for its intelligibility. In other words, the mode-possessor provides its mode's *raison d'être*. This seems clear enough if we inspect the sort of relationship which exists between a class-characteristic as such, say, and its instantiating individual, but it also explains the otherwise puzzling fact of Rāmānuja's willingness to refer to some substantival entities as modes. Rāmānuja maintains that such substances as earrings and staffs are to be reckoned as modes even though, unlike class-characteristics and properties, they are capable of existing apart from their mode-possessor (i.e. the earring-wearer and staff-bearer). If the PSA expression had no more than the existential import analysed above we could not explain the modal nature of substantival things such as staffs and earrings. (This is why the last phrase of the above passage is an explanatory extension of the preceding phrase, i.e. the PSA expression.) In fact, in the case of the relationship between the staff and its bearer, for instance, Rāmānuja is adverting mainly to the epistemological nuance of the PSA expression when he says that this relationship is modal. In other words, though *qua substance* (for example, wood) the staff has an existence independent of the staff-bearer, *qua staff* it has no reason for existing, no intelligibility, apart from the staff-bearer. Such things as staffs and earrings are to be understood for what they are only in relation to staff-bearer and earring-wearer respectively. They exist for the sake of these latter and as such are their modes. The movement to grasp their *raison d'être* flows in one direction only.

In general, it does not really matter whether the mode is a substance or not. For something to be a mode, in Rāmānuja's understanding, it must either be incapable of existing as the thing it is apart from the mode-possessor or be essentially unintelligible for what it is apart from the mode-possessor, or both. The mode, then, in a fundamental sense is a 'hanger-on' of the mode-possessor.

There is a further epistemological nuance to this relationship. It came to the fore in our rendering of Rāmānuja's exegesis of the 'That you are' declaration (see Ch. 2). There it was pointed out that the mode qualifies the mode-possessor by evidencing its distinctive dependence on the latter, and that this qualifying relationship adverts to the underlying existential difference between the two. If the two supportive characteristics identified above emphasise a convergence between mode and mode-possessor (in so far as the former cannot be realised apart from the latter), the qualifying feature brings out their divergence.

Now, for Rāmānuja both the ontological and the epistemological senses of the PSA expression in the context of the mode–mode-possessor relation obtain in the case of the PSA relation between support and thing supported (of the self–body model). In other words, he is saying that the thing supported, as the modal body$_m$ of its support, cannot exist as the thing it is apart from the support (its self$_m$) nor be understood for what it is apart from the latter; further, that, in view of the nature of the overall support, the body$_m$ qualifies the self$_m$ only contingently and not essentially. Thus, where support is concerned, the self$_m$ 'supports' its body$_m$ (relatively or absolutely) both existentially and intelligibly. It is to bring this out that we have translated *pṛthak*-siddhy-*anarha* (PSA) by 'incapable of being *realised* apart from', where 'realised' is intended to bear both the ontological ('realised') and the (supportive) epistemological ('realised') senses isolated above.

Where the microcosmic application of the model is concerned in its epistemological aspect, the finite material body is unintelligible as such apart from the *ātman*. In other words, Rāmānuja's point is that the body has no *raison d'ère qua* body independently of its *ātman*, but exists to serve the *ātman's* ends: first, the outworking of its *karma*; finally, its liberation. And the body, in its human, bovine, piscine or other form, qualifies the *ātman* as its mode by manifesting the kind of dependence it has overall on the *ātman*. Now the *ātman* does not bestow its material body's *raison d'être* in any absolute sense. This is because the *jīvātman*, as a finite entity, is not its own ultimate *raison d'être*. The intelligibility of the *jīvātman*'s being finds its ultimate source and terminus in Brahman alone, who is his own and everything else's final *raison d'être*. In this way the macrocosmic application of the self–body model can complete our understanding of the microcosmic instantiation. Brahman's, as epistemological support of the word, his body$_m$, is its ultimate principle of intelligibility. The world (or, considered separately, its individual substantival components) exists in the last resort to serve Brahman's purposes (purposes which we have shown are neither intrinsically nor extrinsically necessary to Brahman). The world, for its part, qualifies Brahman – that is, marks him out and reveals him to us – in and through its utter dependence on him as his mode. This we perceive with the eyes of a faith opened by understanding scripture aright.

But does not such talk of Brahman's being the finite *ātman*'s ultimate *raison d'être* create a problem? For are we not precluded from saying what in fact we want to say – that in a real sense the *jīvātman* provides its own *raison d'être*, that it is an end-in-itself? And that in virtue of this we can legitimately talk of the material world deriving intelligibility for us in terms of the *jīva*'s own ends? We shall see in due course that Rāmānuja would want to answer both questions in the affirmative. How he attempts to reconcile the finite *ātman*'s being a 'stopping-place' for its own intelligibility (with its consequences for our understanding of the material world) with Brahman's being the ultimate *raison d'être* of the whole finite order we shall also take up when dealing with his theological method.

Thus in the context of Rāmānuja's self–body model the dependence of the thing supported on its support in terms of the PSA relation is a far-reaching one. It is a dependence in which both the ontological and the epistemological aspects are inextricably combined. The dual nature of this dependence can be understood more clearly, I hope, by contrasting it with the kind of dependence the 'thing supported' has on its 'support' in the following illustration. In a normal pregnancy, a very young embryo cannot survive independently of its mother's existential support. If separated from its mother's being it dies. As such, apart from its mother the embryo is incapable of realisation as the entity it is intended to be. But having a *raison d'être* of its own, in due course the embryo becomes viable in its own right, capable of individual existence in terms of its own human ends. It then no longer needs its mother's existential support and is capable of realisation as an individual existing by itself. However, in the context of his self–body model, Rāmānuja does not envisage the PSA relationship between thing supported and its support to be similar to the relationship between the embryo and its mother. The thing supported, unlike the embryo, is not some sort of intrinsically viable and separable addition to its support, but exists as the thing it is and is intelligible for what it is only in terms of its support. Where the finite *ātman* is the support and its material body the thing supported, Rāmānuja describes this intimate heterogeneous relationship thus:

> That the *ātman* is the [body's] sole substrate is known from the body's dissolution upon separation from the *ātman*; that the *ātman* is the [body's] sole goal is known from the [body's] existing for the purpose of the [*ātman*'s] experience of the fruits of its particular *karma*; and that [the body] is the *ātman*'s mode is known from our apprehending [the body] as the qualifier of the *ātman*, which appears either as a god, or as a man, and so on.[15]

In the model's macrocosmic application in this context, the asymmetrical relation between God as support and the world as thing supported is shown in the following paraphrases by Rāmānuja of Kṛṣṇa, the divine *avatāra*'s, words in the *Gītā*: 'all beings are established on Me, their inner Controller . . . but I have no dependence on them, and by their dependence on Me there is nothing that I gain'. Again: 'I am the support of all beings, and there is nothing that I gain by them.'[16]

Indeed, maintains Rāmānuja, it is the peculiar nature of the PSA dependence between the support and the thing-supported as between substances in the framework of the model, that explains linguistically (in the Sanskrit) the difference between the way we talk about the relationship between modes such as staffs and earrings and their mode-possessors (the staff-bearer and the earring-wearer) and the way we talk about the relationship between body$_m$ modes (microcosmically, the material body for instance; macrocosmically, finite substantival entities or their aggregates) and their self$_m$ mode-possessors (the finite *ātman* and the supreme Ātman respectively). In the first case, because only the epistemological nuance of the PSA expression applies, substances such as staffs and earrings being able to subsist independently of their mode-possessors, the relation between mode and mode-possessor is indicated in Sanskrit by substituting the suffix *-in* for the ending of the mode-term. For example, *daṇḍa* ('staff') becomes *daṇḍin* ('staff-bearer'). In the second case, because both the epistemological and the ontological nuances of the PSA expression conjointly apply, the relation between (substantival) mode and mode-possessor is indicated in Sanskrit by way of correlative predication (CP), which we have seen Rāmānuja regards as affirming the distinctive relation of identity-in-difference he is concerned to maintain between the referent of a correlatively predicated statement and its (substance) qualifier term(s). Hence we say, 'I *am* a man', 'Devadatta, owing to bad *karma, is* an ox (in this life)', and so on, or 'Among lights, I (Kṛṣṇa, the Lord) *am* the radiant sun' (*Gītā*, 10.21), and indeed, 'That [i.e. the supreme Self] you *are*.' We have here the inner rationale for Rāmānuja's theory of the extended denotation of words: that all (naming) terms[17] predicated of (finite) substantival entities ultimately terminate in Brahman in their primary sense, for such entities are the supported modal bodies$_m$ of Brahman their supporting ensouler$_m$ (or self$_m$).[18] We can now go on to consider the self–body mode's second component relationship.

(2) *The controller–thing-controlled* (niyantṛ–niyāmya[19]) *relationship*. Carman observes, 'the word ādhāra, like the English translations

support or *ground*, is fundamentally impersonal. It may be, therefore, that Rāmānuja prefers to link this impersonal term with the two other terms used in the definition of the embodied self, niyantā [i.e. controller] and śeṣī [i.e. principal], both of which have a much more personal connotation for him.'[20] This is quite possible, but there is much more to this relationship than the stress on its personal aspect, of course. What sort of control is being spoken of here? It seems that Rāmānuja has in mind two kinds of control, each of which has a microcosmic and a macrocosmic application. In keeping with our earlier observation, it is the person that acts as the paradigm for the controller in every case.

(a) *Control over non-personal entities.* The model here, drawn from everyday experience, is the individual person's control over his voluntary actions in respect of his healthy (prakṛtic) body. Experientially, this control is immediate; further, it is potentially beneficial both to the body – the controlled – in that through 'obedience' to this control the body's health and longevity are likely to be preserved, and to the *ātman*, the controller, for whom the prospect of liberation is enhanced through the dharmic control of its body. This kind of unimpeded, ambivalent control is exercised by the (finite) self$_m$.

An illuminating illustration of the many-sidedness of this control and of its potential for good (and ill) – an illustration which must have weighed in Rāmānuja's mind – arises from the consideration that *niyantṛ* (which we have translated by 'controller') can also mean 'charioteer' (cf., for instance, *Maitri Upaniṣad*, II.6). The charioteer can either keep his horses 'under control' by guiding and restraining them along the recommended path, or he can come to grief by allowing his horses to have their own way. Similarly, in the microcosmic application of the model, the finite *ātman*, the controller, can either keep its bodily chariot (the thing-controlled) on course by guiding and restraining its potentially wayward senses and other prakṛtic faculties along the dharmic path, or it can 'give rein' to these faculties and lose the way to salvation.[21] The ideal, of course, is a fully integrated control between self and body in the latter's different functions and aspects, the sort of control the *Gītā*'s varied use of the term *yam* (and its derivatives) – from which *niyam* and then *niyantṛ* are derived – is intended to explore (a use which no doubt influenced Rāmānuja heavily). In the macrocosmic application of the self–body model under this heading, Brahman is the omnipotent, omniscient and all-providing controller of the non-conscious world, the thing controlled. He exercises this control freely through the regulative force of the universal law of *karma*, which only he can master. And, as we have seen in an earlier chapter, it is essential to Brahman's control of the non-conscious world that the production, disposition, conservation and cessation of every inanimate object fall, absolutely speaking, directly under the command of his effective will (*saṃkalpa*). Well may Rāmānuja quote *Manu*, 12.122, that Brahman is 'the Ordainer of all things' (*sarveṣāṃ praśāsitāram*).[22] However, though for Rāmānuja all things are under Brahman's provident sway, because Vedānta lacks the concept of an eschaton in which the whole of the created order finds its historical consummation he cannot say in the spirit of a Paul that 'the creation waits with eager longing for the revealing of the sons of God' and that under Brahman's guidance 'the creation itself will be set free from its bondage to decay, and obtain the glorious liberty of the children of God' (Romans 8:18f.).

(b) *Control over personal entities*. Here, both in the microcosmic and macrocosmic applications of the relationship we are considering, the controller must not violate the moral autonomy of the personal entity or entities controlled. The model is a community of free agents among whom one rules by consent of the ruled and is responsible to the latter in so ruling. Where the Lord is the controller in this relationship, he exercises control through the application of the karmic law to the situation and circumstances of the controlled. The controlled in response must strive to develop that 'holy will' of which we spoke earlier by which controller and controlled work freely in perfect harmony, at the same time furthering the ends of the former and the salvation of the latter. It is with these various nuances of control in mind that Rāmānuja frequently refers to the Lord as the 'inner Controller' (*antaryāmin*) of the world as a whole and of individual beings separately. Here a problem arises. On the one hand, as a good theist, Rāmānuja is sensible of the need to refer to Brahman as the universal and absolute Controller, upon whose effective will depends the realisation of every action and event in the finite order, regardless of whether these events and actions belong to conscious or non-conscious beings.[23] On the other hand, Rāmānuja is keen to acknowledge, as we have seen, a core of inviolable moral autonomy for the individual self in terms of which the self can be referred to as the 'controller' or determiner of its own destiny in the proper sense. Rāmānuja's response to this tension we shall be considering shortly.

(3) *The principal–accessory* (śeṣin–śeṣa) *relationship*. Rāmānuja says, 'This is, in all cases, the relation between principal and accessory: the accessory is that whose nature [*svarūpa*] it is to be given over to the tendency to render due glory to another; that other is the principal.'[24] Once more the stress is on the personal nature of the principal in the

context of the self–body model. And, again, the accessory may be personal or non-personal. If under the first heading the self$_m$ gives epistemological and ontological support to its body$_m$, providing the latter's *raison d'être*, and under the second heading it directs and restrains its body$_m$, here the self$_m$, by being what it is, gives point to or completes the existence of its body$_m$. In other words, in this relationship of principal and accessory, the body$_m$, by acting out its 'natural' function, voluntarily or involuntarily, i.e. by being what *it* is, 'glorifies' or expresses in some way the due superiority of its self$_m$. Once more, under this relationship, there is a microcosmic and a macrocosmic application.

For Rāmānuja, an important example of the principal–accessory relationship between finite personal agents was the relationship between master and 'born servant'. Today the concept of 'natural' or 'congenital' servitude, i.e. of a person being born to serve another human being, is almost universally found to be morally repugnant, and rightly so. In Rāmānuja's time it seems that the reverse was the case (and not only in India, of course). In any case, the born servant, by compliantly accepting his natural serving-function, and by acting accordingly, exalts his master for what he is – the master – by functioning as what *he* is, the servant. Whether we approve of natural servitude or not, the example brings out what Rāmānuja understood by the principal–accessory relationship: that by duly expressing its nature the accessory glorifies its principal – it throws the spotlight, as it were, on its principal, not on itself. We are now, it seems to me, in the realm of value-discourse: one appreciates the value (as opposed to the intelligibility or the existence) of the accessory, from one or other point of view, only in terms of the principal. In the example above, we estimate the worth, i.e. the dignity and status, of the servant in accordance with the master's. There are further considerations here. Belief in natural servitude is quite compatible with belief in the moral autonomy of the born servant, who can wish freely to carry out the function for which he was born. Certainly Rāmānuja would have held these two beliefs together. The point is that for Rāmānuja the master–servant relationship could be (and ideally was) a loving relationship on the basis of its freedom. (Hinduism traditionally recognised a mutually benign master/mistress–servant relationship as one kind of genuine loving (*bhakti*) relationship.) Thus, the principal–accessory relationship between persons is, ideally, as the master–servant example shows us, a loving relationship.

Rāmānuja applies the master–servant example, *mutatis mutandis*, to the principal–accessory relationship in its theological context. Brahman is the master, the principal, while finite persons (especially human persons) are his servants, his accessories. Rāmānuja adduces in support of this view such scriptural statements as *BĀUp*, IV.4.22: '[The supreme Self] is the patron of all, the master of all.' The point of our existence is to magnify Brahman by acknowledging what we are, by recognising our lowly place relative to him, through a life of devoted service (*kaiṃkarya*).[25] In fact, says Rāmānuja often enough, it is the very savour of our existence to be the Lord's accessories.[26] Ultimately, we derive our value and dignity as persons in our capacity as servants, as accessories, of Brahman the supreme Value. And we realise our value through devoted service, which may none the less be a genuine friendship.

Where non-personal accessories are concerned, the paradigm for the principal–accessory relationship in its finite instantiation is the relation between the *jīvātman* and its material body in the human composite. It is such a body that is best suited to glorify, to 'set off', the jewel that is its inner spirit. This the body does when its multifarious deeds and capacities are allowed to be transparent to the cultivated spiritual beauty of the soul within. And, as the most appropriate empirical vehicle and instrument of the *ātman*, the human body shares in the worth of the human individual, which in and through its *ātman* becomes an end-in-itself, i.e. an intrinsic seat of value. Further, in so far as the whole inanimate world may be regarded as an 'extension' of the human being which grows and develops as the being it is by living in, manipulating and assimilating the world, the human person becomes the summit of visible creation. This means that the 'human' *ātman*, as an end-in-itself, becomes the material world's value-giver in some real sense, i.e. the world is given a value in different respects in so far as it furthers the growth and ends of the human person.

But does this not generate a tension so far as the understanding that it is Brahman who is the supreme Principal of the world (human persons included), the world's final value-giver, is concerned? Brahman alone is that end in terms of which all other ends derive their worth. How then can we say that the *jīvātman* is an end-in-itself and that it is an intrinsic value-bestower to the world? As in the case of similar questions raised under the previous two headings, we shall take this matter up when dealing with the implications of Rāmānuja's theological method.

In fact, we can now go on to examine how the self–body model (in its body-of-God and body-of-the-*jīva* sub-models), under the three constituent relationships considered, can be seen to integrate the various aspects of Rāmānuja's theology. The model does this by a process of identifying and then holding together a 'system of polarities'. It is through the interplay and interrelationships of the various polarities of the two-tiered self–body model that the range and depth of Rāmānuja's 'identity-in-difference' theology are expressed.

By 'polarity' here I mean a more or less stable tension between two (possibly more) poles such that this tension is resolvable into two mutually opposing but synchronous tendencies. One tendency is 'centripetal', whereby the poles are attracted to each other; the other is 'centrifugal', keeping the poles apart. Each tendency by itself is destructive of the polarity as a whole, but as simultaneously corrective of each other the tendencies work towards preserving the dynamic equilibrium of the system. The centripetal and centrifugal tendencies comprising a polarity can each be articulated in terms of a distinctive but mutually complementary mode of discourse. Each polarity itself is translatable into its own appropriate and more or less self-contained pattern of speech which ultimately, through a set of 'universalising factors', must be integrated into the universe of discourse of the polarity-system as a whole. All this is not as complicated as it sounds, and we can explain what we mean by Rāmānuja's 'polarity theology' by illustrating how it works in the context of each of the component relationships of the self–body model.

(1) *The support–thing-supported relationship.* Under this heading, theologically applied in its ontological aspect, Rāmānuja's understanding of Brahman's originative causality in respect of finite being finds its place. We distinguished in an earlier chapter[27] two facets to the divine originative causality: Brahman as finite being's 'substantial cause' (*upādāna kāraṇa*) and Brahman as finite being's 'efficient cause' (*nimitta kāraṇa*). To appreciate how Rāmānuja's polarity-method works under this heading we must recall one or two features of these types of causality. To start which, substantial causality: this generates the 'inherence' mode of discourse to do justice to the scriptural (and experiential) insight that it is *in* Brahman that we live and move and have our being, that apart from Brahman we have no realisation as being. Brahman thus existentially supports the world (the thing supported) as its substantial cause. As part of his method, Rāmānuja gives his understanding of Brahman's substantial causality a distinctive terminology. In so far as this causality may be looked at from Brahman's point of view, as it were, to preserve the ontological intimacy between cause and effect, Rāmānuja, as we have seen, is prepared to talk of Brahman in

his creative aspect as 'the causal Brahman' and of the produced world as 'the effected Brahman'. This accentuates the identity between infinite and finite being in Rāmānuja's theology of 'identity-in-difference'. Now, this way of talking can be said to be 'centripetal' in that it tends to collapse the Brahman-pole and the world-pole into each other by its 'kenotic' emphasis; it empties out, in a manner of speaking, Brahman's reality into the world, identifying the reality of the cause too closely with that of the effect. By seeking to do justice to the utter derivativeness of the world's being, it threatens the transcendence of that being's originative cause. A serious consequence may well be the supreme being's pantheistic involvement with the world's natural limitations and imperfections.

To counteract this, Rāmānuja provided correctives with a 'centrifugal' tendency. The main corrective in this respect was speaking of Brahman, still from a perspective of 'above', as the efficient cause of the world. Now, you will recall that it is a feature of the concept of efficient cause to accentuate the difference in nature between the efficient cause and the effect. Thus Brahman as the world's efficient cause, i.e. as initiating and sustaining the action which brings the world into being, supports the world in the sense that the world cannot be realised as existent apart from him, but at the same time is seen to transcend the world through his sovereign (i.e. unnecessitated) causal action. Such talk is 'centrifugal' since the Brahman-pole and the world-pole are sought to be kept apart. And the stress here is on the difference between infinite and finite being in their 'identity-in-difference' relationship. The way is open for that distinctive theological talk which is mindful of the Lord's essential transcendence, perfection and ontological sovereignty in relation to the world's.

Now, the point is that, within one and the same context of divine originative causality, a polarity is expressed in terms of two modes of discourse: a 'centripetal' one and a 'centrifugal' one. The centripetal mode of discourse emphasises Brahman's identity with the world, the centrifugal way of speaking his difference from the world. Rāmānuja saw no ultimate need to dispense with either mode of discourse within the polarity. This is where he differed from Śaṃkara, for instance. Śaṃkara also accepted that Brahman was both the substantial and the efficient cause of the world – but only in respect of the conditioned (i.e. the *saguṇa*) Brahman: Brahman viewed through the illusory spectacles of duality. From the final standpoint there is no ground for polarity-discourse, since there is but one reality (the *nirguṇa* Brahman) – non-dual, relationless and ineffable. Rāmānuja, by contrast, affirmed the permanent value of polarity-discourse in theology, and developed it methodologically. In fact, it is distinctive of his theological method to identify and to develop, on the basis of an equal hermeneutic status given to the different kinds of scriptural text (dualist, non-dualist, and so forth) and the religious experience grounded on these, a range of polarities, and to use their mutually counterbalancing modes of discourse, within the general framework of the self–body model, to articulate and 'comprehend' the unique sort of identity-in-difference he sought to preserve between his God and the world. Thus, though describing Brahman simultaneously as the world's substantial and efficient causes is not distinctive of Rāmānuja's system (Śaṃkara also calls Brahman the substantial and the efficient cause of the world, though he says this only of the *saguṇa* Brahman), identifying Brahman's originative causality in terms of a polarity is distinctive.

We can appreciate this by considering other polarities that find their home in this schema. Though speaking of Brahman as the world's efficient cause is the main corrective, in Rāmānuja's system, to talk of Brahman as the substantial cause, there is another polarity Rāmānuja uses (within the inherence mode of discourse) which contributes mainly centrifugally to offsetting the centripetal tendency of his understanding of divine substantial causality. This is the part–part-possessor (*aṃśa–aṃśin*) polarity,[28] implying a 'partitive' theological emphasis in contrast to the 'participative' emphasis of the concept of substantial causality. Though one side of the part–part-possessor polarity does assert the identity between Brahman and the world, its main thrust is to differentiate these two poles.

Another polarity we can consider here – this time, in contrast to the part–part-possessor polarity, with an ontologically identifying rather than a differentiating emphasis – is the mode–mode-possessor (*prakāra–prakārin*) polarity.[29] The mode, we recall, is fundamentally a 'hanger-on' (epistemologically and/or ontologically) of the mode-possessor; this makes the corresponding polarity predominantly an identifying one in the context of the self–body model, where Brahman is regarded as the mode-possessor and the world/the substantival individual his mode. It is important to note that both the part–part-possessor and mode–mode-possessor polarities have to do with Rāmānuja's identity-in-difference relation between Brahman and the world 'from below'. There is a further consideration here. In the context of the self–body model – the world/the substantival individual as modal body$_m$ of the self$_m$ – Brahman, the mode-possessor, is simultaneously both ontologically and epistemologically the thing supported. The point is that in its theological application the mode–mode-possessor polarity has, besides the ontological connotations considered above, epistemological implications as well. Here Brahman becomes the epistemological support, the ground of intelligibility, of the world. The world cannot be realised (i.e. understood) for what it is apart from Brahman. Rāmānuja's theory of the extended denotation of (substance) words fits under this heading of the self–body model. Though the tendency coming to the fore here may well be the centripetal one – i.e. in terms of intelligibility the world-pole tends to be swallowed up by the Brahman-pole, the source and terminus of all meaning – there is a counteracting (centrifugal) side to this polarity, as we have seen. Here Brahman as qualificate (*viśeṣya*) becomes the referent of all substance qualifier terms (*viśeṣaṇas*). We have noticed that the result of this is to accentuate the difference between Brahman and the world: Brahman, in so far as he is the self$_m$ of the world his body$_m$, is the ultimate subject qualified (*viśeṣya*) by all qualifier terms referring to substantival, therefore distinguishable, entities.[30]

But what of our problem raised earlier, i.e. that talk of Brahman as the finite self's absolute source of being and meaning threatens the self's substantival reality and intrinsic intelligibility? This is where Rāmānuja's distinctive technique of 'perspectival shift' again comes into effect. From the point of view of the self–body model's second tier, i.e. specifically from the viewpoint of the *jīvātman* as ensouling$_m$ support of its body$_m$ (the material body which is the thing supported), we experience ineluctably our substantival reality in terms of our non-sublatable personal identity. This is where Rāmānuja's analysis of self-consciousness, examined in Chapter 3 in particular, becomes relevant. And it is a consequence of enduring personhood to be, in a real sense, a bestower of meaning and purpose to the materiality in association with which personhood develops and grows. In this way the microcosmic tier of the self–body model counterbalances the macrocosmic, resulting in the dynamic equilibrium of the whole. We can say much more under this heading, but enough has been done in this context, I think, to illustrate how Rāmānuja's polarity method works.

(2) *The controller–thing-controlled relationship.* In its theological application, on one side this relation has as its dominant idea the Lord's absolute sovereignty (*svatantratā*) over the world. Only the Lord can control the world and guide it; this he does by his unique mastery over primal, universal *karma*, as we have seen, and by his indwelling all conscious agents as their inner Controller (*antaryāmin*). This insight

engenders a mode of discourse fully alerted to the sovereign, morally perfect and unthwartable will of the Lord. As a result, the world is in danger of being regarded as a series of predetermined events, and human persons – the true representatives of this world – run the risk of being evacuated of any moral autonomy in the context of a deterministic Calvinist-type ethic. The thrust of things here is centripetal, with little or no room left for genuine chance, contingency and moral freedom in the world: the world has no real 'character' of its own in the face of the Lord's overwhelming sovereignty.

But the controller–thing-controlled relation harbours a genuine polarity in that there is another side to it, a centrifugal side. Here the Lord's control over the world takes into account the vagaries of chance and human freedom. The Lord's elective dealings with man in the context of which divine grace and divine *avatāras* come into play, are based on the freedom of the individual to respond in love (*bhakti*). Such a relationship works only if its personal poles retain their separate, autonomous self-control. If 'centrifugal' distinctions under the support–thing-supported heading allow for Brahman's natural perfection in contrast to the natural limitations of man, 'centrifugal' distinctions under this heading point to Brahman's moral perfection in contrast to man's liability to moral evil. Thus the centripetal and centrifugal sides of the controller–thing-controlled relation set up a polar equilibrium between the Lord and man (and the world), with all the language, behaviour and imagery that this implies. Both sides are to be held together in the life and experience of the devotee, each valid in its own right. And yet another facet of Rāmānuja's identity-in-difference relation between God and the world is exposed to view.

The controller–thing-controlled relation in its microcosmic application reinforces the corrective to the centripetal tendency described above. Here the individual self experiences its genuine moral and physical freedom in its control over its material body, its body$_m$, albeit within the constraints of its karmic heritage. We have seen that Rāmānuja argues for or testifies to the finite self's freedom in more than one context. In other words, he is keen to maintain that the autonomy of the human self is not swamped by God's absolute, universal sovereignty.

(3) *The principal–accessory relationship*. Rāmānuja understands this relation too in terms of the polarity method. In the relation's theological application, the centripetal thrust is provided by the insight (and the theological grammar attendant on it) that the Lord (the principal) is the supreme End, Focus and Value of creation, while the world (the

accessory), personal beings included, exists solely to glorify him.[31] Often enough, especially in his commentary on the *Bhagavadgītā*, Rāmānuja expresses sentiments in accord with the experience and language of monotheists throughout the world – that God is everything and we are nothing; that he must become greater and greater in all things, while we become less and less. The problem here is that, if such talk is taken to its logical extreme, finite persons cease to have any intrinsic value and become mere means, not only in their relationships with God but in their dealings with each other as well. Rāmānuja rejects this extreme. He provides a corrective to the centripetal tendency above by being attentive at the same time to centrifugal insights. In the principal–accessory relation's finite application, the individual *ātman* is assured that it is an end-in-itself, a value-bestower in its own right, through its relationship with its material body, i.e. its body$_m$. This assurance comes not only from scripture but from personal experience in the human individual's dealings with God and with other persons. Rāmānuja's analysis of self-consciousness, complemented by his reading of scripture, is adduced to show that by having a (conscious and blissful) nature essentially similar to Brahman's (cf. Chs. 3 and 5), we reflect in our own right as persons the intrinsic value that characterises Brahman as an end-in-himself. Not even Brahman, as a respecter of his own nature, can violate the essential personhood of our beings. As we have seen already, Rāmānuja's polarity theology demands that both centripetal and centrifugal experiences as distinguished above must be done justice to, held together, in our religious lives: namely, the experience that God is the only final End and Summit of creation, the absolute Value in terms of which we derive our own worth as persons; and the experience that, all things considered, as persons we are inviolable ends-in-ourselves and bestowers of value in our own right to the material world.

We can conclude this chapter with some general remarks on Rāmānuja's polarity method and its implications for theology. First, we have seen that the polarity method as a theological tool is deployed by Rāmānuja in the context of the self–body (ensouler–body) model with its three constitutive relationships. Now, the self–body model functions on two levels, the macrocosmic or theological, and the microcosmic or finite, and though our attention may well be focused on the model in its macrocosmic application we need to take account no less of the model's microcosmic instantiation, for the two levels 'lock into' and complement each other to preserve the equilibrium of the self–body system of polarities as a whole in a theological context. The point of the polarity method is to give due weight to what may at first sight appear conflicting insights (and language) in respect of the polar tension of a relationship. This polar tension, which we have described in the language of 'centripetal' and 'centrifugal' tendencies, is based on authority and/or experience. In the theological context we are considering, it is based on scriptural authority, as well as on religious and this-worldly experience. For example, Śaṃkara and Rāmānuja had to come to terms with scriptural authority which referred to Brahman as the world's substantial and efficient cause with the conflicting tensions of language and experience these concepts implied in the Vedāntic tradition. Śaṃkara resolved the tension by ultimately doing away with it in the context of his unconditioned or *nirguṇa* Brahman.[32] Rāmānuja took a radically different approach. Committed as he was to genuine theism, with its complexities of language and experience, he sought to preserve the tension on the grounds that this did justice both to the declarations of scripture and to the believer's religious experience. He did not seek to collapse, as a final solution, one pole of the tension into the other to come up with either an absolute transcendentalism (as Śaṃkara did, stifling the theistic consciousness in the process) or a gross pantheism (as the Bhedābhedavādins criticised by Rāmānuja seemed to have done, unwittingly making of their supreme being an object of ridicule).

On the other hand, Rāmānuja did not glory in paradox, theological or otherwise, for its own sake; his method holds out no invitation to wallow in 'soft thinking', to indulge in a logic of irrationality or contradiction. There is nothing of the *Credo quia absurdum* in Rāmānuja the theologian. Even a cursory reading of the Summary or of the Commentary (and, I hope, a reading of this book) will show beyond doubt the respect Rāmānuja had for reason and logic and the vigour with which he pursued logical argument. But a 'seamless logic', if you will, did apply *within* the confines of a particular mode of discourse in a polarity, not necessarily across the polarity-tension or between the various polarities. And, again, the same strict rules of logic applied within the polarity-system but not the same premisses. Rāmānuja's credit lies in seriously and humbly recognising the place of paradox in our necessarily limited human experience and understanding of the meaning of life and human fulfilment in the light of the Transcendent, and in then developing a comprehensive method to articulate this paradoxical grasp of mystery. We have seen that his method is the 'polarity method', and the polarity method is likely to work best precisely where human experience comes up ineluctably against paradox: in the face of mystery. And the *mysterium tremendum et fascinans* (and, we may add, *necessarium*) *par excellence* is the supreme being or God. This is why Rāmānuja's polarity method is ideally a theological method.

Because Rāmānuja's polarity theology acknowledges as unavoidable the age-old tensions between authority and faith and between the experience and reason of the mature believer, and seeks to 'comprehend' and reconcile them within the framework of a dynamic equilibrium, it is both creative and fertile. This framework is, of course, the self–body model as described. The theology it expresses is creative because it first recognises and then reconciles in an original way the various tensions mentioned. It is fertile in so far as it is open-ended and yet structures reason and experience in their theological articulation. The two most overarching structural factors are the concepts of 'self' (or 'ensouler') and 'body', in the specialised yet allegedly literal senses Rāmānuja gave to them. (The specialised literal bias to my mind betokens a healthy evaluation of the relation between the literal and the metaphorical use of words in theology.) The two concepts of 'self' and 'body' are made to inform a universal mode of theological discourse in terms of which the three constitutive relationships of the model with their more particular modes of discourse function polarity-wise as a system. A further feature binding the whole together is the setting-up of 'resonances' among the polarities. For example, the 'resonance' between the ontological and the epistemological nuances of the supportive mode–mode-possessor polarity helps one appreciate better the unitive function exercised by the dominant 'support' and 'thing-supported' ideas of the first constituent relationship of the self–body model. Again, all three of the model's constitutent relationships have distinctive emphases which 'resonate' together to form a perception of the human person as an inviolable end-in-itself, and so on. This idea of 'resonance' awaits further analysis.

What, we may now ask very briefly, is Rāmānuja's main contribution to the theological enterprise (not excluding especially the dialogue between Hinduism and Christianity[33])? Historically, in the Mīmāṃsaka or exegetical tradition it offered the first serious, orthodox scripture-based theistic challenge to the onslaughts of Śaṃkarite non-dualism on the one hand, and of Pūrvamīmāṃsaka on the other. In time, Rāmānuja's theology restored respectability to devotional theism and encouraged other innovative thinkers to follow suit. In general, as I hope this book has shown, Rāmānuja has made an original contribution to theology in respect of both content and method. As to content, there are a number of new and stimulating ideas as well as a fertile development of earlier (sometimes germinal) views: for example, his theory of the denotation of naming-words extending to Brahman, the conception of the divine supernal form, and indeed the substance of the self–body model itself, comprising as it does the dominant ideas of the three constituent relationships. But Rāmānuja's outstanding original contribution to theology is, as indicated, his implicit proposal of the polarity method, which we have spelt out and analysed. Surely here Rāmānuja is offering theologians the world over something which, because of the unique nature of theology's proper object, they could ponder with much profit.

One final point. Is there a suitable label we can use to describe Rāmānuja's theology? In the Sanskrit, though Rāmānuja himself does not use it, the expression most often used later by his followers and critics to refer to his system is *viśiṣṭādvaita* (i.e. the non-duality of qualified or differentiated beings).[34] This seems an apt-enough description for Rāmānuja's distinctive thinking on the relation of identity-in-difference between Brahman and finite being – especially in view of his repeated and characteristic use of the participle *viśiṣṭa* ('qualified') in this context. But is there a suitable English equivalent? The favoured contender seems to be 'panentheism' (the being all-in-(one)God).[35] But this will hardly do. For one, while 'panentheism' seems to approximate satisfactorily to Rāmānuja's central teaching that the deity comprehends all of reality within itself, it quite fails to adequate to another equally central concern of Rāmānuja's: that the deity indwells all of reality, controlling and fulfilling it as its inner Self. But my main objection against the 'panentheism' description is that apparently its aim is to describe Rāmānuja's theology in respect of content rather than method. And the whole thrust of the discussion in the latter half of this chapter makes it evident, in the light of the pivotal role of Rāmānuja's method in his theology, that this is inappropriate. This is why I have sought to describe Rāmānuja's theology in terms of his method, i.e. as a 'polarity theology'. But in the end, of course, it is unwise in such matters to lay too much store by labels: one finds that for creative minds they are apt to come unstuck.

Glossary

ācārya	Learned teacher, master scholar.
Advaita	Non-duality; the philosophical-theological system of non-dualism in which ultimately there is but one reality, Brahman–Ātman, homogeneous, relationless and ineffable. From this viewpoint the pluralistic world is sublated away into the non-dualism of the Ultimate. The greatest *ācārya* of Advaita is Śaṃkara (c. eighth century CE).
Āgama	Sacred (especially sectarian) teachings or writings.
ākṛti	Independently real 'concrete universal', the formal object of 'naming' words (see Ch. 1).
Āḷvār	One of a select group of innovative Tamil *bhakti* saints of the Vaiṣṇavas (c. sixth–ninth centuries CE).
aṃśa	Part or aspect.
aṃśin	Part-possessor.
ānanda	Bliss, the affective side of consciousness, and usually contrasted with *sukha*: (worldly) pleasure.
aṇu	Literally, atom or minute particle, but also connotes spatio-temporal limitation in general (see Ch. 4).
apauruṣeya	Non-personal.
ātman	The spiritual centre of an individual.
avatāra	Literally, descent (i.e. the descent of the deity or a liberated soul into *saṃsāra*).
bhāṣya	Written commentary.
Bhedābheda	Literally, difference/non-difference; philosophical–theological position maintaining some relation of identity-in-difference between the supreme being and finite reality.
bhoktṛ(-tā)	Experiencer (empirically).
dharma	Code of right conduct socially and religiously; law, virtue.

guṇa	Constituent strand of *prakṛti*; quality, property.
guru	Spiritual preceptor.
jīva	Individual finite self (or *ātman*).
jña(*-ātṛ,-ātā*)	Knower.
jñāna	Knowledge.
karma	Meta-empirical, personal deposit of (morally) meritorious and unmeritorious unenlightened action, to be expended in *saṃsāra*.
karman	Action, deed.
kartṛ(*-tā*)	Doer, performer of *karman*.
mahāvākya	'Great' (i.e. weighty) utterance.
mokṣa	Liberation, salvation.
phala	'Fruit', i.e. the (usually scripturally prescribed) consequence of *karman*.
pradhāna	The primal material cause, in Sāṃkhya a synonym for *prakṛti*.
prakāra	Mode, determiner.
prakārin	Mode-possessor.
prakṛti	In Sāṃkhya, the primordial, insentient principle of material, changeable being, comprising the three *guṇas* of *sattva*, *rajas* and *tamas* – the counterpart of *puruṣa*; in Vedānta, *mutatis mutandis*, in essence the same (cf. Ch. 2, n. 28).
pramāṇa	Epistemologically, a distinctive source of knowledge.
prasthānatraya	'The three foundations' of Vedāntic theory: the classical *Upaniṣads*, the *Bhagavadgītā* and the *Brahma Sūtras*.
purāṇa	A *smṛti* text of religious stories and miscellaneous information.
puruṣa	Person. In Sāṃkhya one of an indefinite number of homogeneous, conscious centres – in essence the spiritual counterpart of *prakṛti*; in Vedānta, usually synonymous with *ātman*.
Pūrvamīmāṃsā	The Earlier or Prior School of Exegesis, concentrating on those areas of scripture concerned with the sacred ritual.
pūrvapakṣa	The position of the opponent in a debate; (*-ṣin*) the opponent.
Sāṃkhya	An orthodox dualist school of thought, in which *puruṣa* and *prakṛti* are the first principles.
saṃpradāya	Teaching-tradition.
saṃsāra	The round of rebirth.

saṃskāra	(Usually mental) impression or trace.
śarīra	Body.
śarīrin	Ensouling self.
śāstra	(Often religious) authoritative text.
smṛti	Sacred text, authoritative in so far as it supports or illuminates *śruti*.
śruti	Canonical scripture (i.e. the Vedas).
suṣupti	Dreamless sleep.
sūtra	Aphorism.
svarūpa	Proper form: form belonging to some entity *qua* that entity.
tejas	Fire, lustre.
Veda(s)	Canonical scripture (see *śruti*).
viśeṣaṇa	Qualifier.
viśeṣya	Qualificate.
yoga	Union, bonding, discipline; (Yoga) an orthodox dualist school of thought like Sāṃkhya, emphasising meditative techniques and postures.

Abbreviations

AitĀr	*Aitareya Āraṇyaka.*
BĀUp	*Bṛhadāraṇyaka Upaniṣad.*
BG11	*The Bhagavad-Gītā with Eleven Commentaries*, 3 vols, ed. Shastri G. S. Sadhale.
BRG	*Śrī Bhagavad-Rāmānuja-Granthamālā*, ed. Sri Kanchi P. B. Annangaracharya Swamy.
BrSū	*Brahma Sūtra.*
BSBh	Śaṃkara's *Brahmasūtrabhāṣya*, rev. Wāsudev Laxmaṇ Shāstrī Paṇśīkar, 2nd edn.
ChāndUp	*Chāndogya Upaniṣad.*
Gītā	*Bhagavadgītā.*
KaṭhUp	*Kaṭha Upaniṣad.*
KauUp	*Kauṣītakī Upaniṣad.*
MuṇḍUp	*Muṇḍaka Upaniṣad.*
ShBh	*Śrī-Bhāshya by Rāmānujāchārya*, ed. Vasudev Shastri Abhyankar. [The Commentary.]
ŚveUp	*Śvetāśvatara Upaniṣad.*
TaiUp	*Taittirīya Upaniṣad.*
Th	G. Thibaut, *The Vedānta-Sūtras with the Commentary by Rāmānuja.*
VedDīp	Rāmānuja's *Vedāntadīpa* (text taken from the *BRG*).
VedS	*Rāmānuja's Vedārthasaṃgraha*, ed. J. A. B. van Buitenen [The Summary.]
VedSār	Rāmānuja's *Vedāntasāra* (text taken from the *BRG*). [The Essence of the Vedānta.]
ViPu	*Viṣṇu Purāṇa.*

Notes

CHAPTER ONE: LANGUAGE AND MEANING

1. In his *The Theology of Rāmānuja*, p. 27, J. B. Carman proposes a modification of these dates.

2. 'God' is being used not as a proper name but as a descriptive term for the supreme being.

3. In some circles, not least among modern Hindu thinkers, 'theology' has acquired a pejorative sense, and implies dogmatism. This is unfortunate and unwarranted and some recent works have done much to rehabilitate the term in its Hindu context. See, for instance, R. V. De Smet's *The Theological Method of Śaṃkara*, esp. ch. 1, and Carman's *The Theology of Rāmānuja*; also G. Gispert-Sauch's fine article 'Shankaracarya and our Theological Task', *Vidyajyoti*, Sep. 1978, pp. 348–55. It is hoped that this book too will contribute towards establishing that at least in Rāmānuja's case theology was a serious and systematic inquiry into matters of enduring truth and value for man in the light of the transcendent.

4. For information about Rāmānuja's life, cf. for example A. Govindacharya, *The Life of Ramanujacharya*; C. R. Srinivasa Aiyengar, *The Life and Teachings of Sri Ramanujacharya*. For briefer versions, see Carman, *The Theology of Rāmānuja*, ch. 2; and K. D. Bharadwaj, *The Philosophy of Rāmānuja*, ch. 1.

5. The Sanskrit text followed in this book is from *Rāmānuja's Vedārthasaṃgraha*, ed. J. A. B. van Buitenen (*VedS*).

6. Sanskirt text taken from *Śrī-Bhāshya by Rāmānujāchārya*, ed. Vasudev Shastri Abhyankar (*ShBh*). Though, as noted already, all translations from the Sanskrit in this book are my own, I give page references to G. Thibaut's English translation, *The Vedānta-Sūtras with the Commentary by Rāmānuja* (*Th*), for those who wish to consult an English translation in wider context.

7. All quotations from Sanskrit commentaries on the *Gītā* are taken from *The Bhagavad-Gita with Eleven Commentaries*, 3 vols, ed. Shastri G. S. Sadhale (*BG11*).

8. References to the *Vedāntasāra* (*VedSār*) and *Vedāntadīpa* (*VedDīp*) are taken from the Sanskrit text in *Śrī Bhagavad-Rāmānuja-Granthamālā*, ed. Sri Kanchi P. B. Annangaracharya Swamy (*BRG*). (This volume contains the Sanskrit text of the nine works traditionally ascribed to Rāmānuja.) The *VedSār* and *VedDīp* are shorter commentaries on the *Brahma Sūtras* than the *Śrī Bhāṣya* and rarely have a neater turn of phrase or original material.

9. The Sanskrit text of these last four works is in the *BRG*. They await good English translations.

10. There is useful material in this book on the development of Śrī Vaiṣṇava thought after Rāmānuja.

11. Carman, *The Theology of Rāmānuja*, p. 49.

12. For more on this see ibid., ch. 3, pp. 57–60, and ch. 17, esp. n. 1.

13. Why did Rāmānuja write these two – compared to the *Śrī Bhāṣya* much shorter, unoriginal – commentaries on the *Brahma Sūtras*? Conversely, why did he not write individual commentaries on the classical *Upaniṣads* as Śaṃkara and Madhva did, for instance? To consider the second question first: it was central to Rāmānuja's exegetical approach to treat the classical *Upaniṣads* as a single body of revealed truth and to show the overall coherence of their teaching by a proper application of the rules of exegesis. In this light the traditional demarcation of the *Upaniṣads* under different names was a division of convenience not of function. To make separate commentaries of the individual *Upaniṣads* might give the impression of fragmenting their unitary nature. Further, so far as Rāmānuja was concerned it was unnecessary, for one of the chief ends of the Summary and of the Commentary was to show the coherence and unitariness of Upaniṣadic teaching. As to the first question (why three commentaries on the *Brahma Sūtras*?): the *Sūtras* as centring round key Upaniṣadic texts were generally thought by Vedāntins to encapsulate teachings of vital concern. Three commentaries on them was a measure of their importance for Rāmānuja. The Commentary or *Śrī Bhāṣya* was no doubt meant to act as Rāmānuja's *magnum opus*, establishing his credentials as an authoritative exponent of the sacred texts and setting out in detail the chief features of his system. The two lesser commentaries may well have been intended as handy summaries, ready-reference manuals, or the like, each in its own way, for the serious but less academic members of Rāmānuja's sect, especially at a time when the sect offered a serious alternative to Śaṃkara's theological system. Contrary to the view that the two shorter commentaries are not authentic works of Rāmānuja, they seem to bear the unmistakable stamp of his intellect. For a treatment of Rāmānuja's analysis of individual *Upaniṣads*, see S. S. Raghavachar's *Śrī Rāmānuja on the Upanishads*.

14. We can disregard S. R. Bhatt's view that Rāmānuja was not a Śrī Vaiṣṇava, that his predecessor Yāmuna was not the author of the *Ātmasiddhi* and *Gītārthasaṃgraha*, and indeed that the Āḷvārs probably post-dated Rāmānuja(!). Bhatt has not really substantiated these claims. See the Introduction to his *Studies in Rāmānuja Vedānta*, and pp. 69, 138, 156, 172, 180.

15. Carman writes, 'both branches [of the sect] regard Rāmānuja as the *third* great teacher (ācārya) of the distinct Śrī Vaiṣṇava tradition' (*The Theology of Rāmānuja*, p. 24, emphasis added). Perhaps the operative term here is *ācārya* or authoritative teacher, and Carman is distinguishing it from *guru* or spiritual preceptor (though not infrequently the roles of *ācārya* and *guru* merged).

16. *VedS*, para. 2, p. 73. 'Scripture and reason': *śrutinyāya-*.

17. Cf., for example, *ShBh*, I.1.3 (p. 142, l.19; *Th*, p. 169). 'Scripture': *śāstra*. This Sanskrit term has the general meaning of sacred or authoritative text. Its sense is broader than either *śruti*, meaning 'canonical scripture or statement', or *smṛti*, which refers to a text that has authority only in so far as it supports or illuminates *śruti*.

18. Thus *svarūpa*, (strictly) the nature or form proper to some entity *qua* that entity.

19. *ShBh*, I.1.3 (p. 145, l. 17 – p. 146, l. 2; *Th*, p. 173). From 'proper form' to 'repugnant': *nikhilaheyapratyanīkasvarūpam*; 'comprising omniscience, omnipotence and so on': *sarvajñasatyasaṃkalpatvādimiśra-*.

20. Cf. Śaṃkara's *Brahmasūtrabhāṣya*, I.1.2 (pp. 7–8), from the text revised by Wāsudev Laxmaṇ Shāstrī Paṇśīkar (*BSBh*). 'Inference': *anumāna*, 'argument': *tarka*.

21. *ShBh*, I.1.13 (p. 187, l. 19; *Th*, p. 216).

22. For a more detailed analysis of sources influencing Rāmānuja's thought, cf. E. Lott's *God and the Universe in the Vedāntic Theology of Rāmānuja*; also see Bharadwaj, though here one must bear in mind that as a committed follower of Rāmānuja's school Bharadwaj often blurs the distinction betwen Rāmānuja's own views and those of his disciples.

23. W. G. Neevel, *Yāmuna's Vedānta and Pāñcarātra*, pp. 74–5. This book also has a good treatment of the conceptual interplay among Rāmānuja's precursors in the tradition; see esp. chs 4–5.

24. In the *VedSār* and *VedDīp* Rāmānuja's commentary on these *sūtras* is slight compared to that on many other *sūtras*. He did not go out of his way to give them prominence.

25. Carman, *The Theology of Rāmānuja*, p. 48.

26. On this point Lott comments, 'is this absence of explicit sectarian material so curious? . . . It was not merely a matter of expediency but the need for clarity of articulation and effective communication that precluded an explicit sectarian orientation' (*God and the Universe*, p. 25).

27. See P. N. Srinivasachari's *The Philosophy of Bhedābheda* for more information about this approach.

28. Much remains to be done in determining the conceptual relationship between Bhāskara, Yādavaprakāśa and Rāmānuja.

29. By Rāmānuja's time Śaṃkara's theology was fast becoming the most influential Vedāntic interpretation of the scriptures.

30. This was in sharp contrast to the view of the Nyāya Vaiśeṣika school, which maintained that it was Īśvara or the Lord who determined the denotativeness of Vedic words and taught this to the primeval seers; also, it was the Lord who composed the Vedas, and as such, they were *pauruṣeya* or 'personal'. Here we must issue a warning that it was not any sort of Vedic word Rāmānuja had in mind when treating of the relationship between Vedic words and their objects. He had in mind so-called 'naming' words (referring in the main to types of material substantival entities). We shall return to this, but this qualification must be kept in mind during the ensuing discussion.

31. See n. 17.

32. *ShBh*, I.3.29 (p. 318, l. 9–15; *Th* pp. 333–4). 'The Blessed One': *bhagavān*; 'the previous configuration': *pūrvasaṃsthānam*; 'previously collapsed in himself as but his residual power': *svasmiñ chaktimātrāvaśeṣaṃ pralīnam*; 'traditional order': *pūrvānupūrvī-*.

33. Cf. *ShBh*, I.3.28 (p. 317, ll. 9–15; *Th*, pp. 332–3).

34. The term is appropriate here in so far as the knowledge concerned is a direct (unmistaken) awareness of past events and objects. However, unlike memory proper, it does not necessarily entail a former *first-person experience*

(absent in the case of secondary promulgators such as Brahmā and the primeval seers). In the context of a partial dissolution, for instance, where roles rather than specific events are repeated, the present (promulgating) seer Viśvāmitra (for instance) is unlikely to be the same individual as the previous one and so cannot 'remember' by way of a first-person experience the previous transmission of the Vedas. In this connection, the tradition speaks of the sages depending on innate impressions (*saṃskāras*) of the Vedas in their pre-established form. Rāmānuja explicitly exempts Brahman from this dependence since Brahman's knowledge is perfect. For these reasons the use of *smṛ* ('remember') here is a special one; note also Rāmānuja's special use of *anu-smṛti*) to describe the imageful cognition constituting the highest *bhakti* or devotion to the Lord (see Ch. 6).

35. We may note a contrast here between the Vedāntic view and that of the Pūrvamīmāṃsakas. In order to preserve the absolute independence of the Vedas, the Pūrvamīmāṃsakas affirmed their eternity by rejecting the periodic dissolution of the world.

36. *VedS*, para. 139 (p. 168). 'Injunctions, explanations and chants': *vidhyarthavādamantra-*.

37. Literally, 'the being one statement' of meaning.

38. *VedS*, p. 200, n. 134. In his pioneering but still practically inaccessible work *The Theological Method of Śaṃkara*, Fr De Smet illustrates (pp. 207–8) how these exegetical factors come into play in determining the sense and coherence of a text.

> (1) upakramopasaṃhārau (beginning and end): it is the mention in the beginning as well as the end, of the topic treated in the section; for instance, C[hāndogya] U[paniṣad] 6 begins with the words 'One only, without a second' (6.2.1)' and ends with the sentence 'All this is identical with that; that is truth; that is Ātman; that art thou, O Śvetaketu' (6.6.13). Such clear beginnings and ends are the best sign of the intention of the śruti.
> (2) abhyāsa (repetition): it is the statement, now and again in the course of a section, of the matter to be taught in it; for instance, the ninefold repetition of the sentence, 'That thou art', in the course of CU 6. This is also a very clear sign of the intention of the śruti.
> (3) apūrvatā (novelty): it is the unknowability through the other pramāṇas, such as perception etc. of the matter taught in the section; for instance, the transcendent secondless Brahman in CU 6. Such a sign suggests that it must be the topic intended by the śruti.
> (4) phala (fruit): it is the usefulness, referred to here and there, of the knowledge of the matter taught; see, for instance, CU 6.14.1(and 2).
> (5) arthavādas (secondary passages): it is either the commendation or the condemnation by secondary passages of the subject taught or blamed in the section; for instance, the extolling of the secondless Braham in CU 6.1.3.
> (6) upapatti (consistency): it is shown by (analogical) reasoning stated now and then in order to establish the truth of the matter taught; see, for instance, CU 6.1.4–6.

39. *ShBh*, I.3.29 (p. 318, ll. 15–19; *Th*, p. 334). 'Mental impression': *Saṃskāra*.

40. See *VedS*, para. 139 (pp. 168–9).
41. In Sanskrit, *autpattikas tu śabdasyārthena saṃbandha iti*. The technical Sanskrit expression for the word–object relation we are considering is *śabdārthasaṃbandha*.
42. *VedS*, para. 137 (p. 167). 'The natural power': *-śaktiyogaḥ svābhāvikaḥ*; 'the natural power to denote': *bodhanaśaktiḥ svābhāvikī*.
43. See ibid.
44. 'Of its own accord': *svātmanā*; van Buitenen's suggested correction, *svātmanām*, i.e. 'belonging to the words themselves' (?) (cf. *VedS*, p. 268, n. 612) seems not only unnecessary but more obscure. The *BRG* has, strangely, *svātmanām* for the *Śrī Bhāṣya* and *svātmānam* for the *VedDīp*, under I.1.1. In any case, the point of this expression is that the Vedic words, by their inherent capacity to denote objects, spontaneously generate their meanings as the veil of such impediments as lack of a competent teacher, defective cognitive faculties, and the like, is progressively removed.
45. *ShBh*, I.1.1 (p. 127, ll.5–11; *Th*, p. 150). 'Personal determiner': *saṃketayitṛpuruṣa-*. See also *VedS*, para. 116 (p. 146).
46. *ShBh*, I.1.1 (p. 125, ll.17–21; *Th*, p. 148). 'Use by (one's) elders': *vṛddhavyavahāra-*; 'cognition of what-is-to-be-done': *kāryabuddhi-*; *'full-blown (entity)': pariniṣpann(a)-*.
47. The three basic categories into which sacred language was divided were *arthavāda* or explanatory statement, *mantra* or sacrificial formula, and *vidhi* or injunction.
48. For a clear statement of terms and positions in this debate see esp. ch. 1 of John Hick's *God and the Universe of Faiths*.
49. We give the substance of a discussion in *VedS*, para. 119 (p. 147f).
50. Cf. *VedS*, para. 116 (p. 146). In a later example, in the Commentary, the message is changed to 'Your father is keeping well' – *ShBh*, I.1.1 (p. 127, ll.15f; *Th*, p. 150). As van Buitenen points out (*VedS*, p. 268, n. 611), the first (i.e. stick) example could without too much difficulty be interpreted as a covert injunction, prompting the messenger or Devadatta to fetch the stick and so intimate to the bystander the meaning of the message. The example would thus run counter to Rāmānuja's reasoning. He seems to have been aware of this and to have changed the example in the Commentary to the much more satisfactory father-example.
51. *VedS*, para. 137 (p. 167).
52. In Sanskrit, *yathābhūtavādi hi śāstram*.
53. Cf. *VedS*, para. 118 (p. 147).
54. Cf. *ShBh*, I.1.4 (p. 169; *Th*, p. 199).
55. In his *Brahmasūtrabhāṣya* Śaṃkara makes a clear statement in this connection: 'Their *ākṛtis* do not come into being when individual oxen etc. do, for only individual instances of substances, qualities and actions come into being, not *ākṛtis*. The [innate] relation of words is with the *ākṛtis*, not with the individuals. This relation cannot obtain [between word and individuals] because the individuals are infinite [in number as to time and place]' – *BSBh*, I.3.28 p. 123).
56. M. Biardeau, *Théorie de la connaissance et philosophie de la parole dans le Brahmanisme classique*, p. 32f. A detailed discussion on the Pūrvamīmāṃsaka view on the relation between word and object is given, from p. 156.
57. The word *artha* can mean both 'object' and 'meaning', and sometimes

Rāmānuja exploits this ambiguity (as here). Nevertheless, in Vedāntic no less than in Pūrvamīmāṃsaka discussions on the specific relation between word and its *artha* (*śabdārthasaṃbandha*), *artha* always means (natural) object. In the Pūrvamīmāṃsā context Biardeau writes, 'Quand il s'agit du sens du mot ou de l'objet signifié par le mot, le terme sanskrit *artha* ne désigne jamais autre chose dans la Mīmāṃsā que l'objet lui-même en tant que perçu et non une idée de l'objet, un concept abstrait des objets, ou simplement un object-de-pensée' (ibid., p. 161). In his *Śabdaprāmaṇyam in Śabara and Kumārila*, Francis D'Sa's discussion on *ākṛti* is confused in places because he does not clarify whether *ākṛti* is some external thing or a part of the cognitive process. Thus on p. 87 we have: 'Strictly speaking ākṛti and vyaktiḥ [i.e. individual] are two closely related moments in the process of knowing'; on p. 89 it is said, 'ākṛtiḥ . . . in its concrete existence is never found to be without its correlative, namely, the irrepeatable individual'. This confusion rests on the prior confusion as to whether *artha* means '(external) object' or 'meaning'.

58. *VedS*, para. 21 (p. 83). 'Kinds of being': *-padārthān*; 'applied as names': *nāmatayā prayuktāḥ*; 'find their fulfilment in the supreme Self': *paramātmaparyant(a)-*.

59. *VedS*, para. 103 (p. 135). 'Root': *prakṛtiḥ*; 'transformation': *vikāra-*; 'he (alone) who is expressed by the A, the root of the whole collection of words': *sarvavācakajātaprakṛtibhūtākāravācyaḥ*; 'Nārāyaṇa . . . the [ontological] root of the whole collection of beings': *sarvavācyajātaprakṛtibhūtanārāyaṇ(aḥ)*.

60. *ShBh*, II.2.42 (p. 512, ll.8–15; *Th*, p. 531 [under II.2.43]. 'Principles of being': *tattva-*: 'essence': *svarūpam*.

61. See *ShBh*, I.1.1 (p. 27, ll.17f.; *Th*, p. 39).

62. *BSBh*, I.1.1 (p. 6). '[Sound] reasoning and quotation mixed with the appearance only of these': *yuktivākyatadābhāsasamāśrayāḥ*.

CHAPTER TWO: PREDICATION AND MEANING

1. Rāmānuja does consider a post-Śaṃkara Advaitic view that the object of perception is pure being (*sanmātra*) but rejects it on the grounds that it is contrary to experience. Cf. *ShBh*, I.1.1 (p. 31f.; *Th*, p. 44f.).

2. For more information on the ways of knowing in Hindu philosophy see, for example, D. M. Datta's *The Six Ways of Knowing*.

3. One must remember that Rāmānuja had Sanskrit in mind here.

4. *ShBh*, I.1.1 (p. 28, ll.19–24; *Th*, pp. 40–1). The Sanskrit in full:

> *śabdasya tu viśeṣeṇa saviśeṣa eva vastuny abhidhānasāmarthyam. padavākyarūpeṇa pravṛtteḥ. prakṛtipratyayayogena hi padatvam. prakṛtipratyayayor arthabhedena padasyaiva viśiṣṭārthapratipādanam avarjanīyam. padabhedaś cārthabhedanibandhanaḥ. padasaṃghātarūpasya vākyasyānekapadārthasaṃsargaviśeṣābhidhāyitvena nirviśeṣavastupratipādanāsāmarthyān na nirviśeṣavastuni śabdaḥ pramāṇam.*

Similarly in the *VedS*, para. 27 (pp. 86–7), we have:

> Because language, possessed as it is of words and sentences formed respectively in relation to difference in objects and through the knowledge of

particular groups of differenced objects, receives its pramāṇic nature only in virtue of the sort of essence it has, language is incapable of making known a non-differentiated entity. Therefore language cannot be a *pramāṇa* for a non-differentiated entity. Words such as 'non-differentiated' signify by denying of a particular entity known to be determined by some differentiation the differentiation belonging to another entity. Otherwise such words could not signify at all. [Our point about language is carried] because the *word* is impregnated with numerous differentiations in virtue of its form of radical element and suffix, and the *sentence* makes known a group of various kinds of object.

In Sanskrit:

api cārthabhedatatsaṃsargaviśeṣabodhanakṛtapadavākyasya svarūpatālabdhapramāṇabhāvasya śabdasya nirviśeṣavastubodhanāsāmarthyān na nirviśeṣavastuni śabdaḥ pramāṇam. nirviśeṣa ityādiśabdās tu kenacid viśeṣeṇa viśiṣṭatayāvagatasya vastuno vastvantaragataviśeṣaniṣedhaparatayā bodhakāḥ. itarathā teṣām apy anavabodhakatvam eva. prakṛtipratyayarūpeṇa padasyaivānekaviśeṣagarbhatvād anekapadārthasaṃsargabodhakatvāc ca vākyasya.

5. The term *jñapti* as a designation for the Absolute is used by Śaṃkara. Thus, in his *Taittirīya Upaniṣad Bhāṣya*, under II.1.1, when commenting upon the *jñānam* ('knowledge') of the text, he says, '*jñānam* means "knowing" [*jñapti*] or "awareness" [avabodha]' (p. 49).

6. *VedS*, para. 28 (p. 87). In fact knowing is said to be self-established . . . something else: *anyasādhanasvabhāvatayā hi jñapteḥ svataḥsiddhir ucyate.*

7. In this connection Śaṃkara says in *BSBh*, I.3.25 (p. 120), 'The Vedānta statements have a twofold function: sometimes to describe the proper form of the supreme Self, sometimes to teach the unity [*ekatva*] of the supreme Self with the [individual] knowing self [*vijñānātma-*].

8. All Upaniṣadic references follow the text in S. Radhakrishnan's *The Principal Upaniṣads*.

9. *VedS*, para. 26 (p. 86). In Sanskrit, *bhinnapravṛttinimittānāṃ śabdānām ekasminn arthe vṛttiḥ sāmānādhikaraṇyam iti hi tadvidaḥ*. See also *ShBh*, for instance under I.1.1 (p. 59, *Th*, p. 79) and I.1.13 (p. 191; *Th*, p. 220).

10. Or as O. Lacombe comments in his *La doctrine morale et métaphysique de Rāmānuja*, p. 232, n.83, 'Le texte: tasya eṣa eva śārīra ātmā, "Il (le Brahman) est le Soi incorporé de celle-ci (l'âme individuelle)" [*TaiUp*, II.3.1], peut fournir un exemple du . . . vaiyadhikaraṇya: les termes se rapportant au Brahman sont au nominatif, tandis que le mot désignant l'âme individuelle est au génitif. – Tattvamasi est un exemple du . . . sāmānādhikaraṇya'. Cf. Śabara's commentary on the *Mîmâṃsâ Sûtra*, III.1.12: 'We know that correlative predication obtains from the [words having the] same case-ending, as in the example, "The lotus is blue" ' (*ekavibhaktinirdeśāt sāmānādhikaraṇyam avagamiṣyāmaḥ, yathā nīlam utpalam iti*). Even in this example, where, in accordance with Western logic there appears to be but one qualifying predicate, 'blue', Rāmānuja's definition that in CP more than one differentiating word is applied to a single referent is justified. For according to Hindu logic 'lotus' and 'blue' are both regarded as predicates describing the referent (the external lotus). In other words, through

these two terms appropriately inflected in the Sanskrit (here, in the nominative), this existential statement is saying that there is an object out there which instantiates the synthetic co-presence of 'lotusness' and 'blueness'. Subsequently, when clarity seems to require it, we shall call the term standing for the referent in existential statements the 'referent term' ('lotus' in our example), and the other terms predicated of the referent 'qualifier terms' (e.g. 'blue').

11. *ShBh*, I.1.13 (p. 191, ll.16–17; *Th*, p. 220). In Sanskrit, *tattadviśeṣaṇaviśiṣṭam eva brahma.*

12. See *ShBh*, I.1.1 (p.19, ll.10ff.; *Th*, p. 26ff.).

13. Ibid. (p. 20, ll.6–14; *Th*, p. 28). From 'The word "reality"' to end:

tatra satyapadaṃ vikārāspadatvenāsatyād vastuno vyāvṛttaparam. jñānapadaṃ cānyādhīnaprakāśāj jaḍarūpād vastuno vyāvṛttaparam. anantapadaṃ ca deśataḥ kālato vastutaś ca paricchinnād vyāvṛttaparam . . . evam ekasyaiva vastunaḥ sakaletaravirodhyākāratām avagamayad arthavattaram ekārtham aparyāyaṃ ca padatrayam iti. tasmād ekam eva brahma svayaṃjyotir nirdhūtanikhilaviśeṣam ity uktaṃ bhavati.

14. The expression used is *svārthaprahāṇena*; cf. Śaṃkara's *svārthasya hy aprahāṇena* is his exegesis of *tat tvam asi* (*Upadeśa Sāhasrī*, ch. 18, v. 173) and his *svārthāparityāga* in his *Taittirīya Upaniṣad Bhāṣya*, p. 50, on *satyaṃ jñānam anantaṃ brahma.*

15. Indeed the cockiness of the opponent in Rāmānuja's description of his view is remarkable, and indicates how self-assured and developed the Advaitic interpretation of this and other key scriptural texts had become by Rāmānuja's time. Śaṃkara's own exegesis of the two texts we are considering does not explicitly tackle all the objections raised by the objector against the developed (Advaitic) position; in any case the tone of Śaṃkara's language is restrained.

16. *ShBh*, I.1.1 (p. 21, ll.7–8; *Th*, p. 29). 'All agree . . . unity': *sāmānādhikaraṇyasya hy aikya eva tātparyam iti sarvasaṃmatam.*

17. Cf. Ibid. (p. 59, ll.12–13; *Th*, p. 79).

18. See under I.1.2. Thibaut's translation, though generally good, is sometimes both inaccurate and incomplete here.

19. The definitional character of Brahman's essential qualities for Rāmānuja is evident from the following extract from *ShBh*, III.3.13 (p.625, l.16 – p. 626, l.2; *Th*, p. 638):

Those qualities adequating to an object in that they are tied to the apprehension of the object itself in so far as their characteristic is to describe the proper form of the object, are always present in the manner of the object's proper form. And these qualities are reality [*satya*], knowledge [*jñāna*], bliss [*ānanda*] and purity [*amalatva*]. Now, by such texts as 'Whence these beings are born . . .' [*TaiUp*, III.1.1], Brahman is described through secondary characteristics [*upalakṣitaṃ brahma*], as cause of the world and so on; but by 'Brahman is reality, knowledge, infinite' and 'Brahman is bliss' [*TaiUp*, III.6.1] etc., Brahman is described essentially [*svarūpato*] through the words 'bliss' and so on. 'Those qualities adequating' to the proper form of the object': *ye tv arthasamānā arthasvarūpanirūpaṇadharmatvenārthapratityanubandhinas.* The first-order (essence-) defining quality of our *Taittirīya* text is not really impaired by the addition of 'bliss' and 'purity' in the extract above, for, as we shall see later, Rāmānuja makes 'bliss' the obverse of 'knowledge', while 'purity' as a negative, is functionally and semantically interdependent with 'infinitude'.

20. Not strictly required by the grammar of the Sanskrit. Thus *satyaṃ jñānam anantaṃ brahma* could, for example, be rendered *satyaṃ, jñānam anantaṃ brahma*, i.e. 'Truly, Brahman is boundless knowledge'. Here *satyaṃ* is taken as an adverb ('truly') and is not correlatively predicated with the other terms.

21. *ShBh*, I.1.2 (p. 135, ll.6–7; *Th*, pp. 159–60). 'The word 'reality' declares Brahman as possessing being without circumscription': *tatra satyapadaṃ nirupādhikasattāyogi brahmāha*. Note the use of *āha* ('declares') here and *nirūpaṇa* and *nirūpyate* ('describe') in n. 19 to indicate that, unlike in Śaṃkara's exegesis, the positive qualifier terms do positively describe Brahman. Also, the use in this context of *vyāvṛt* (to be set apart) can be traced back to Śaṃkara's exegesis.

22. Ibid. (p. 135, ll.8–10; *Th*, p. 160). 'A nature solely of eternal and uncontracted knowledge': *nityāsaṃkucitajñānaikākāram* . . .'.

23. Ibid. (p. 135, ll.10–13; *Th*, p. 160). From 'the word "infinite"' to 'proper form and qualities': *anantapadaṃ deśakālavastuparicchedarahitasvarūpam āha. saguṇatvāt svarūpasya svarūpeṇa guṇaiś cānantyam.*

24. *ShBh*, III.3.15 (p.627, ll.9–10; *Th*, p. 639). 'But metaphor': *rūpaṇamātram.*

25. See *ChāndUp*, VI.8.7ff.

26. For Rāmānuja the infinite Brahman as the fullness of being must comprehend, in some way, the whole of reality, including finite being as we know it. The problem then becomes one of accommodating the finitude of being within the perspective of the infinite without explaining away its reality as Śaṃkara had done.

27. Cf., for instance, the discussion under *ShBh*, I.4.23 (p. 386, ll.18–22; *Th*, p. 399), where we have:

> The highest Brahman, in all cases the self of all, in as much as he has all conscious and non-conscious being for his body, sometimes is possessed of differentiated name and form, sometimes of undifferentiated name and form. When he is possessed of differentiated name and form he is known as manifold and as effect; when he is possessed of undifferentiated name and form he is known as the one cause, without a second . . . .

From 'When he is possessed of' till end: *yadā vibhaktanāmarūpaṃ tadā tad eva bahutvena kāryatvena cocyate. yadāvibhaktanāmarūpaṃ tadaikam advitīyaṃ kāraṇam iti ca.*

28. Note that *prakṛti* (sometimes interchangeable with *pradhāna*) is a key term in the seminal religious literature (e.g. *Upaniṣads, Bhagavadgītā*) of the Hindus, and is central to the influential classical Sāṃkhya system. Suitably interpreted it was incorporated into the Vedāntic systems. In Sāṃkhya it stands for all that we call material and more; in short, it is the changeful, insentient, unitary causal principle of all the world's forms and mutiplicity. In essence it is the contrary of, yet at the same time is subservient to, the infinite number of *puruṣas* or spirits. The nature of these *puruṣas* is to be changeless, impassive,

homogeneous consciousness and bliss. Through the interplay of *puruṣa* and *prakṛti* we have the universe we live in and its denizens. This broad scheme was assimilated into the various systems of Vedānta in accordance with the particular monistic or theistic cast of each system.

29. For this see Ch. 1.

30. *ShBh*, I.1.13 (p. 199, ll.4–9; *Th*, p. 227). The Sanskrit in full:

śarīrasya śarīriṇaṃ prati prakāratvāt, prakāravācināṃ ca śabdānāṃ prakāriṇy eva paryavasānāc śarīrābhidhāyināṃ śabdānāṃ śarīriparyavasānaṃ nyāyyam. prakāro hi nāmedam ittham iti pratīyamāne vastunīttham iti pratīyamāno' ṃśaḥ. tasya tadvastvapekṣatvena tatpratītes tadapekṣatvāt tasminn eva paryavasānaṃ yuktam iti tasya pratipādako'pi śabdas tasminn eva paryavasyati.

31. The discussion here centres around words designating 'substances' understood in the loose sense of substantival entities, i.e. entities, including aggregates of entities, having a relatively stable and independent existence in their own right (man, body, fish, flower, water, fire, river, mountain, and so on).

32. *VedS*, para. 75 (p. 113): 'all words expressing . . . such being apply in their primary sense to the supreme Self'. In Sanskrit, *paramātmani mukhyatayā vartante sarve vācakāḥ śabdāḥ*.

33. Cf. *ShBh*, I.1.5–6 (p. 172, l.17–p. 173, l.16; *Th*, pp. 202–3). 'Figurative': *gauṇa*; 'literal': *mukhya*.

34. *VedS*, para. 21 (p. 83). 'Types of being: *padārthāḥ*; from 'Worldly persons think' till end: *tatra laukikāḥ puruṣāḥ śabdaṃ vyāharantaḥ śabdavācye pradhānāṃśasya paramātmanaḥ pratyakṣādyaparicchedyatvād vācyaikadeśabhūte vācyasamāptiṃ manyante. vedāntaśravaṇena ca vyutpattiḥ pūryate.*

35. It may not have escaped the reader's attention, and the examples given here confirm this, that scriptural correlatively predicated terms with Brahman as their referent seem, paradigmatically, to have the nominative case-ending. But the reader may be puzzled as to how the terms 'That' and 'you' in the *Chāndogya* refrain have the same case-ending. The answer is that 'you' (*tvam*) in the Sanskrit here is inflected in the nominative.

36. *BG11*(3), p. 19. The Sanskrit in full:

yathā kṣetraṃ kṣetrajñaviśeṣaṇataikasvabhāvatayā tadapṛthaksiddheḥ tatsāmānādhikaraṇyenaiva nirdeśyam, tathā kṣetraṃ kṣetrajñaś ca madviśeṣaṇataikasvabhāvatayā madapṛthaksiddheḥ matsāmānādhikaraṇyenaiva nirdeśyau viddhi . . . pṛthivyādisaṃghātarūpasya kṣetrasya kṣetrajñasya ca bhagavaccharīrataikasvabhāvasvarūpatayā bhagavadātmakatvaṃ śrutayo vadanti . . . idam evāntaryāmitayā sarvakṣetrajñānām ātmatvenāvasthānaṃ bhagavatas tatsāmānādhikaraṇyena vyapadeśahetuḥ.

37. *BG11*(3), 13.3 (pp. 24–5). From 'This being so' till end: . . . *iti kāraṇāvasthaparamātmavācinā śabdena kāryavācinaḥ śabdasya sāmānādhikaraṇyam mukhyavṛttam . . . cidacitoḥ sarvāvasthayoḥ paramapuruṣaśarīratvena tatprakāratayaiva padārthatvāt tatprakāraḥ paramapuruṣa eva kāraṇaṃ kāryaṃ ca; sa eva sarvadā sarvaśabdavācya . . . .*

38. *VedS*, para. 20 (pp. 82–3). From 'Thus it is Brahman' till end:

. . . *tattvam iti sāmānādhikaraṇyapravṛttayor dvayor api padayor brahmaiva vācyam. tatra ca tatpadaṃ jagatkāraṇabhūtaṃ sakalakalyāṇaguṇagaṇākaraṃ niravadyaṃ nirvikāram ācaṣṭe. tvam iti ca tad eva brahma jīvāntaryāmirūpeṇa saśarīraprakāraviśiṣṭam ācaṣṭe. tad evaṃ pravṛttinimittabhedenaiksamin brahmaṇy eva tattvam iti dvayoḥ padayor vṛttir uktā.*

39. 'For', he argues, 'correlative predication has to do with one entity conditioned by two [or more] modes. If one abandoned the [plurality] of modes, correlative predication itself would have to be abandoned in that there would be no difference of grounds [in the referent] for the application of terms [to it]' – *ShBh*, I.1.1 (p. 110, ll.15–17; *Th*, p. 130). In Sanskrit, *prakāradvayāvasthitaikavastuparatvāt sāmānādhikaraṇyasya. prakāradvayaparityāge pravṛttinimittabhedāsaṃbhavena sāmānādhikaraṇyam eva parityaktaṃ syāt.*

40. I would submit, though this needs to be argued elsewhere, that Śaṃkara's own exegesis of *tat tvam asi* did not require both substance terms to be understood by way of *lakṣaṇā* – only *tvam* needed to be so purified. However, Śaṃkarites later on did interpret both *tat* and *tvam* obliquely in their reading of the text; evidently Rāmānuja has this view in mind here. On this account both *tat* and *tvam* had to be purified of their empirical, pluralistic connotations in order to produce an identity-judgement of the form, 'That [the pure, non-differentiated underlying causal Self of the world] is identical with the [inner] you [the pure, non-differentiated inner Self].'

41. Cf. *ShBh*, I.1.1 (ll.19–21; *th*, p. 131).

CHAPTER THREE: THE ESSENTIAL SELF

1. *VedS*, para. 3 (p. 73). 'True nature': *yāthātmya*; 'individual self': *jīvātman*.

2. Rāmānuja refers to the spiritual principle of the spirit–matter composite variously as *jīva*, *jīvātman*, *ātman* and (sometimes) *puruṣa*. He uses the first two expressions interchangeably (we shall follow his example in this book) to denote the individual spiritual principle (i.e. the finite *ātman*) in so far as it is in the general condition of being naturally associated with a prakṛtic body or parts thereof. The latter two terms have a broader connotation and, suitably qualified, may refer to the supreme being itself. It is important to note that Rāmānuja's use of *jīva* (and *jīvātman*) is quite different from Śaṃkara's. For the Advaitin this term denotes the empirical self, i.e. the ego or false centre of 'I-consciousness' essentially prakṛtic in nature, in contrast to the inner or 'true' underlying spiritual self (the *pratyagātman*) ultimately to be identified with the supreme Self or Brahman. For Rāmānuja the *jīva* is the individual spiritual principle itself, i.e. the finite *ātman* (potentially or actually naturally associated with *prakṛti*). Note too that when we speak of the self–body composite in this book the human individual is to be understood as the paradigm.

3. For example under *Gīta*, 2.12 ('Never ever was I not, nor you, nor these kings . . .') he comments (*BG11* [1], pp. 83–4),

> . . . the distinction between the [individual] selves [i.e. *ātmans*] and the Lord God of all, and between the [individual] selves themselves is final [*pāramārthika*]. . . . For at a time for teaching the truth [as at the solemn hour of the

Great Battle] it is not right to teach this distinction if, as in the doctrine that the distinction of self is superimposed only, this distinction were not really true.

4. In this context Rāmānuja uses the various Sanskrit cognates for knowledge interchangeably. Thus he says, 'Consciousness [*anubhūti*, elsewhere *caitanya* and *cit* are used] which is a special characteristic [*dharmaviśeṣa-*] of the *ātman* as experiencing subject [*anubhavitur*], goes by such other names as *jñāna, avagati, saṃvid* and so on' – *ShBh*, I.1.1 (p. 39, ll.9–11; *Th*, p. 56). However, *saṃvedana* is more appropriately translated 'act of consciousness'. Thus in the ensuing discussion our own use of 'knowledge', 'consciousness', 'awareness', and so on, especially as translations, is meant to reflect the synonymity of the Sanskrit terms intended by Rāmānuja, and must not be given the varying nuances they sometimes assume in Western philosophy.

5. (1) *ShBh*, I.1.1 (p. 34, ll.10–11; *Th*, p. 48). In Sanskrit, *anubhūtitvaṃ nāma vartamānatādaśāyāṃ svasattayaiva svāśrayaṃ prati prakāśamānatvam.*

(2) Ibid. (p. 34, ll.11–12; *Th*, p. 48). In Sanskrit, *svasattayaiva svaviṣayasādhanatvaṃ vā.*

(3) Ibid. (p. 38, ll.12–13; *Th*, p. 55).

(4) Ibid. (p. 39, ll.9–10; *Th*, p. 56). In Sanskrit, *anubhūtir iti svāśrayaṃ prati svasadbhāvenaiva kasyacid vastuno vyavahārānuguṇyāpādanasvabhāvo* . . . .

6. In Sanskrit: *yaḥ prakāśasvabhāvaḥ so'nanyādhīnaprakāśo dīpavat* – *ShBh*, I.1.1 (p. 41, l.11; *Th*, p. 58–9); . . . *evam ātmā cidrūpa eva caitanyaguṇa iti. cidrūpatā hi svayaṃprakāśatā* – ibid. (p. 42, l.7–8; *Th*, p. 59–60). In connection with 'illumination for its essence' (*prakāśasvabhāva*), Neevel (*Yāmuna's Vedānta*, esp. pp. 122–9) has an interesting discussion on the meaning of *svabhāva* (esp. in relation to consciousness) in contrast with *svarūpa* in Yāmuna's usage. He says, 'Thus, one aspect of consciousness's being a *svabhāva* is its being a special property (*asādhāraṇa-dharma*) of the *ātmā*, i.e. something that distinguishes an *ātmā* alone and no other category of reality' (p. 125; see also p. 128). This seems also to have been the view of Rāmānuja (who was influenced by Yāmuna, of course), but Neevel's further observation that, apropos of Yāmuna's technical distinction between *svabhāva* and *svarūpa*, this was 'a distinction that was also maintained and developed by Rāmānuja' (p. 124), is, to say the least, misleading. Rāmānuja may have maintained the distinction, but he hardly developed it. Nor does Neevel's recourse to Ch. 6 of Carman's *The Theology of Rāmānuja* for support have the desired effect. If anything, this chapter forces us to recognise the semantic fluidity of the terms *svabhāva* and *svarūpa* in Rāmānuja's thought.

7. On 'analogy': 'La comparaison de la connaissance et de la lumière physique a toujours joué un rôle de premier plan dans les explications que l'Inde s'est données à elle-même touchant la nature de la pensée' – Lacombe, *La Doctrine*, p. 198, n. 369. Note too that 'Yāmuna employs what is his favourite example (*dṛṣṭānta*) or analogy for the relationship between the *ātmā* and consciousness, i.e. that between the sun and its luminosity (*tejasvitva*, *prakāśa*) or light (*āloka*)' – Neevel, *Yāmuna's Vedānta*, p. 126. It is important to get the terms of Rāmānuja's analogy right, else confusion ensues. Strictly speaking, the comparison applies between consciousness (in the form of the conscious subject, the *ātman*, and conscious acts) and *tejas*, the fire-stuff (in the form of luminous

matter, the flame, and radiant light). We shall go on to explain this in the text. Various interpreters of this analogy give an unclear rendering of its terms (cf., for instance, C. Sharma, *A Critical Survey of Indian Philosophy*, p. 343).

8. Cf. *ShBh*, I.1.1 (pp. 41–2; *Th*, p. 59).

9. Sanskrit, *tejodravya*. Fire (*tejas*): 'substance élémentaire, principe du feu, de la lumière et de la chaleur' – Lacombe, *La Doctrine*, p. 198, n. 370.

10. 'Although light exists as a quality of a substance, i.e. the light-possessor [or flame], it is nevertheless the *tejas* substance' – *ShBh*, I.1.1 (p. 41, ll. 15–16; cf. *Th*, p. 59). In Sanskrit, *yadyapi prabhā prabhāvaddravyaguṇabhūtā tathāpi tejodravyam eva.*

11. Ibid. (p. 41, ll. 18–19; *Th*, p. 59).

12. Ibid. (p. 45, ll. 13–14; *Th*, p. 63). In Sanskrit, *jña iti . . . jñānaguṇāśrayatvam . . . svābhāvikam iti.*

13. Ibid. (p. 39, ll. 15–18; *Th*, p. 56). 'Permanence of the producer': *kartuḥ sthiratvam*; 'directly perceived': *pratyakṣam īkṣyante*; 'recognition': *pratyabhijñā.*

14. Ibid. (p. 39, ll. 18–22; *Th*, pp. 56–7). From 'If it were accepted' till end: *evaṃ kṣaṇabhaṅginyāḥ saṃvida ātmatvābhyupagame pūrvedyur dṛṣṭam idam aparedyur idam aham adarśam iti pratyabhijñā ca na ghaṭate. anyenānubhūtasya na hy anyena pratyabhijñānasaṃbhavaḥ.*

15. *VedSār*, I.1.2 (p. 399).

16. *ShBh*, I.1.13 (p. 184, l. 17 – p. 185, l. 2; *Th*, p. 213). From 'and because the knower's proper form' till end: *jñānaikanirūpaṇīyatvāc ca jñātuḥ svarūpasya. svarūpanirūpaṇadharmaśabdo hi dharmamukhena dharmisvarūpam api pratipādayati* . . . . See also *ShBh*, II.3.29 (p. 530, ll. 6–7; *Th*. p. 550) and 30 (p. 530, ll. 18–22; *Th*, p. 550). We note that Rāmānuja distinguishes here (and elsewhere) between the *ātman*'s 'essential nature' or 'proper form' (i.e. its *svarūpa*) and its (essential) qualities or *guṇas* (e.g. knowledge). Does this mean that he thought of the *ātman*'s nature as comprising two radically different sorts of things, inseparably related but rigidly distinct from each other – namely, a substantial indefinable substrate existing by itself, a 'something I know not what' (i.e. the *svarūpa*), and existentially dependent but defining essential properties or *guṇas* (e.g. knowledge)? According to my understanding of Rāmānuja's philosophy of the self, no. This precisely is the point of his self–lamp analogy and the articulation that its terms function simultaneously as substance and property. In other words, Rāmānuja spoke in the same breath, so to speak, of the *ātman*'s nature in terms of *svarūpa* and *guṇa* partly, no doubt, because he inherited this terminology from the Vedāntic philosophical tradition in general and his *ācārya* predecessors in particular, but mainly because he wanted to make the point (against, by and large, the Buddhists, for instance) that the *ātman* had a substantial reality of its own and could not simply be reduced to its essential properties, i.e. that it was not the sum total of a bundle of properties (hence the contrast between *svarūpa* and *guṇa*). But to correct the impression of the *ātman* as a substance–property dichotomy as described above, he spoke of the *ātman*'s being 'of the form of consciousness', i.e. of ātmanic consciousness functioning simultaneously as substance and property in the way we have described (hence the 'fusion' between *svarūpa* and *guṇa* in terms of consciousness). Consciousness is best suited to bring out this *sui-generis* relationship between *svarūpa* and essential quality because it is the most distinctive

'characteristic' (perhaps the least misleading translation of *guṇa* here) of the *ātman qua ātman*.

17. 'Self-luminosity': *svayaṃprakāśatā*. We recall Rāmānuja's observation, 'For to have consciousness for one's form is self-luminosity' (cf. n. 6). See also *ShBh*, I.1.1 (p. 41, l.10; *Th*, p. 58), and cf. ibid. (p. 38, ll.13–14; *Th*, p. 55): 'self-luminosity is the illumining to one's own substrate by one's own existence alone'. In Sanskrit, *svayaṃprakāśatā tu svasattayaiva svāśrayāya prakāśamānatā*. Note the close similarity of this description with that of consciousness (1).

18. Ibid. (p. 45, ll.2–4; *Th*, p. 62). 'An object, outward, and for-the-sake-of-something-else': *-dṛśyatvaparāktvaparārthatva-*; 'and because knowerhood has consciousness specifically for its essence': *cetanāsādhāraṇasvabhāvatvāc ca*.

19. For Rāmānuja consciousness is essentially inward or auto-transparent (*pratyak-*) in contrast to the products of *prakṛti*, which are essentially outward or non-reflexive (*parāk-*). This characteristic of inwardness or reflexivity of consciousness manifests itself in I-awareness, distinctive to *ātmans* alone. See further below.

20. *ShBh*, I.1.1 (p. 41, ll.7–10; *Th*, p. 58). In Sanskrit, *ahaṃpratyayasiddho hy asmadarthaḥ. yuṣmatpratyayaviṣayo yuṣmadarthaḥ. tatrāhaṃ jānāmīti siddho jñātā yuṣmadartha iti vacanaṃ jananī me vandhyetivad vyāhatārthaṃ ca. na cāsau jñātāhaṃartho'nyādhīnaprakāśaḥ. svayaṃprakāśatvāt. caitanyasvabhāvatā hi svayaṃprakāśatā*.

21. This chapter will show that for Rāmānuja the nature of consciousness is such as to make it *a priori* necessary that the *ātman* is, at least minimally, self-aware in every (transitive) act of awareness. In other words, in so far as the *ātman* is aware of the 'other' *qua* 'other' it is necessarily aware of itself *qua* 'I'. However, we shall see that Rāmānuja allows for the possibility of purely reflexive conscious acts in which the *ātman* is aware only of itself (the 'I') and nothing else.

22. As was maintained, for instance, in the rival school of Nyāya-Vaiśeṣika. The view of this school was that the self could not be self-aware and other-aware in the same cognitive act. Self-identity could be grasped, in fact recognised, only through a subsequent act of awareness (called 'after-cognition' or *anuvyavasāya*).

23. *ShBh*, I.1.1 (p. 40, ll.13–14; *Th*, p. 58). In Sanskrit, *ahamartho na ced ātmā pratyaktvaṃ nātmano bhavet/ ahaṃbuddhyā parāgarthāt pratyagartho hi bhidyate*.

24. 'We have said that in the absence of I-awareness [*ahaṃbhāvavigame*] the inwardness of knowing too cannot be established' – ibid. (p. 49, ll.8–9; *Th*, p. 67).

25. Ibid. (p. 44, ll.16–17; *Th*, p. 62). 'Illusion': *mithyā*.

26. A discussion of Rāmānuja's theory of error would take us too far afield. For his view in this respect see, for instance, ibid. (pp. 94f., 96f.; *Th*, pp. 117f., 119f.).

27. First published in the *Proceedings of the First Indian Philosophical Congress* (1925) and subsequently in M. Hiriyanna's posthumously published work *Indian Philosophical Studies (I)*, from which the given extract is taken. This article seems to have been influential, judging by, for example, the explicit reference to it in P. N. Srinivasachari's *The Philosophy of Visishtadvaita*, p. 29, and the implicit reference in Sharma's *Critical Survey*, p. 343, where Hiriyanna's precise terminology is used.

28. Ibid., p. 54.
29. See *ShBh*, I.1.1 (p. 26, ll.14f.; *Th*, p. 37).
30. Ibid. (p. 49, ll.19–21; *Th*, p. 68).
31. Rāmānuja says, ibid. (p. 49, ll.9–11; *Th*, p. 67), 'In spite of the absence of a clear and distinct presentation of the I-reality [in *suṣupti*] because of the predominance of the quality of *tamas* and the absence of awareness of external objects, there is no loss even in suṣupti of I-awareness right up to wakefulness, on account of the *ātman* flickering [to itself] in its sole form as the "I".' From 'there is no loss' till end: *ā prabodhād aham ity ekākāreṇātmanaḥ sphuraṇāt suṣuptāv api nāhaṃbhāvavigamaḥ*.
32. Ibid. (p. 50, ll.14–18; *Th*, p. 69). Note that Rāmānuja is prepared to distinguish the self as the 'object of knowledge'.
33. In such awareness our distinction between the 'implicit object of awareness' and the 'explicit object of awareness' collapses in upon itself in so far as existentially subject and object of awareness are one and the same thing.
34. Cf. n. 31.
35. *ShBh*, I.1.1 (p. 63, ll.10–16; *Th*, p. 84). 'Bliss is said to be the agreeable [aspect] of knowledge: *jñānam eva hy anukūlam ānanda ity ucyate*; 'For to be a knower is to be one who experiences bliss': *jñātṛtvam eva hy ānanditvam*.
36. *ShBh*, III.2.9 (p. 588, l.19 – p. 589, l.2; *Th*, p. 606).
37. 'There no chariots exist, nor teams of horses, nor roads. Then he produces chariots, teams of horses and roads. There no joys exist, nor pleasures, nor delights. Then he produces joys, pleasures and delights. There no ponds exist, nor pools of lotuses, nor rivers. Then he produces ponds, pools of lotuses and rivers. For it is he who is the maker.'
38. Cf. *ShBh*, I.1.1 (p. 97, ll.12–20; *Th*, pp. 120–1).
39. Ibid. (p. 98, ll.13–15; *Th*, p. 121).

CHAPTER FOUR: THE CONTINGENT SELF

1. For example, under *BrSū*, II.4.6, he says, 'The vital breaths are limited in size since scripture speaks of them as going out, and so on; this being so, they must be minute [aṇava-] because they are not observed by bystanders when they do go out [of the body at death]' – *ShBh*, p. 551, ll.12–14; *Th*, p. 572. In Vedāntic theory the vital breaths (*prāṇas*) are prakṛtic. Rāmānuja also refers to the Vaiśeṣika view that atoms (*paramāṇus*) constitute the material world (cf. *ShBh*, II.2.10). These atoms have a *sui-generis* nature: while they are themselves eternal, impartite and inextended, in combination they give rise to the perishable, spatially extended material objects that we know. However, since Rāmānuja does no more than show up the internal contradiction of the Vaiśeṣika notion of *paramāṇu*, his ciriticism does not tell us what he himself understands positively by the term *aṇu*. The gist of Rāmānuja's criticism is that these atoms must be themselves extended and part-possessing if by their combination spatially extended objects are produced: 'otherwise, if the *paramāṇus* lack spatial divisions, there could be no such thing as smallness, shortness, largeness or length, even if a thousand *paramāṇus* were in conjunction, for the extension of one such atom would not differ [from that of the thousand]' –*ShBh*, II.2.10 (p. 479, ll.20–2; *Th*, p. 495).

2. *ShBh*, I.1.1 (p. 2, ll.8–10; *Th*, p. 4). The Sanskrit in full: *sarvatra bṛhattvaguṇayogena brahmaśabdaḥ. bṛhattvaṃ ca svarūpeṇa guṇaiś ca yatrānavadhikātiśayaṃ so 'sya mukhyo' rthaḥ. sa ca sarveśvara eva.*

3. Says Carman, 'This distinction between the 'atomicity' of the finite self and the pervasiveness (vibhutva) of the Supreme Self is taken by Rāmānuja's followers as one of the primary distinctions between the two' – *The Theology of Rāmānuja*, pp. 102–3.

4. *ShBh*, II.3.20, (p. 527, l.5; *Th*, p. 546).

5. For instance, *ChāndUp*, III.14.3: 'This Self of mine within the heart . . .'; and VIII.1.1: 'Now in this city of Brahman there is this dwelling, a small lotus: within it there is a Small Space . . . .' For Rāmānuja both 'Self' (*ātmā*) and 'Small Space' (*dahara ākāśaḥ*) refer to Brahman.

6. On this topic see the discussion under *ShBh*, I.2.7 and 3.13.

7. Under *ShBh*, I.2.7, we have: 'The supreme Self is described as thus minute [*aṇīyān*] as a means of devout meditation [*nicāyyatvena*]. . . . In fact its proper form is not minute [*na punar aṇīyastvam evāsya svarupam iti*]' – p. 242, ll.4–6; *Th*, p. 264. Further on it is said, 'the highest Brahman is resident in our hearts out of his supreme compassion with the desire to enliven us' (*paraṃ brahma paramakāruṇyenāsmadujjijīviṣayāsmaddhṛdaye saṃnihitam*) – p. 243, ll.6–7; *Th*, p. 265.

8. For Vedānta in general the heart was the symbol and physical focus of the embodied self. However, the *ātman* is not to be thought of as coming into physical contact with its cardiac abode, a view seemingly espoused by the Jainas. According to the Jaina position the individual self pervaded, in a physical sense, the whole body it tenanted, in that it expanded or contracted to fit the varying volumes of the different bodies it inhabited during the round of rebirth. No doubt it was to counter this physicalist picture of the self that the Vedāntic tradition spoke of the individual self as being 'atomic' and dwelling in the 'cave of the heart'.

9. See under *ShBh*, I.3.13, esp. p. 299, ll.13–15: 'Though this Small Space resides within the heart which is a part of the body, and though the body is liable to old age and destruction, [the Small Space] is immutable for as the supreme Cause it is ultra-subtle.' In Sanskrit, *tasya daharākāśasya dehāvayavabhūtahṛdayāntarvartitve'pi dehasya jarāpradhvaṃsādau saty api paramakāraṇatayātisūkṣmatvena nirvikāratvam* . . . . Thibaut's translation here (p. 316) is not strictly accurate.

10. Rāmānuja makes this point by contrasting the *ātman*-reality *as conscious* (*yenātmatattvena cetanena*) with all non-conscious reality (*acetanatattvaṃ sarvam*); see *BG11* (1), p. 110.

11. Cf. Śaṃkara's *BSBh*, II.3.29 (p. 286). 'The real *ātman*': *sata ātmanaḥ*; 'on account of' till end: *buddhyupādhidharmādhyāsanimittam*.

12. *Kārikā* 19 of G. Jha's *The Tattva-kaumudī* (p. 38 of Sanskrit text). In Sanskrit, *tasmāc ca viparyāsāt siddhaṃ sākṣitvam asya puruṣasya/kaivalyaṃ mādhyasthyaṃ drastṛtvam akartṛbhāvaś ca.*

13. Ibid., *kārikā* 20 (p. 40). 'The non-conscious subtle body . . . becomes conscious as it were': *acetanaṃ cetanāvad iva liṅgam*; 'dispassionate': *udāsīnaḥ*.

14. In Śaṃkara's case, we have seen that, though his theory of divine predication was essentially apophatic, he was constrained to acknowledge a minimal literal sense for scriptural positive descriptive terms of Brahman, the supreme Self. For only thus could his theology be taken seriously, i.e. as one

conforming to the basic rule of Vedic hermeneutic that positive terms could be given non-literal senses, not in any systematic way, but only as a last resort where the individual context demanded it.

15. *ShBh*, I.1.1 (p. 45, ll.15–16; *Th*, p. 63). In Sanskrit, *svayam aparicchinnam eva jñānaṃ saṃkocavikāsārham ity* . . . .

16. See *ShBh*, I.4.16 (p. 365, ll.19–20: *Th*, p. 378). 'Meritorious or unmeritorious nature': *puṇyapāparūpa*. Rāmānuja is in the midst of a debate here and this is the opponent's description of action. However, Rāmānuja accepts it as obviously correct and does not challenge it.

17. Another vexed area in Hindu ethics is the precise demarcation of an action in relation to its fruit/result.

18. *ShBh*, I.1.1 (p. 45, ll.17–21; *Th*, p. 63). In Sanskrit, *kṣetrajñāvasthāyāṃ karmaṇā saṃkucitasvarūpaṃ tattatkarmānuguṇataratamabhāvena vartate. tac cendriyadvāreṇa vyavasthitam. imam indriyadvārē jñānaprasaram apekṣyodayāstamayavyapadeśaḥ pravartate. jñānaprasare tu kartṛtvam asty eva. tac ca na svābhāvikam. api tu karmakṛtam ity avikriyasvarūpa evātmā.*

19. *ShBh*, II.3.40 (p. 536, l.14–15; *Th*, p. 556–7). In Sanskrit, *yo hi svabuddhyā pravṛttinivṛttyārambhaśaktaḥ sa eva niyojyo bhavati.*

20. *VedS*, para. 90, (p. 125). 'Equitably': *sāmānyena*; 'all the equipment' to 'and so on': *cicchaktiyogaḥ pravṛttiśaktiyoga ityādi sarvaṃ pravṛttinivṛttiparikaram*; 'the consenter': *anumantṛ*; 'The supreme Self [merely] witnesses the doing and remains impartial': *evaṃ kurvāṇam īkṣamāṇaḥ paramātmodāsīna āste.*

21. Under *BrSū*, II.3.41. See the discussion in *ShBh*, p. 537; *Th*, p. 557.

22. Ibid.

23. *BG11*(2), 9.25 (p. 179). In Sanskrit, *aho mahad idaṃ vaicitryaṃ, yad ekasminn eva karmaṇi vartamānāḥ saṃkalpamātrabhedena kecid atyalpaphalabhāginaḥ cyavanasvabhāvāś ca bhavanti; kecanānavadhikātiśayānandaparamapuruṣaprāptirūpaphalabhāgino' punar āvartinaś ca bhavanti.* The contrast between SI and ST action, which devolves around the intention underlying the action, is well brought out by Rāmānuja in his exegesis of *Īśa Upaniṣad*, v. 11: 'He who knows both knowledge and non-knowledge, with non-knowledge having overcome death, attains the Immortal by knowledge.' Here 'non-knowledge' (*avidyā*), says Rāmānuja, refers to action prescribed by one's caste and stage in life (i.e. dharmic action). If this action is performed with a pure intention – in other words, without desire for its fruit – then 'death', i.e. one's previous *karma* inimical to the origination of liberating knowledge (or *vidyā*), is overcome and the immortal Brahman is attained by the liberating knowledge. If dharmic action, however, is performed for its fruit, then in so far as it is fruit-oriented (even if this fruit is pleasant) it is similar to fruit-oriented *a*dharmic action for it perpetuates its agent in the round of *saṃsāra*, where the fruit must needs be experienced. In other words, meritorious (fruit-intended) action and unmeritorious (fruit-intended) action have this in common: that, as self-seeking and therefore unenlightened in nature, they both oppose the origination of liberating knowledge. As such, observes Rāmānuja, in contrast to (dis-interested) ST action which is 'good' in the absolute sense, meritorious and unmeritorious action can both be said to be 'evil' (*pāpa*). Cf., *ShBh*, I.1.1 (esp. p. 12; *Th*, p. 18).

24. In his discussion of the nature of dreamless sleep in *ShBh*, I.1.1 (see esp.p. 97; *Th*,p. 120–1).

25. For example, in *ShBh*, I.4.16, (p. 368, 11.7–8; *Th*, p. 380), in glossing

KauUp, IV.19 – 'O Bālāki, he indeed must be known who is the maker [kartā] of these persons, whose work [i.e. *karman*] that is' – Rāmānuja maintains that 'maker' refers to Brahman and 'work' not to merit or demerit or to action as such but to 'the whole world as an effect'.

26. *BG11*(1), p. 191. From 'Where' to 'as desired': *nitye naimittike kāmye ca . . . śrūyamāṇe karmaṇi*; from 'your responsibility' to 'the action alone': *nityasattvasthasya mumukṣos te karmamātre dhikāraḥ*; 'non-doer': *akartṛ-* .

27. *BG11*(1), 3.27 (p. 320) and 29 (p. 324). 'The ātman deluded by the ego': *ahaṃkāravimuḍātmā*; from 'by discriminating' till end: *prāptāprāptavivekena.*

28. *ShBh*, II.3.33 (p. 533, ll.18–20 and p. 534, ;l.2; *Th*, pp. 553–4). In Sanskrit *śāstrāṇi hi yajeta svargakāmaḥ, mumukṣur brahmopāsītety evamādīni svargamokṣādiphalasya bhoktāram eva kartṛtve nijuñjate. na hy acetanasya kartṛtve cetano niyujyate . . . ataḥ śāstrāṇām arthavattvaṃ bhoktuś cetanasyaiva kartṛtve bhavet.*

29. *VedS*, para. 5 (p. 74). From 'this much we can say' till end: *svarūpabhedo vācām agocaraḥ svasaṃvedyaḥ, jñānasvarūpam ity etāvad eva nirdeśyam. tac ca sarveṣām ātmanām samānam.*

30. *ShBh*, I.1.1 (p. 40, ll.13–20; *Th*, p. 58). The Sanskrit of the first part of this quotation is given in Ch. 3, n. 23. From 'He who seeks liberation' till end: *nirastākhiladuḥkho'ham anantānandabhāk svarāṭ/bhaveyam iti mokṣārthī śravaṇādau pravartate. ahamarthavināśaś cen mokṣa ity adhyavasyati/apasarped asau mokṣakathāprastāvagandhataḥ. mayi naṣṭe'pi matto'nyā kācij jñaptir avasthitā/ iti tatprāptaye yatnaḥ kasyāpi na bhaviṣyati.*

31. Cf. the point Rāmānuja is making in the discussion corresponding to Ch. 3, n. 32. Note that our discussion of personal identity here is being conducted in terms of the human paradigm. The question is greatly complicated if it is made to incorporate, as Rāmānuja no doubt believed it did, non-human, particularly sub-human, 'identity-sets' belonging to the *ātman* in its journey through saṃsāric rebirths. That Rāmānuja accepted the traditional Hindu belief that owing to its past *karma* the *ātman* may be united to non-human (including sub-human) bodies is clear from *VedS*, para. 4 (pp. 73–4):

> The collection of Vedāntic statements functions . . . to destroy the fear of inevitable [re-] becoming [*bhava*] which is produced by the [*ātman*'s] misconception [*abhimāna*] [of its true nature] through its entry into one of the four kinds of body – i.e. either of a celestial such as Brahmā, or of a man, animal or plant. [The entry of the *ātman* into a particular kind of body is] caused by the flow of *karma* in the form of the individual self's merit and demerit amassed through beginningless ignorance.

It is not clear how Rāmānuja would account for the *ātman*'s sub-human experiences in his total picture of the *ātman*'s personal identity. What we can say is that Rāmānuja theologises as if human embodiment has a significance and value intrinsically superior to those of other kinds of embodiment.

32. Many questions arising from Rāmānuja's view of the nature of personal identity in *saṃsāra* are hereby left unanswered (for instance, the moral and philosophical viability of a continuum of personal identity over a number and range of rebirths, the integration of the *ātman*'s sub-human identities into the overall picture, and so on). Since Rāmānuja himself for one reason or another does not attend to these questions, to discuss them would take us too far afield in

relation to his thought. I intend in due course to take up these questions in another work.

33. *ShBh*, I.1.1 (p. 52, ll.10–12; *Th*, p. 71). In Sanskrit, *brahmātmabhāvāparokṣanirdhūtaniravaśeṣāvidyānām api vāmadevādīnām aham ity evātmānubhavadarśanāc . . ..*

CHAPTER FIVE: BRAHMAN

1. In *The Theology of Rāmānuja*, Ch. 6, Carman has examined this distinction. But see above, Ch. 3, n. 6.
2. Cf. *ShBh*, III.3.13. See also Ch. 2, n. 19.
3. In *ShBh*, I.1.1: See Ch. 3, n. 35.
4. In Ch. 3, n. 16.
5. *ShBh*, III.2.11 (p. 590, ll.17–23; *Th*, p. 608). From beginning to 'illustrious qualities': *sarvatra śrutismṛtiṣu paraṃ brahmobhayaliṅgam ubhayalakṣaṇam abhidhīyate. nirastanikhiladoṣatvakalyāṇaguṇākaratvalakṣaṇopetam ity arthaḥ.* The quotation from the *ViPu*: *samastakalyāṇaguṇātmako'sau svaśaktileśoddhṛtabhūtasargaḥ/ tejobalaiśvaryamahāvabodhasuvīryaśaktyādiguṇaikarāśiḥ / paraḥ parāṇāṃ sakalā na yatra kleśādayaḥ santi parāvareśe.*
6. See, for example, Carman, *The Theology of Rāmānuja, passim.*
7. For instance, De Smet, 'Theological Method', p. 343, says, 'Indeed, it is on the basis of the few Upaniṣadic passages which he recognized as "great sayings" that Śaṃkara built up his advaitavāda . . . .'
8. See, for instance, *ChāndUp*, VI.2.1–3; *AitĀr*, II.4.1; *TaiUp*, II.6.1. Both Śaṃkara and Rāmānuja resort to 'great sayings' (*mahāvākyas*) in the sense that both use certain Upaniṣadic texts as interpretative keys for their theologies. Nevertheless, as van Buitenen has pointed out (*VedS*, p. 57), for Rāmānuja the *mahāvākya* is not a primary scriptural statement in terms of which other scriptural statements may be adjudged to be secondary and exegetically sublatable. However, van Buitenen's choice of the statement, 'All *śrutis* are equally authoritative', to represent Rāmānuja's position in contrast to Śaṃkara's here is perhaps unfortunate. Both Śaṃkara and Rāmānuja would agree that all *śrutis* are equally authoritative in that all equally derive from the same authoritative source.
9. To support, for example, the view that *advaita* is false (i.e. 'May I be *many*'); that Brahman is both substantial and efficient cause; and so on.
10. *ShBh*, I.1.1 (p. 60, 1.10–13; *Th*, p. 80). 'He wishes to create '*sisṛkṣu-;* from 'it occurs' to 'rejects [this notion]': *kāryotpattisvābhāvyena buddhisthaṃ nimittāntaram iti tadevādvitīyapadena niṣidhyata ity avagamyate.*
11. Sometimes translated 'material cause' in the (Christian) Scholastic sense of 'that from which something becomes' (*id ex quo aliquid fit*).
12. Cf. our comments in Ch. 1 on the scope of reason in Vedānta.
13. The 'inherence' mode of discourse derives from the relation of inherence between two things – that is, the ontological relation between thing inhering and thing-inhered-in such that there is a non-reversible flow of being between the two: the thing-inhered-in (relatively or absolutely) bestowing being, the thing inhering receiving being. In due course this idea will become clearer with the help of appropriate examples.

14. See Ch. 2 in connection with Rāmānuja's exegesis of the text 'That you are'.

15. *ShBh*, I.4.23 (p. 385, ll.5–6; *Th*, p. 398). In Sanskrit, *kāraṇam evāvasthāntaram āpannaṃ kāryaṃ na dravyāntaram iti*. See the whole discussion under this *sūtra*, which concerns Brahman as substantial cause of the world. Under *ShBh*, II.1.15, Rāmānuja discusses the concept of substantial cause in general with the use of examples, two of the more telling of which are: (1) a lump of clay transformed into a jar for the storing or fetching of water (here the clay-substance is not destroyed; 'it only becomes possessed of another name ["jar"] and configuration [*saṃsthāna*] for the purpose of accomplishing a particular operation [*vyavahāraviśeṣa-*], i.e. fetching water, and the like'); and (2) the same Devadatta becoming the object of different ideas and words as he passes through the different stages of life, from boyhood to old age.

16. For a comparative discussion in the context of Hindu and Christian thought on this subject in general, see J. Lipner, 'The Christian and Vedāntic Theories of Originative Causality: A Study in Transcendence and Immanence', *Philosophy East and West*, Jan 1978, pp. 53–68.

17. Cf. *VedS*, para. 59.

18. For this idea cf. Ch. 2, pt. II.

19. *ShBh*, II.3.18 (p. 522, l.13–p. 523, l.2; *Th*, p. 542). The Sanskrit of this important passage in full:

ataḥ sarvadā cidacidvastuśarīratayā tatprakāraṃ brahma. tat kadācit svasmād vibhaktavyapadeśānarhātisūkṣmadaśāpannacidacidvastuśarīraṃ tiṣṭhati. tat kāraṇāvasthaṃ brahma. kadācic ca vibhaktanāmarūpasthūlacidacidvastuśarīram. tac ca kāryāvastham. tatra kāraṇāvasthasya kāryāvasthāpattāv acidaṃśasya kāraṇāvasthāyāṃ śabdādivihīnasya bhogyatvāya śabdādimattayā svarūpānyathābhāvarūpavikāro bhavati. cidaṃśasya ca karmaphalaviśeṣabhoktṛtvāya tadanurūpajñānavikāsarūpavikāro bhavati. ubhayaprakāraviśiṣṭaniyantraṃśe tattadavasthatadubhayaviśiṣṭatārūpavikāro bhavati. kāraṇāvasthāyā avasthāntarāpattirūpo vikāraḥ prakāradvaye prakāriṇi ca samānaḥ.

See also Ch. 2, n. 27.

20. *ShBh*, II.3.45 (p. 543, l.3; *Th*, p. 563). In Sanskrit, *ekavastvekadeśatvaṃ hy aṃśatvam*. See also *VedSār*, I.1.2.

21. See *VedS*, para. 87.

22. *VedSār*, II.1.2 (p. 400). From 'for in all cases' till end: *sarvatra viśeṣaṇaviśeṣyayoḥ svarūpasvabhāvabhedāt*.

23. While the *aṃśa–aṃśin* duality in respect of Brahman and the world is not unimportant it is not central to Rāmānuja's theology. It is especially interesting as a facet of his unique theological method, which will be discussed in Ch. 7.

24. Though Brahman's originative causality in Rāmānuja's theology is different in important respects from the divine act of creation as described in traditional Christian thought (see the article referred to in n. 16 for an indication of these differences), it may still be regarded as 'creative' in the strong sense if it is essential to this sense that produced being depends existentially totally, from the point of view of its ultimate origin and continuance, on the supreme being. As this chapter unfolds we shall see that Rāmānuja did maintain this view.

25. Cf. Ch. 2, n. 28.

26. Sanskrit, *īkṣāpūrvikā*. Cf. *ShBh*, I.1.5.

27. The unenlightened souls awaiting rebirth, who in their past births produced the pending regulative *karma* of the world-to-be, remain during the dissolution in a disembodied state of 'suspended animation'.

28. See Ch. 1 for a discussion of this point.

29. In Sanskrit, *bahu syāṃ prajāyeya*. The mood is the *vidhiliṅ*.

30. See Ch. 4, pp. 70f.

31. *ShBh*, I.1.21 (p. 212, ll.8–12; *Th*, p. 239). The Sanskrit in full: *apahatapāpmatvaṃ hy apahatakarmatvaṃ karmavaśyatāgandharahitatvam ity arthaḥ. karmādhīnasukhaduḥkhabhāgitvena karmavaśyatā hi jīvāḥ. ato'pahatapāpmatvaṃ jīvād anyasya paramātmano eva dharmaḥ. tatpūrvakaṃ svarūpopādhikaṃ lokakāmeśatvaṃ satyasaṃkalpatvādikaṃ sarvabhūtāntarātmatvaṃ ca tasyaiva dharmaḥ.* I have here translated *satyasaṃkalpa* as 'having a will for the real' and *satyakāma* as 'having a desire for the real', instead of the more natural 'with intentions realised' and 'with wishes come true', respectively, in view of Rāmānuja's exegeses of these terms, following in the text.

32. Sanskrit, *śeṣataikarati-*. This expression occurs regularly in two of the hymns attributed to Rāmānuja, the *Śaraṇāgatigadya* and the *Śrīraṅgagadya*.

33. For instance, in the *ShBh*, I.1.1 (p. 121, ll.19–20; *Th*. p. 143), we have: 'Brahman, through his will, is conditioned by the various modes whose proper forms are the different mutable and immutable entities' (*brahmaiva svasaṃkalpād vicitrasthiracarasvarūpatayā nānāprakāram avasthitam iti*); the *Gītābhāṣya*, under 9.5, says simply, in Kṛṣṇa's name; 'My supportiveness [of being] is not like that of jars of water. Then how [am I supportive]? By my will' (*na ghaṭādīnāṃ jalāder iva mama dhārakatvam. katham – matsaṃkalpena*).

34. It cannot be the case then that Brahman 'is in need of the universe which is a necessary phase of His self-realisation' – Bhatt, *Studies in Rāmānuja Vedānta*, p. 53.

35. *ShBh*, II.3.14 (p. 518, ll.7–8; *Th*, p. 537). In Sanskrit, *mahadādikāryāṇām api tattadanantaravastuśarīrakaḥ sa eva puruṣottamaḥ kāraṇam.*

36. *ShBh*, II.3.15 (p. 519, l.5; *Th*, p. 538). In Sanskrit, *sarvasya brahmaṇaḥ sākṣāt saṃbhavottambhanam.*

37. *ShBh*, II.1.32 (p. 461, ll.20ff.; *Th*, pp. 476f.)

38. Cf. *ShBh*, Intro. to I.2 (p. 233, ll.8–9; *Th*, p. 256): '[the Lord] has a supernal form, non-prakṛtic, not caused by *karma*, and peculiar to him alone'. In Sanskrit, *sa cāprākṛtākarmanimittasvāsādhāraṇadivyarūpa iti* . . ..

39. A description which, as van Buitenen points out, is rooted in scripture. For a more general description of the supernal form see the introductory section of the *Gītābhāṣya*.

40. *ShBh*, I.2.2 (p. 239, l.20–p. 240, l.2; *Th*, p. 262). 'Objects of [the Lord's] enjoyment': *svabhogyabhūtāḥ*.

41. Less wisely his followers speculated and even argued about its nature: the industry of scholastic disputation on the words and ideas of the master was well under way.

42. It is in this broad sense of 'proper form' that Rāmānuja also includes the heavenly abode and the heavenly attendants of the Lord. Further, the supernal form, heavenly attendants and abode belong to Brahman's 'proper form' in the sense that they were eternally with him in an unchanging condition, in contrast to the world and its inhabitants, whose state is continually changeable as the

world is regularly produced, 'comes to its fruition' and is then dissolved.

43. *ShBh*, I.1.21 (p. 215, ll.1–3; *Th*, p. 241). In Sanskrit, *tadidaṃ svābhāvikam eva rūpam upāsakānugraheṇa tatpratipattyanuguṇākāraṃ devamanuṣyādisaṃsthānaṃ karoti svecchayaiva paramakāruṇiko bhagavān.*

44. *To Christ through the Vedānta* originally appeared serially in the little magazine *The Light of the East*, published by G. Dandoy SJ (Calcutta, 1922–46), in which Johanns participated for some years. The extract is taken from the December 1923 issue, p. 4(b). The work appeared later in a French edition, *Vers le Christ par le Vedānta* (2 vols).

45. In so far as his philosophy seeks to support and illuminate his theology, Rāmānuja may be called a philosophical theologian.

46. Cf. *VedS*, para. 134.

CHAPTER SIX: THE WAY AND JOURNEY'S END

1. Sanskrit, *smṛti.* We shall take note of this peculiar usage later. To give *smṛti* its usual translation of 'memory' would be misleading here.

2. *ShBh*, I.1.1 (p. 10, ll.5–20; *Th*, pp. 15–16). From 'In other words' to end: *ataḥ sākṣātkārarūpā smṛtiḥ smaryamāṇātyarthapriyatvena svayam atyarthapriyā yasya sa eva pareṇātmanā varaṇīyo bhavatīti tenaiva labhyate para ātmety uktaṃ bhavatīti. evaṃrūpā dhruvānusmṛtir eva bhaktiśabdenābhidhīyate.*

3. *ShBh*, III.4.26 (p. 696, ll.13–14; *Th*, p. 699). 'Through the grace of the supreme Person': *paramapuruṣaprasādadvāreṇa.*

4. One must bear in mind that the saṃsāric world comprises the three levels of (1) the celestial realms, (2) the manifest world in which we live, and (3) the nether regions; further, that there is the traffic of rebirth between all three levels.

5. *ShBh*, II.2.3 (p. 471, ll.14–16, and p. 472, l.11 – p. 473, l.2; *Th*, pp. 487–8). In Sanskrit,

> *[śāstraṃ] ca paramapuruṣārādhanatadviparyayarūpe karmaṇī puṇyāpuṇye tadanugrahanigrahāyatte ca tatphale sukhaduḥkhe iti vadati . . . sa ca bhagavān puruṣottam[o] . . . etāni karmāṇi samīcīnāny etāny asamīcīnānīti karmadvaividhyaṃ saṃvidhāya tadupādānocitadehendriyādikaṃ tanniyamanaśaktiṃ ca sarveṣāṃ kṣetrajñānāṃ sāmānyena pradarśya svaśāsanāvabodhi śāstraṃ ca pradarśya tadupasaṃhārārthaṃ cāntarātmatayānupraviśyānumantṛtayā ca niyacchaṃs tiṣṭhati. te kṣetrajñās tu tadāhitaśaktayas tatpradiṣṭakaraṇakalevarādikās tadādhārāś ca svayam eva svecchānuguṇyena puṇyāpuṇyarūpe karmaṇī upādadate. tataś ca puṇyarūpakarmakāriṇaṃ svaśāsanānuvartinaṃ jñātvā dharmārthakāmamokṣair vardhayate. śāsanātivartinaṃ ca tadviparyayair yojayati. ataḥ svātantryādivaikalyacodyāni nāvakāśaṃ labhante.*

6. Carman, in *The Theology of Rāmānuja*, pp. 39f., recounts a story in which Rāmānuja is reputed to have climbed a temple-tower and announced openly to one and all in the courtyard below his guru's secret teaching to him concerning salvation. There is doubt as to whether the recipients of this largesse were only duly initiated Śrī Vaiṣṇavas or the public at large, but that this doubt exists at all is tribute to the memory of Rāmānuja's openness. Then again, one must not

forget that by the very writing of his works for public dissemination Rāmānuja gives evidence of his inclusive salvific concern.

7. On this last point Rāmānuja, in *VedS*, para. 107 (p. 138), says,

> We have to understand that the Lord's dwelling within an effect [in the form of an *avatāra*] . . . is the descent of One who, from his own desire and for his own play, completes the number of those realities which are his own effects for the welfare of the world: as when, out of play, the Highest completes the number of gods [in his descent] as Upendra, or when the highest Brahman's descent, from his own desire, completes the number of kings of the Solar Dynasty in the form of Rāma, the son of Daśaratha, or when, from his own desire, the Blessed One's descent into the house of Vasudeva [as Kṛṣṇa] for removing the burden [of evil] from the earth completes the number of the Lunar Dynasty.

From beginning to 'for the welfare of the world': *yaḥ punaḥ . . . kāryamadhye niveśaḥ sa svakāryabhūtatattvasaṃkhyāpūraṇaṃ kurvataḥ svalīlayā jagadupakārāya svecchāvatāra ity avagantavyaḥ*. 'Play' here must be understood in the appropriate sense of the discussion in Ch. 5.

8. As the previous note and Ch. 5, n. 43, for example, make abundantly clear.

9. *ShBh*, I.3.1, (p. 277, l.21 – p. 278, l.2; *Th*, p. 297). In Sanskrit, *devādīnāṃ samāśrayaṇīyatvāya tattajjātīyarūpasaṃsthānaguṇadharmasamanvitaḥ svakīyaṃ svabhāvam ajahad eva svecchayā bahudhā vijāyate paraḥ puruṣa iti* . . . .

10. The so-called 'law of similitude' (*kratu-nyāya*) between intention (*kratu*) and one's existential condition is here implicitly invoked; that is, as one desires so one becomes.

11. *GB11*(1), p. 6 'Has decended repeatedly in the various worlds': *teṣu teṣu lokeṣv avatīryāvatīrya*.

12. Commenting on *Gītā*, 4.8 ('For the protection of the righteous . . . I come into existence [in avatāric form] age after age'), Rāmānuja writes, 'The "righteous" are the foremost among the Vaiṣṇavas . . . occupied in taking refuge in me [i.e. Kṛṣṇa] . . .' – *BG11*(1), p. 373.

13. Rāmānuja comments (ibid.) 'for establishing the waning Vedic law [*kṣīṇasya vaidikasya dharmasya*] . . . I come into existence age after age in the form of god, man, and so on'.

14. Under 4.11 Rāmānuja says that whoever turns to the Lord will be granted access to him in the appropriate way; again, Rāmānuja interprets 9.23 to mean that all sincere worship directed to beings other than Kṛṣṇa in the end finds Kṛṣṇa in that, as Lord of all, he ensouls all other beings. Further, the name of every other being worshipped as divine ultimately finds its terminus and full significance in Kṛṣṇa as Lord.

15. Under 4.5 Rāmānuja says that *avatāras* have 'reality' (*satyatva*).

16. And observes, 'Then the Blessed One . . . showed [Arjuna] his own four-armed form, and assuming his familiar gentle body, comforted him' – *BG11*(2) 11.50 (p. 333).

17. For Rāmānuja, and this contrasts with the Christian view, there may be historicity to the *avatāra*, but not necessarily realism.

18. *ShBh*, I.1.1 (p. 3, ll.7–10; *Th*, p. 6).

19. In Thibaut the commentary begins under I.3.32, midway on p. 337.

20. In this connection Rāmānuja says in *ShBh*, I.3.33 (p. 323, ll.5–7; *Th*, p. 338), specifically with reference to the Śūdra,

> It is not possible for one untutored in what Brahman's proper form is, and in the kinds of worshipful meditation on that form, and also having no right to perform the various things ancillary to the preceding, such as recitation of the Veda, the [ordained] sacrifices, and so on, to be equipped to bring the worshipful meditations to a [successful] conclusion. Even though one may be desirous [of following the above discipline], without the [proper] qualification one cannot have the right [to embark upon it].

This non-qualification applies equally to Śūdras, twice-born Śrī-Vaiṣṇava women, and Hindu and non-Hindu outcastes. From 'cannot have the qualification' to end: [*na hi*] *upāsanopasaṃhārasāmarthyaṃ saṃbhavati. asamarthasya cārthitvasadbhāve'py adhikāro na saṃbhavati.*

21. For an interesting and promising synthesis in this respect see J. Hick, *Death and Eternal Life*.

22. *BG11*(2), p. 65. Gītārthasaṃgraha, v. 12: *aiśvaryākṣarayāthātmyabhagavaccharaṇārthinām / vedyopādeyabhāvānām aṣṭame bheda ucyate.*

23. Cf. Rāmānuja's commentary on 7.28. It is important to note, as we shall see, that for Rāmānuja this threefold distinction is descriptive rather than prescriptive. That is, he is describing the kinds of devotees there are rather than prescribing how they ought to be.

24. *BG11*(1), p. 512. In Sanskrit, *vigatecchābhayakrodho . . . mokṣaikaprayojano muniḥ ātmāvalokanaśīlo yaḥ sadā mukta eva saḥ sādhyadaśāyām iva sādhanadaśāyām api mukta eva sa ity arthaḥ.* In his sub-commentary Vedāntadeśika notes (ibid.), '"he is liberated" means, "he is on the way to being liberated"' (*mukta eva muktaprāya ity arthaḥ*).

25. *ShBh*, IV.3.14 (p. 754, ll.18–19; *Th*, p. 752). In Sanskrit, *api tu ye paraṃ brahmopāsate ye cātmānaṃ prakṛtiviyuktaṃ brahmātmakam upāsate tān ubhayavidhān nayati.*

26. *BG11*(2), p. 115. In Sanskrit, *ātmayāthātmyavidaḥ paramapuruṣaniṣṭhasya ca, 'sa enān brahma gamayati' iti brahmaprāptivacanād acidviyuktam ātmavastu brahmātmakatayā brahmaśeṣataikarasam ity anusaṃdheyam . . . .*

27. Will not the *yogin* if he studies and contemplates scripture as required realise that his goal is not the final one and is inferior to the *jñānin*'s? Would he not then cease to be a *yogin* in this sense? Rāmānuja would answer either (1) that the *yogin*, knowing this, could still for temperamental and other circumstantial reasons choose as his first (limited) goal the first-level *ātmā*-vision, by the more difficult path of withdrawal from works (this would be a strategic choice to arrive at a stage in his spiritual journey at which his final goal, i.e. second-level *ātmā*-vision, could securely be achieved); or (2) that the yogin's scriptural study, even though theologically defective, could yet be adequate for him to embark upon his misguided spiritual discipline.

28. Traditionally between three and five such obligations were recognised: (1) to the seers or *ṛṣis* (fulfilled by study of the Vedas); (2) to the gods or celestials (fulfilled by sacrifice); (3) to the ancestors, i.e. the fathers (fulfilled by the procreation of a son); (4) to the world, to mankind, to one's society (fulfilled by benevolence and good example to all concerned); and (5) to guests (fufilled by the appropriate hospitality). In our context Rāmānuja seems to have had primarily the fourth in mind.

29. This paragraph contains the gist of Rāmānuja's remarks on (esp.) *Gītā*, 3.8, 21–4.

30. Cf. S. N. Dasgupta, *A History of Indian Philosophy*, vol. III, p. 214.

31. See J. A. B. van Buitenen, *Rāmānuja on the Bhagavadgītā*, p. 154, n. 596; for R. C. Lester's agreement, cf. his *Rāmānuja on the Yoga*, p. 14, n. 3.

32. *BG11*(1), p. 524. In Sanskrit, *idānīṃ jñānayogakarmayogasādhyātmāvalokanarūpayogābhyāsavidhir ucyate.*

33. Ibid., p. 529. In Sanskrit, *yogam ātmāvalokanaṃ prāptum icchor mumukṣoḥ karmayoga eva kāraṇam ucyate.*

34. *BG11*(3) pp. 181–2. In Sanskrit *smṛtiḥ pūrvānubhūtaviṣayam anubhavasaṃskāramātrajaṃ jñānam. jñānam indriyaliṅgāgamayogajo vastuniścayaḥ.*

35. Thus the term *yoga* is used in various senses by Rāmānuja, i.e. *ātmā*-vision, the discipline of works, knowledge, or love, and so on. Lester cannot be right then when he says that when Rāmānuja 'speaks of Yoga he has specifically in mind that Yoga systematized by Patañjali for the Yoga school' (*Rāmānuja on the Yoga*, p. 30). Lester undermines his own thesis by proceeding substantially to modify it. He acknowledges that Rāmānuja rejects the Patañjalian metaphysics as well as the last member of the original eight-limbed technique, and radically reinterprets the seventh member (*dhyāna*). After this one may reasonably wonder how, when Rāmānuja speaks of *yoga*, he has the Patañjalian Yoga specifically in mind.

36. *ShBh*, I.2.23 (p. 262, l.18–p. 263, l.12; *Th*, pp. 284–5). From the beginning to 'and this takes on the nature of *bhakti*': *brahma prepsunā dve vidye veditavye brahmaviṣaye parokṣāparokṣarūpe dve vijñāne upādeye ity arthaḥ. atra parokṣaṃ śāstrajanyaṃ jñānam. aparokṣaṃ yogajanyaṃ jñānam. tayor brahmaprāptyupāyabhūtam aparokṣajñānam. tac ca bhaktirūpāpannam.* From 'But by "Now the higher [knowledge] . . ."' to end: *atha parā yayā tad akṣaram adhigamyate ity upāsanākhyaṃ brahmasākṣātkāralakṣaṇaṃ bhaktirūpāpannaṃ jñānam ucyate.* Note the occurrence of *yoga* here, which means *yoga* proper, i.e. 'second-level' *ātmā*-vision. For another full description of the way to salvation, cf. *VedS*, para. 91.

37. See his comments under *BrSū*, III.4.19–20, for instance: yet further evidence of his positive outlook on this material world and its relationships.

38. This idea corresponds to the Sanskrit expression *aśeṣaśeṣataikarati* which occurs not infrequently in the *Gītābhāṣya* and in the devotional hymns ascribed to Rāmānuja. In connection with this point Rāmānuja says in *VedS*, para. 142 (p. 171), 'When the highest Brahman is realised as the object of untainted and unexcelled love on the grounds that, being the Principal of everything, he is thus related to the *ātman* which is his accessory, then the highest Brahman himself leads the *ātman* on to the attainment of its goal.' In Sanskrit, *tadevaṃ parasya brahmaṇo . . . . sarvaśeṣitvād ātmanaḥ śeṣatvāt pratisaṃbandhitayā anusaṃdhīyamanam anavadhikātiśayaprītiviṣayaṃ sat paraṃ brahmaivainam ātmānaṃ prāpayatīti.* See also next para.

39. See, for instance, n. 2.

40. *ShBh*, I.1.1 (p. 9, ll.11–19, and p. 10, ll.19–20; *Th*, pp. 14–15, 16). From 'Now this meditation' till end: *dhyānaṃ ca tailadhārāvad avicchinnasmṛtisaṃtānarūpam. dhruvā smṛtiḥ . . . sa ca smṛtir darśanasamānākārā . . . bhavati ca smṛter bhāvanāprakarṣād darśanarūpatā . . . . evaṃrūpā dhruvānusmṛtir eva bhaktiśabdenābhidhīyate.*

41. Hence the use in the note above of *(anu)smṛti*, which ordinarily connotes remembering on the basis of a cognitive impression (*saṃskāra*) of some sort. Though the image-based *bhakti* experience of the Lord about which Rāmānuja

speaks here is not an ordinary remembrance, it is to contrast its *re*presentational (*saṃskāra*-dependent) nature with direct apprehension of the Lord that Rāmānuja refers to it as (*anu*)*smṛti*. Nevertheless, he insists that it is a steady (and extremely vivid) experience. Its steadiness is indicated by the prefix *anu* sometimes used; this prefix suggests continuity (among other things). To highlight this feature, the experience is compared to the steady flow of oil, so familiar and striking an image not only of classical but also of contemporary India. Compare this use of *anu-* in *anusmṛti* with the use of *anu-* in *anuvṛtti* in Rāmānuja's commentary on *Gītā*, 2.12, for example, where he discusses in the guise of the Advaitin *pūrvapakṣin* the 'knowledge of difference . . . in the form of the *continuance* of what has been sublated' (*bādhit*ānuvṛtti*rūpam . . . bhedajñānam*). See also Ch. 1, n. 34.

42. Carman, *The Theology of Rāmānuja*, ch. 18, has a good if short discussion of Rāmānuja's and his disciples' references to Śrī.

43. See, for instance, Carman's discussion (ibid., ch. 17) and Lester's *Rāmānuja on the Yoga* (appendix II).

44. The powers of the *jīvātman*, including multilocation, (non-prakṛtic) embodiment at will, (relative) all-knowingness, and above all transcendence over *karma* – unexpressed in *saṃsāra* – can now be given full rein. It is important to note, however, that in *mokṣa* these powers are manifest in a way appropriate to the *jīva*'s finite nature and as participative in the Lord's sovereignty over cognitive and volitional limitations.

45. *ShBh*, I.3.41 (p. 332, ll.19–21; *Th*, p. 348). In Sanskrit, *parabrahmāsādhāraṇaṃ sarvatejasāṃ chādakaṃ sarvatejasāṃ kāraṇabhūtam anugrāhakaṃ . . . jyotir dṛśyate.*

46. Cf. *KaṭhUp*, II.3.15; *MuṇḍUp*, II.2.11; *ŚveUp*, VI.14.

47. There is scope here for points of contact between Rāmānuja's picture of the liberated state and the Christian understanding of the resurrection of a (spiritual) body in the eschaton.

48. *ShBh*, I.3.7 (p. 287,ll.7–12; *Th*, p. 306). In Sanskrit, *karmavaśyānāṃ kṣetrajñānāṃ brahmaṇo'nyatvenānubhūyamānaṃ kṛtsnaṃ jagat tattatkarmānurūpaṃ duḥkhaṃ ca parimitasukhaṃ ca bhavati. ato brahmaṇo'nyatayānubhūyamānam anyatayā parimitasukhatvena duḥkhatvena ca jagadanubhavasya karmanimittatvāt karmarūpāvidyāvimuktasya tad eva jagad vibhūtiguṇaviśiṣṭabrahmānubhavāntargataṃ sukham eva bhavati.*

49. As an instance of this, Rāmānuja allows for certain individuals who have attained the liberating knowledge (e.g. Vasiṣṭha) to undergo fresh embodiments in this world after death, in order to complete the function/service their previous *karma* merited. Cf. *ShBh*, III. 3.30–1.

CHAPTER SEVEN: THE ONE AND THE MANY: OBSERVATIONS ON RĀMĀNUJA'S THEOLOGICAL METHOD

1. In this context 'model' is being understood in the sense of a conceptual structure or framework in terms of which a complex, multifaceted reality can be opened up to the understanding. 'Model' is not being used in its current more technical senses. Cf., for example, Ian Barbour's *Myths, Models and Paradigms*.

2. Cf. Ch. 2. p. 37.

3. This chapter is an enlarged version of a similar discussion contributed by

the author to the H. D. Lewis *Festschrift* issue of *Religious Studies* (Mar 1984), ed. Prof. S. Sutherland with the assistance of the author. However, the *Festschrift* contribution has a section on the potential for dialogue with Christian theology in general (and Indian Christian theology in particular) of Rāmānuja's theological method.

4. *BĀUp*, III.7.15 (Kāṇva recension). Cf. the whole section.
5. For some discussion on this, Cf. Lott, *God and the Universe*, Ch. 3.
6. *ShBh*, II.1.8 (p. 409, ll.8–10; *Th*, 419–20. In Sanskrit, *śarīraṃ hi nāma karmaphalarūpasukhaduḥkhopabhogasādhanabhūtendriyāśrayaḥ pañcavṛttiprāṇādhīnadhāraṇaḥ pṛthivyādibhūtasaṃghātaviśeṣaḥ.*
7. II.1.9 (p. 413, ll. 14–16; *Th*, p. 424). In Sanskrit, *ato yasya cetanasya, yaddravyaṃ sarvātmanā svārthe niyantuṃ dhārayituṃ ca śakyam taccheṣataikasvarūpaṃ ca tat tasya śarīram iti śarīralakṣṣṇam āstheyam.* From this definition we see that for Rāmānuja it was not necessary that a substance be capable of existing (relatively) independently.
8. See Ch. 2, pp. 37.
9. See A. Farrer, *Faith and Speculation*, Ch. 10 ('Anima Mundi').
10. See, for instance, Lott, *God and the Universe*, p. 31: 'The texts . . . illustrate Rāmānuja's thesis of organic relationship as the principal characteristic of the unity of God and universe. That they were the original inspiration for Rāmānuja in his adopting this organic viewpoint is clearly a strong possibility. . . .'
11. *VedS*, para. 76 (p. 114). In Sanskrit,

ayam eva cātmaśarīrabhāvaḥ pṛhaksiddhyanarhādhārādheyabhāvo niyantṛniyāmyabhāvaḥ śeṣaśeṣibhāvaś ca. sarvātmanādhāratayā niyantṛtayā śeṣitayā ca – āpnotīty ātmā sarvātmanādheyatayā niyāmyatayā śeṣatayā ca – apṛthaksiddhaṃ prakārabhūtam ity ākāraḥ śarīram iti cocyate. evam eva hi jīvātmanaḥ svaśarīrasaṃbandhaḥ. evam eva paramātmanaḥ sarvaśarīratvena sarvaśabdavācyatvam.

12. Not, of course, in so far as its material body is material, i.e. prakṛtic, or has its distinctive shape, or functions in its characteristic biological ways, and so on, but in so far as it is related to its *ātman* in the technical sense of the self-body model.
13. *VedS*, para. 62 (p. 107). In Sanskrit, *jātyāder vastusaṃsthānatayā vastunaḥ prakāratvāt prakāraprakārinoś ca padārthāntaratvaṃ prakārasya pṛthaksiddhyanarhatvaṃ pṛthaganupalambhaś ca . . . .*
14. Cf. following note.
15. *ShBh*, I.1.1 (p. 114, l.21 – p. 115, l.2; *Th*, pp. 136–7) In Sanskrit, *ātmaikāśrayatvam ātmaviśleṣe śarīravināśād avagamyate. ātmaikaprayojanatvaṃ ca tattatkarmaphalabhogārthatayaiva sadbhāvāt. tatprakāratvam api devo manuṣya iti ātmaviśeṣaṇatayaiva pratīteḥ.*
16. First quotation, on *Gītā*, 9.4: *BG11*(2), p. 137. In Sanskrit, *sarvāṇi bhūtāni mayy antaryāmiṇi . .;. ahaṃ tu na tadāyattasthitiḥ. matsthitau tair na kaścidupakāra ity arthaḥ.* The second, on *Gītā*, 9.5: *BG11*(2), p. 138. 'I am the support': *bhartāham.*
17. '(Naming) terms': understood in the technical sense mentioned in Ch. 1 (see p. 14).
18. See the discussion in Ch. 2, pp. 39ff.

19. The rules of grammar demand *niyamya*, but the best textual authorities have *niyāmya*. No doubt this was a use peculiar to Rāmānuja.

20. Cf. Carman, *The Theology of Rāmānuja*, p. 135.

21. In classical Hindu thought control of a chariot in its various aspects provided a particularly potent illustration of integrated and integrating forces in personal relationships. A well-known example in this context occurs in *KaṭhUp*, I.3.3f. Indeed, to my mind the key relationships of the *Bhagavadgītā* itself are structured with the model of control over a (war) chariot in view. In neither case, however, taken as a whole, is there an exact parallel with Rāmānuja's controller – thing-controlled relationship.

22. And *BĀUp*, III.8.9, that it is by Brahman's command that 'the sun and moon stand firm, set apart'. Cf. *VedS*, paras 13f.

23. On the unnecessitated sovereignty of Brahman's will, see Ch. 5, pp. 89f.

24. *VedS*, para. 121 (p. 150). In Sanskrit, *ayam eva hi sarvatra śeṣaśeṣibhāvaḥ. paragatātiśayādhānecchayopādeyatvam eva yasya svarūpaṃ sa śeṣaḥ paraḥ śeṣī.*

25. As a docrinal concept *kaiṃkarya* was developed in the theology of Rāmānuja's followers. Rāmānuja himself seems to give it a general, non-technical meaning, though it may well be thought that the hymns ascribed to him suggest otherwise. However, there is no doctrinal elaboration of *kaiṃkarya* in the hymns.

26. See Ch. 6, n. 38.

27. See Ch. 5, pp. 83f.

28. See Ch. 5, pp. 85f.

29. See Ch. 2, pp. 38f., and earlier sections of this chapter.

30. The contrast between the two aspects of the polarity can be pointed to linguistically by noting the *pra-* prefix in *prakāra–prakārin* (suggesting convergence) and the *vi* – prefix in *viśeṣya–viseṣaṇa* (suggesting divergence). Hence under *ShBh*, I.1.1 (p. 30, ll. 8–9; *Th*, pp. 42–3) Rāmānuja can say of the latter feature, 'Whenever we apprehend the qualifier – qualificate relation the sharp distinction between the two is perceived as obvious.' In Sanskrit, *sarvatra viśeṣaṇaviśeṣyabhāvapratipattau tayor atyantabhedaḥ pratītyaiva suvyaktaḥ.*

31. Interpreting words of Kṛṣṇa, Rāmānuja says in this vein, '[Serve and worship] Me . . . as illumining the whole world by My unlimited and surpassing lustre, gladdening the universe by the beauty of My self' – *BG11*(1), 6.47 (p. 592). In Sanskrit, . . . *mām* . . . *anavadhikātiśayatejasā nikhilaṃ jagad bhāsayantam ātmakāntyā viśvam āpyāyayantaṃ bhajate sevata upāsta ity arthaḥ.*

32. See pp. 135–6.

33. For some ideas in this regard see my article mentioned in n. 3.

34. On the meaning of this compound, see J. A. B. van Buitenen, *Rāmānuja on the Bhagavadgītā*, p. 1, n. 1 (there seems to be an omission here: read, 'but it is a ṣaṣṭhī tatpuruṣa'). Also see V. Varadachari's article 'Antiquity of the Term Visishtadvaita', in *Visishtadvaita: Philosophy and Religion*, pp. 109f.

35. An intriguing discussion on this description in connection with Rāmānuja's thought was initiated by R. V. De Smet when in 'Rāmānuja and Madhva', in *Religious Hinduism*, ed. De Smet and J. Neuner, he referred, quite inappropriately, to Rāmānuja's 'definite pantheism' (p. 69). Fr Anthony replied with 'Is Rāmānuja a Pantheist?', in *Indian Ecclesiastical Studies*, vol. V, no. 4 (Oct 1966) pp. 283–313. This was followed by De Smet's 'Rāmānuja, Pantheist or Panentheist?' in *Annals of the Bhandarkar Oriental Research Institute*,

Diamond Jubilee Volume (1977–8) pp. 561–71. Lott says, 'Brahman contains the universe within his total being, transcending it by his inclusiveness. This may properly be termed *pan-en-theistic* Vedānta' (*God and the Universe*, p. 85). Comparisons and indeed contrasts may be made between Rāmānuja's and A. N. Whitehead's (and Whitehead-derived) theological views, especially in connection with 'pan-en-theism', but, as indicated earlier, explicit dialogue is not to my purpose in this book.

Bibliography

Comprising works cited in this book and other relevant titles.

RĀMĀNUJA'S WORKS AND TRANSLATIONS/RENDERINGS OF THE SAME

NB. Versions listed under editor(s)/translator(s).

Abhyankar, Vasudev Shastri, *Śrī-Bhāshya of Rāmānujācharya* (Bombay: Government Central Press, 1914). Sanskrit text.

Annangaracharya Swamy, Sri Kanchi P. B., *Śrī Bhagavad-Rāmānuja-Granthamālā* (Kancipuram; Granthamala Office, 1956). Sanskrit text of the complete works.

Govindacharya, A., *Śrī Bhagavad-Gītā, with Rāmānuja's Commentary in English* (Madras: Govindacharya, 1898).

Krishnamacharya, Pandit V., and Narasimha Ayyangar, M. B., *Vedāntasāra of Bhagavad Rāmānuja*, Adyar Library Series, vol. LXXXIII, 2nd edn (Madras: Adyar Library and Research Centre, 1979). Sanskrit text and English translation.

Lacombe, O., *La doctrine morale et métaphysique de Rāmānuja* (Paris: Adrien-Maisonneuve, 1938). Abhyankar's Sanskrit text, plus French translation with notes, of *Śrī Bhāṣya*, I.1.1.

Raghavachar, S. S., *Vedārthasaṃgraha of Śrī Rāmānujācārya* (Mysore: Sri Ramakrishna Ashrama, 1956). Sanskrit text with English translation.

Sadhale, Shastri G. S., *The Bhagavad-Gītā with Eleven Commentaries*, 3 vols (Bombay: Gujarati Printing Press, 1935–8). Sanskrit text.

Sampatkumaran, M. R., *The Gitabhasya of Ramanuja* (Madras: Professor M. Rangacharya Memorial Trust,1969). English translation.

Srinivasan, S. V., 'Ramanuja's Saranagati Gadya', in *Visishtadvaita: Philosophy and Religion* (Madras: Ramanuja Research Society, 1974) pp. 64f. English translation.

Thibaut, G., *The Vedānta-Sūtras with the Commentary by Rāmānuja*, The Sacred Books of the East Series, ed. F. Max Müller, vol. 48 (Oxford: Clarendon Press, 1904). English translation.

Van Buitenen, J. A. B., *Rāmānuja on the Bhagavadgītā* (The Hague: H. L. Smits, 1953). Condensed English rendering.

—— (ed.), *Rāmānuja's Vedārthasaṃgraha* (Pune: Deccan College Postgraduate and Research Institute, 1956). Sanskrit text plus English translation with notes.

OTHER WORKS

Fr Antony, 'Is Ramanuja a Pantheist?' in *Indian Ecclesiastical Studies*, vol. v, no. 4 (Oct 1966) pp. 283–313.
Barbour, I. G. *Myths, Models and Paradigms* (London: SCM, 1974).
Bharadwaj, K. D., *The Philosophy of Rāmānuja* (New Delhi: Sir Shankar Lall Charitable Trust Society, 1958).
Bhatt, S. R., *Studies in Rāmānuja Vedānta* (New Delhi: Heritage, 1975).
Biardeau, M., *Théorie de la connaissance et philosophie de la parole dans le Brahmanisme classique* (Paris: École Pratique des Hautes Études, Sorbonne, 1964).
Carman, J. B., *The Theology of Rāmānuja* (New Haven, Conn., and London: Yale University Press, 1974).
Dasgupta, S. N., *A History of Indian Philosophy*, vol. III (Cambridge: Cambridge University Press, 1940).
Datta, D. M., *The Six Ways of Knowing* (London: Allen and Unwin, 1932).
De Smet, R. V., 'The Theological Method of Śaṃkara' (PhD thesis, Pontifical Gregorian University, Rome, 1953).
—— and Neuner, J. (eds), *Religious Hinduism*, 3rd rev. edn (Allahabad: St Paul Publications, 1968).
——, 'Rāmānuja, Pantheist or Panentheist?', *Annals of the Bhandarkar Oriental Research Institute*, Diamond Jubilee Volume (Pune, 1977–8), pp. 561–71.
Devasthali, G. V., *The Vākya-Śāstra of Ancient India* (Bombay: Booksellers' Publishing, 1959–60?).
D'Sa, F., *Śabdaprāmāṇyam in Śabara and Kumārila* (Vienna: De Nobili Research Library, 1980).
Farrer, A., *Faith and Speculation* (London: A. & C. Black, 1967).
Gispert-Sauch, G., 'Shankaracharya and our Theological Task', *Vidyajyoti: Journal of Theological Reflection* (Delhi) Sep 1978, pp. 348–55.
Govindacharya, A., *The Life of Rāmānujāchārya* (Madras: S. Murthy, 1906).
Hick, J., *God and the Universe of Faiths* (London: Macmillan, 1973).
—— *Death and Eternal Life* (London: Collins, 1976).
Hiriyanna, M., *Indian Philosophical Studies (I)* (Mysore: Kavyalaya, 1957).
Hohenberger, A., *Rāmānuja – ein Philosoph indischer Gottesmystik* (Bonn: Selbstverlag des Orientalischen Seminars der Universität Bonn, 1960).
Jha, G. *The Prābhākara School of Pūrvamīmāṃsā* (Allahabad, 1911).
—— *The Tattva-Kaumudī*, Poona Oriental Series, no. 10 (Pune: Oriental Book Agency, 1934).
Johanns, P., *Vers le Christ par le Vedānta* (2 pts) (Louvain: Museum Lessianum, 1932).
Kumarappa, B., *The Hindu Conception of the Deity, as Culminating in Rāmānuja* (London: Luzac, 1934).
Lacombe, O., *L'Absolu selon le Vedānta: les notions de Brahman et d'Ātman dans les systèmes de Ćankara et Rāmānoudja* (Paris: Librairie Orientaliste Paul Geuthner, 1937).
Lester, R. C., *Rāmānuja on the Yoga*, Adyar Library Series, vol. CVI (Madras: Adyar Library and Research Centre, 1976).
Lipner, J., 'The Christian and Vedāntic Theories of Originative Causality: A Study in Transcendence and Immanence', *Philosophy East and West*, vol. XXVIII, no. 1 (Jan 1978) pp. 53–68.

—— 'Through a Prism Brightly', *Vidyajyoti: Journal of Theological Reflection*, Apr 1980, pp. 150–67.

Lott, E., *God and the Universe in the Vedāntic Theology of Rāmānuja* (Madras: Rāmānuja Research Society, 1976).

—— *Vedantic Approaches to God* (London: Macmillan, 1980).

Neevel, G., *Yāmuna's Vedānta and Pāñcarātra: Integrating the Classical and the Popular*, Harvard Dissertations in Religion, no. 10 (Montana: Scholars Press, 1977).

Radhakrishnan, S., *The Principal Upaniṣads* (London: Allen and Unwin, 1953).

Raghavachar, S. S., *Śrī Rāmānuja on the Upanishads* (Madras: Prof. M. Rangacharya Memorial Trust, 1972).

Śaṃkarācārya, *Taittirīya Upaniṣad Bhāṣya with Ānandagiri's Ṭīkā*, Ānandāśrama Sanskrit Series, vol. XII (Pune: Ānandāśrama, 1977).

——, *Brahmasūtrabhāṣya*, rev. Wāsudev Laxmaṇ Shāstrī Paṇśīkar, 2nd edn (Bombay: Pāndurang Jāwajī, 1927).

——, *Upadeśa Sāhasrī* (Madras: Sri Ramakrishna Math, 1970). Sanskrit text, plus English translation by Swāmī Jagadānanda.

Sen Gupta, A., *A Critical Study of the Philosophy of Rāmānuja*, Chowkhamba Sanskrit Studies, vol. LV (Varanasi: Chowkhamba Sanskrit Series Office, 1967).

Sharma, C., *A Critical Survey of Indian Philosophy* (Delhi: Motilal Banarsidass, 1964).

Srinivasa Aiyengar, C. R., *The Life and Teachings of Sri Ramanujacharya* (Madras: R. Venkateshwar, n.d.).

Srinivasachari, P. N., *The Philosophy of Viśiṣṭādvaita*, Adyar Library Series, vol. XXXIX, 2nd edn (Madras: Adyar Library and Research Centre, 1946).

——, *The Philosophy of Bhedābheda*, Adyar Library Series, vol. LXXIV, 2nd edn (Madras: Adyar Library and Research Centre, 1950).

Varadachari, V., 'Antiquity of the Term, Visishtadvaita', in *Visishtadvaita Philosophy and Religion (A Symposium)*, pp. 109–12.

Visishtadvaita: Philosophy and Religion (A Symposium) (Madras: Rāmānuja Research Society, 1974).

Yāmunācārya, *Gitārthasaṃgraha*: Sanskrit text and English translation in J. A. B. van Buitenen's *Rāmānuja on the Bhagavadgītā*, pp. 177–82.

Index